CITY SLICKERS

WILLIAM E. GEIST

PENGUIN BOOKS

PENGUIN BOOKS
Published by the Penguin Group
Viking Penguin Inc., 40 West 23rd Street,
New York, New York 10010, U.S.A.
Penguin Books Ltd, 27 Wrights Lane,
London W8 5TZ, England
Penguin Books Australia Ltd, Ringwood,
Victoria, Australia
Penguin Books Canada Ltd, 2801 John Street,
Markham, Ontario, Canada L3R 1B4
Penguin Books (N.Z.) Ltd, 182–190 Wairau Road,
Auckland 10, New Zealand

Penguin Books Ltd, Registered Offices:
Harmondsworth, Middlesex, England

First published in the United States of America by Times Books 1987
Reprinted by arrangement with Times Books, a division of Random House, Inc.
Published in Penguin Books 1989

10 9 8 7 6 5 4 3 2 1

The essays in this book originally appeared in the column "About New York" in
The New York Times. Copyright © 1983, 1984, 1985, 1986, 1987 by The New
York Times Company. Reprinted by permission. All rights reserved.

Grateful acknowledgment is made to Warner Bros. Music for permission to
reprint excerpts from the lyrics to "Ten Cents a Dance" by Richard Rodgers and
Lorenz Hart. © 1930 Warner Bros. Inc. (Renewed) All Rights Reserved. Used
by permission.

LIBRARY OF CONGRESS CATALOGING IN PUBLICATION DATA
Geist, William.
City slickers/William E. Geist.
p.   cm.
ISBN 0 14 01.1580 3
1. New York (N.Y.)—Anecdotes.   2. New York (N.Y.)—Humor.
I. Title.
[F128.36.G45   1989]
974.7'1—dc19   88–21891

Printed in the United States of America by
R. R. Donnelley & Sons Company, Harrisonburg, Virginia

Drawings by Naomi Osnos from photographs by Jeremy Shatan

*For Mom and Dad
and brother Dave*

CONTENTS

INTRODUCTION

The trouble with working at *The New York Times* is that people at parties are always trying to pin you down on Botswana. When I was working there, I always had to explain to them that I was writing about people who lived in trees in Central Park, sold bullwhips on streetcorners, hit chip shots out of abandoned cars on New York City golf courses — that type of thing. By choice.

I suspect New York is as different from mainland America as Botswana. For the longest time after moving here from the Midwest, I thought everybody in New York was just running a fever — some sort of tsetse fly deal. Here in the nation's thyroid, people scurry about at a frenzied pace. Drivers routinely run red lights. People walk and talk too fast, and many of them eat lunch walking. They eat peculiar things, too: knishes, kasha varnishkes, fried kreplach — stuff that might not even be food, I don't know.

I still think people are talking to me on the street when they're just talking to themselves. A lot of people do that in New York. Sometimes when I'm at the bank or in a department store, someone will just start yelling at a teller or a clerk. It seems like this happens more in August, when everyone's psychoanalyst is on vacation.

On a single day (not April Fools') in New York, I discovered a trendy hair salon giving lion urine hair treatments; a man selling "Bob's Lucky Potatoes" on Wall Street, and investors buying them for luck; 150 "retro runners" competing in a backward mile race to bring attention to their new and apparently serious sport; and a man introducing a line of dog hair clothing.

All facilities in New York are inadequate. The city always seems one minor fender bender away from total collapse yet somehow muddles through. Speaking of collapse, I noticed how they finally determined that a road was bad enough to need repairing. One day a truck fell right through an elevated roadway, and they closed it for repairs. Some motorists complained about the closing.

While waiting for a WALK light one day, I couldn't help noticing the man next to me was eating fire. He turned out to be a street performer, working for tips. He said he made $37,500 a year. In New York, you don't know if that's bragging or complaining.

The fire-eater said he came here to juggle for tips but soon found that it is not enough just to juggle in New York. No one notices you. You must also eat fire.

He said he took a course in fire-eating. I didn't know if he was kidding or not. I wouldn't be too surprised if there is a New York Fire-Eating Academy. There are courses in hot-coal walking and a course in "How to Lose Your Noo Yawk Accent" and a course in how to live in Manhattan on $100,000 a year.

No one seems to have enough money in New York. A night security guard at the newspaper won a million dollars in the lottery. It worked out to twenty annual payments of about $30,000 or so, after taxes; so of course he can't quit his job, not in New York.

No one has enough time or space either. When you go to someone's apartment in Chicago, they always offer to show you around. In New York people live in tiny, NASA nose-cone-sized apartments, and at NASA line-item prices. They have loft beds, necessary because they can't get a bed *and* a chest of drawers in a New York bedroom – should they happen to actually have a separate bedroom. Convertible couches are an industry here. Futons, the combination chair-bed that hails from another cramped island, Japan, are popular, and so are Murphy beds and Pullman kitchens.

A guy told me recently he was having his closets analyzed, by one of the many professional closet analysis firms in Manhattan. Space is so critical, and expensive, that proper closet space utilization is obligatory. The floor space in the closet, if the guy breaks it out of the overall bill, is probably running him a couple hundred a month.

People search maniacally for apartments, the way people elsewhere search for kidnapped children: putting up posters, offering rewards, knocking on doors, checking the obituaries. One woman I know quit her job to devote more time to the search. When people here finally find some claustrophobia-inducing apartment in a bloodcurdling neighborhood, they seem pleased.

For obvious reasons New Yorkers don't seem to spend much time at home. Cramped apartments may be one reason they are such film and restaurant devotees. A new restaurant seems to open every night, a new dance club every week and a new magazine every month. On trendy Columbus Avenue, a friend poked his head in a restaurant under construction and found one of the workmen taking reservations. The place was booked for the entire first month after its scheduled opening date.

They also like to get out of the congested city, but seemingly all at the same time, on their way to all the same places. Gridlock reigns. My son and I were in a two-hour traffic jam on the way to the opening game of the World Series and listened to the first two innings on the radio. What other city is even capable of a common, everyday two-hour traffic jam?

Many people want to go to the Hamptons — by train, car, bus, jitney, helicopter and seaplane — all at the same time, so rents there are likewise astronomical. To make it affordable, a custom of "summer shares" has developed, whereby one can buy a half share or a quarter share in a summer house. A quarter share, for example, is one of two twin beds in the same bedroom of a large house, every other weekend. Some shares are on couches.

New Yorkers have special ways of folding their newspapers to take up less room on buses and trains. They read the back of your newspaper while you read the front, and they read your watch on subways and in restaurants, where tables are sometimes two inches (by actual measure) apart. Two lovers quarreled and cried one day just inches from my bacon-cheeseburger, and I didn't know what to do after I had offered her my napkin to dry her eyes.

New Yorkers walk farther and faster than any other Americans I've seen. For one reason they can often walk faster than a taxicab in traffic can travel. (An estimated 800,000 cars enter midtown and downtown every day.) And the walking is always interesting. Visitors to New York always complain that they've never walked so far and that their feet are killing them.

New Yorkers are not like other people. Many of them don't have cars. I've met people who have no idea how to drive, some of them while driving. Others have never driven at all.

Many New Yorkers don't have TV sets either. A surprising number of them don't watch the Super Bowl. You'd think they would worry about being subpoenaed by the House Un-American Activities Committee for this kind of behavior. Instead of watching TV, they go, they claim, to operas, museums and ballet and orchestra performances. And they read. Juliette Benton, eighty-eight years old, proudly put an end to the Wednesday Book Group she had headed for fifty-five years — with a big wingding in her son's loft this year.

Yet many New Yorkers haven't a clue as to who Vanna White might be. Sad, yet one of the things I like best about New York is that it has not yet completely given in to the twentieth century.

Those without TV sets miss a lot. There is a nude talk show on New York cable television. "Some people up on Eighty-fifth Street called to complain," the talk show host said to a female guest, "that the last time you were on the show they didn't get to see your rear end." She stood up and showed it.

One reason people don't have cars is that a garage space costs $300, $400 or more a month in a lot of places; $22 for three hours in others. I've just met someone who is paying $407 a month in mortgage and monthly maintenance fees for the $30,000 parking space he purchased. It's called a "car condominium."

Alternate side of the street parking means constantly having to move the damned car, if you have one. A man on the Upper West Side described his job to me as a "car shepherd": Neighborhood residents give him the keys to their cars, and he keeps them parked where they won't get tickets. They have no idea where their cars might be; they just come to him when they need them.

Otherwise they may find themselves among the mob of angry motorists paying $100 to retrieve their towed vehicles, shouting and cursing and throwing things at city clerks, who duck and weave behind the counter.

The subways have 3.5 million riders a day. Remarkably few, considering the reputation of the subway system, are killed. Many more die of natural causes than are killed, and a few are born and occasionally named after the nearest station. The subways frightened me at first. All the graffiti made me wonder just who was in charge down there anyway. Now many of the cars don't have graffiti, and I have heard tourists voice disappointment at the sight of clean cars.

Other New Yorkers prefer thrill rides in the city's twelve thousand taxis, driven largely by non-English-speaking immigrants, it seems. Other New Yorkers ride in style in the city's ten thousand to fifteen thousand limousines — reportedly more limousines than exist throughout the rest of the world. Style is critical to New Yorkers.

Friends come to visit New Yorkers a lot, because New York is a nice place to visit, but the hotel-room prices are prohibitive. Friends of ours arrive with plans to see Carnegie Hall, the Carnegie Deli, Plaza Hotel, Central Park, Columbus Avenue, Chinatown, Little Italy, Little Odessa, Hasidic Williamsburg, South Street Seaport, Trump Tower, the Garment District, Fur District, Diamond District, Ralph Lauren's department store, the Village, the East Village, World Trade Center, Wall Street, Harlem, Brooklyn Heights, Little Italy, SoHo, Times Square, Bloomingdale's, Statue of Liberty, Metropolitan Museum, Rockefeller Center, Empire State Building, Zabar's, United Nations, St. Patrick's Cathedral, Lincoln Center and the Palladium.

They want to take a Circle Line cruise, shop Fifth Avenue and Madison Avenue, ride the Staten Island ferry and Roosevelt Island tram, attend the Letterman show, watch punk haircuts, go to quaint art galleries, eat lunch at "21," have a drink in the Algonquin lobby, eat dinner at Elaine's, have dessert in Little Italy at one of the places where a Mafia chieftain was shot, dance in the Rainbow Room and have a nightcap at an after-hours spot that serves refreshing cocktails until 11:00 A.M. (really) — and if possible, to get away from the tourist traps and see The Real New York.

If possible, they'd also like to go where they might run into Jackie O., Yoko O., Rodney D., Madonna, Woody, Mia, Bianca, Baryshnikov, Garbo, Hepburn, Kissinger, Bacall, Rather, Jennings, Brokaw, Pauley, Donahue or somebody.

It takes a while to get used to seeing famous actors and actresses and playwrights and painters and composers and dancers — not just at Elaine's, but at the A&P.

Walking in New York, some Soviet defectors told me that there was nothing in their line of vision that reminded them of home; a family of five visiting from Snohomish, Washington, told me the same thing. Walking on the sidewalks, both groups gawked at street musicians and three-card-monte players, panhandlers outside exclusive shops and restaurants, people selling fake Rolex watches and children's coloring books, and people selling drugs and women — convenience shopping. Outside a porno shop they saw men you could pay to play chess with, who were most accomplished.

Another impediment to pedestrian traffic is an outbreak of sidewalk cafés, where boulevardiers try to maintain a veneer of sophistication while suffering honking and panhandlers as well as exhaust fumes from the tail pipe of a Buick parallel parking two feet away.

And there are the sidewalk schmoozers. Schmoozing is a Yiddish word for standing and — how to say it? — kibitzing. No other city has so many Yiddish words in its working vocabulary. Schmoozing usually takes place on the sidewalks after lunch and sometimes involves doing a little business during the course of the discussion — perhaps because New York restaurants are too small for a private conversation.

The litter on the sidewalks and streets can be ghastly. But what should you expect on a streetcorner that might host more people every day than Giants Stadium holds for a football game? Take a look at a football stadium after a game. Also, there are unsightly piles of trash bags in front of buildings, because there is no room in Manhattan for alleys.

Another use for the sidewalks is sleeping and setting up

housekeeping. The homeless are everywhere, the shame of the city.

People here have the most unusual occupations. Most people seem to do more than one thing: waitress-actress, writer-philosopher-plumber, that type of thing. I met the car shepherd one morning, and that afternoon I met a man who stands in lines for a living.

Like Poland, there are lines for everything in New York: for cabs, buses, cash machines, parking garages, restaurants – anything desirable in the least. In New York they call it standing "on line" not "in line." I was shocked to see on TV during last season's New York Mets–Houston Astros baseball playoff series that Astros fans were just loading their families into their station wagons, driving out to the Astrodome on game day, buying some tickets at the door and walking in. In New York, after a couple of thousand playoff tickets went on sale by telephone, New Yorkers placed 1.5 million calls per hour to the number, and phone stores sold out of GTE 2200 phones with auto-redial capability.

New York women seem quite different from those I'm accustomed to, far more independent and self-assured. They walk faster and more erect. Casual empiricism suggests they are also more beautiful. On any given WALK light in midtown, you are likely to see one or more women fairer by far than any in the homecoming court in your hometown.

As for men, women friends tell me there are not enough of them – at least not enough heterosexuals. One said she believes New York is "a city of nerds," brainy men, type-A's, making lots of money and getting the good-looking women. I think she's right.

It is an intellectual city, the capital of the publishing world, a city of museums and libraries and colleges and nearly eight hundred thousand college graduates. Education is so important that parents in Manhattan enroll their two-year-olds in courses that prepare the kids for interviews by the "right" pre–nursery school programs, which parents believe lead to the "right" nursery school, then to the "right" prep school, and then on to Harvard. Otherwise, the child might just as well not have been born.

It is also the nation's capital for fashion designers, painters, sculptors, writers, stage actors and, along with Los Angeles, for actors and television performers. The three network news shows emanate from New York, and this is the headquarters for the Associated Press, *Time* and *Newsweek* and *The Wall Street Journal* and home of the leading critics in film, theater, dance, art and music. Pegeen Fitzgerald's local talk show emanates from her apartment, as it has for the past fifty years, with the sound of Mrs. Woo, the cleaning lady, vacuuming in the background.

It is a city for writers, a city where newspaper reporters have agents. Must have. You write a good newspaper article in New York, and agents call to ask if you have adequate representation, book publishers call to ask if you want to do a book on the subject, film producers call to ask about obtaining rights to the material or to ask if you would like to participate in the writing of a "treatment" or a screenplay. The Letterman show calls to see if this goofy guy you wrote about is entertaining enough in real life to have on his show or if you made him sound good. I wrote about a shy, introverted young man who built tree houses in Central Park, and within hours he had a lawyer and an agent. The last I heard, Disney was doing a film on his life.

It is a city of thousands of writers (using the term loosely), where scenes of plays, chapters of novels, soap-opera scripts, magazine pieces, newspaper articles and screenplays are written on computers and race around town from one terminal to the next on wires beneath the streets. A man named Bruce Stark, doing business as Bruce the Computertutor, races around town on his scooter, catering to one writer's emergency after another's, saving prose, for better or worse, from wherever it goes when computers eat it.

The newspapers and TV news talk about crime all the time. It's not terribly difficult coming up with a juicy crime story every day in a metropolitan area of seventeen million people. So a lot of people live in fear, even though New York doesn't even rank in the top ten cities in any major crime category. In six years of working and traveling around the city, I have yet to witness any crime, whatsoever. Having said this, I expect this book to be published posthumously.

In New York you are always unintentionally walking through

scenes being shot on the streets for films, TV movies, commercials and music videos. Norman Jewison, the director, tells a typical story of taking over a bakery in New York for a scene and having it filled with lighting crews, sound crews, camera crews and actors when a man walked in and demanded to buy his customary four loaves of bread. He told the director he didn't care if they were filming, and they sold him four loaves of bread for $2.20 each. "Pay the woman at the counter," Mr. Jewison told him, and the man gave the $8.80 to Cher, the actress, and left with his bread.

Most of the movies show New York to be a grimy, scary place. In other cities, chambers of commerce and city council members raise objections about how their city is depicted. Here no one seems to care very much.

With New York's image as a crime capital, I enjoyed a day spent watching motorists from out of state coming through the Lincoln Tunnel only to be scared out of their wits as their cars were immediately set upon by swarms of black teenagers at the first stoplight. The teenagers brandished squeegees and set about washing windshields, just some of the city's entrepreneurs, who try to sell you a product or service whenever you stop or even slow down. One man told me of standing at an intersection waiting for a WALK light and looking down to see an entrepreneur putting polish on his shoes.

I notice further that New Yorkers are far more friendly than I expected, willing to offer advice, directions and occasionally even a little money to complete strangers. I think this is because so many New Yorkers have been new to New York themselves and, indeed, still get lost in it sometimes. About one in three New Yorkers is foreign born, and there are the multitudes of immigrants from throughout America, as well, come to seek their fortune. Two Soviet defectors burst into tears when they glimpsed the Manhattan skyline from their taxi on the way in from the airport. The man who had met them at the airport began to cry, too, recalling his arrival when he emigrated from Cuba. Then their cabdriver burst into tears, too, and told them of his emigration from Yugoslavia.

Many restaurants are staffed entirely by aspiring actors and actresses, some of whom have spent their last dollars on the bus fare to New York. Really. And there are many alumni of the restaurants who have hit it big. At The Lion's Head the manager said: "Yeah, Jessica Lange worked here. She was the second prettiest waitress on her shift."

I came to New York to work for *The Times*. I had never seriously entertained the idea of coming to New York, which I regarded as an essentially unlivable city that was dirty, crime-ridden and exciting, yes, but in a terrifying kind of way. At work, however, was some notion that I was being invited to be a writer in New York, home at one time or another of nearly every great American writer, to include the homespun variety, such as Mark Twain.

I found *The Times* to be as different from any other newspaper as New York was different from any other city.

"And what," the patrician former editor of *The New York Times* is said to have asked the job applicant, "makes you think you are qualified to work at *The New York Times*?"

The applicant, a Pulitzer Prize winner (now deceased, so I won't give his name), was a bit taken aback by the question, which he pondered silently for a moment before answering.

"Well," he said, "I once screwed a member of the Junior League."

"That's right," said his wife. "He did."

. He got the job. I had no such recommendation. I submitted a batch of my clippings that included a column on the results of a suburban garage-door art contest I had run in Chicago and a column on a "zucchini plague" in my neighborhood. Lucky for me, a *Times* editor, Peter Millones, read them on the beach under a hot, dizzying sun and invited me for an interview.

When I was hired, Abe Rosenthal, the former executive editor, took me into the inner sanctum, the little Japanese garden of his in the bowels of his office. He expressed doubts about me but then stood abruptly and shook my hand, saying: "I am offering you a position at *The New York Times*. Congratulations!"

He told me that there are three great days in a person's life: birth, marriage and getting a job at *The Times*. I told him I was deeply honored but that I had promised to relate word of any job offer to my employer, *The Chicago Tribune*, before accepting.

"Of course," Mr. Rosenthal said with a warm smile, "I fully understand. I wish to tell you, however, that if you do not accept my offer, you will be making the biggest goddamned mistake of your life."

The Chicago Tribune's editor, the late Bill Jones, had told me: "When Abe takes you to the mountaintop, don't forget to look down on the shit below" — meaning New York in general and Times Square in particular.

But the heights in New York proved dizzying. The city looked like a dream world as I flew in on a night flight, up the East River past the glittering skyscrapers and bridges festooned with lights.

And I am finding it endlessly fascinating, which is not to say I don't hate the goddamned place at times, I really do.

GAMERS

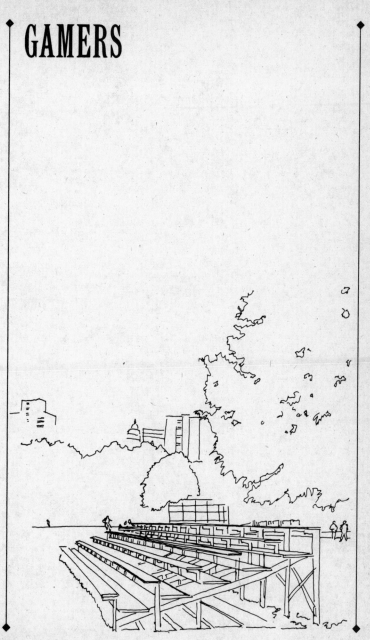

GUERRILLA GOLF

Ⓘɴ ɢᴏʟꜰ, ᴀs in life, almost everything is a little different in New York.

Take golf-course hazards, for example, which tend to be of the sand and water variety elsewhere but are far more diverse on New York City's public courses.

Out on the Pelham Golf Course in the Bronx this week, Don L. Jerome told of one of his tee shots recently bouncing into an abandoned car on the fairway, costing him a stroke.

On another occasion a friend of Mr. Jerome's was robbed while lining up an approach shot, costing him no strokes but $65 and his credit cards. "Something like that disrupts a golfer's concentration," Mr. Jerome noted.

New York's beleaguered golfers are returning to city courses in droves this year — in twice the numbers as last year at some courses — after fleeing to suburban courses or giving up the game altogether because of hazards that ranged from waist-high weeds to muggers.

"I know a guy who used to take his guard dog with him to the golf course," said James McDonald, who recalled yet another golfer who carried a can of Mace in his bag alongside the woods and irons.

Charlie Pessoni said that instead of twosomes or foursomes, he and his friends found it a smart idea to play in eightsomes and even sixteensomes.

"I was never bothered," James Murphy commented.

"You carried a gun," Mr. Pessoni replied.

These guerrilla golfers blamed the city's fiscal crisis of the 1970s for all of this and said course conditions have been improving rapidly and dramatically under a new program where the city has licensed private golf course companies to operate nine of the thirteen municipal courses.

"We are in a mild state of shock," said Kimble Knowlden, who came to New York last year to oversee the operation of six of the city's courses for the American Golf Corporation of Los Angeles. "You have to remember that we're from California," said Mr. Knowlden, who was once the head golf pro at Pebble Beach, one of the world's grandest courses.

"Here," said the tanned Mr. Knowlden, "there were assaults and robberies right on the courses. If you left your car in the lot while you played, it would probably be gone when you returned. Graffiti was all over everything. The well water at a course on Staten Island was so polluted from the nearby landfill that when we used it to water the course, all the grass turned black! And people were using the courses as trash dumps."

"Tell about the bodies, Kimble," said John DeMatteo, another American Golf supervisor. "We get a certain number of dead bodies. I try not to be the first one out on the course in the morning."

"At the Dyker Beach course in Brooklyn," said Mr. DeMatteo, "it was lovely in the morning, mowing the tall grass and watching the rats hop here and there like bunnies." He said area residents complained about the cleanup, because the rats were moving off the courses and into their homes.

Although crime has diminished with the return of more golfers, many problems of city golfing persist. Youths still run out of the bushes and steal golf carts while players are putting. The manager of the Clearview course spends a good deal of time roaming the streets of Queens retrieving the carts and driving them back to the course on the expressways. At Clearview youths broke into the golf-cart barn recently and played demolition derby with about twenty-five carts.

"Abandoned automobiles on the courses are a perpetual

problem," Mr. Knowlden said. "Auto thieves love to drive them out on the courses, and they get stuck in the sand traps."

At first, Mr. Knowlden employed armed guards at the golf courses. But crime has diminished, and in the interest of providing a "country-club atmosphere," he has replaced uniformed guards with a force of "marshals" that is made up largely of retired men who like to play golf. They patrol the courses, checking for people sneaking on and such. Mr. Knowlden has also done away with high-security cashier cages, which were most un-country-club-like.

"New Yorkers love to beat the system," he said. "We catch people sneaking onto the courses, and they say, 'So try to stop me.' We call the cops, and they say: 'What? We got three murders over here we're working on.'"

With so few open spaces in the city, the golf courses are used as soccer fields, picnic areas, dirt-bike courses, lovers' lanes and what have you. "They usually get out of the way," said Jane Angelo, one of the many women golfers reappearing on city courses. "They stopped what appeared to be a gang fight once to let us play through."

"We try to live and let live now," said Mr. Knowlden. At Clearview, American Golf bulldozed a sophisticated dirt-bike track that local youths had built on the course, only to have the kids retaliate by tearing up the greens. "So," he said, "we rebuilt their track, off to the side." He said that a number of people had taken up residence in tents on golf-course property but were allowed to stay so long as they were out of the way.

Mr. Knowlden said that when American Golf took over, it had to hire "ex-cops or large firemen" as starters at the course because of all the arguments over who was next. "Before they took over," said Lou Avon, who has played Bronx golf courses for twenty years, "we had to come here at 1:00 A.M. to get in line to play. That makes people irritable. They have a phone reservation system now, and there aren't as many fistfights. It is becoming a country club for the average man."

Mr. Knowlden sees the golf course as a microcosm of the city. "It was a frightening place to come to from California," he said, "and I still won't ride the subways, but I see improvements all over this park and in the roads around the city and in other aspects of life."

Where there had been rats on the Pelham and neighboring Split Rock courses, this week one could observe foxes, rabbits and colorful birds, including pheasants, quail and a mother duck hatching some eggs fifty yards from Pelham's seventh hole.

Perhaps as importantly, out in the nearly filled parking lot that was once a nearly abandoned weed field, one could observe the return of expensive cars, including the occasional Mercedes convertible with "MD" license plates.

A NO-SWEAT ALTERNATIVE TO RUNNING THE MARATHON

For A LITTLE different perspective on New York's imminent marathon, we take you now to the La-Z-Boy recliner-chair store in Queens and Ralph Sansone.

"Marathon runners are crazy," said Mr. Sansone, who had come to the La-Z-Boy Showcase Shoppe on Northern Boulevard in Flushing during this week of marathon mania to look for yet a third recliner chair for his den.

"They say that jogging is healthy and relieves stress — well, this is how I do it," he said, pulling back the lever that flipped up the footrest on a recliner, then tilting back — all the way back, to a position suitable for root-canal work — and closing his eyes.

There are issues that continue to divide this nation, and running is one of them. When 18,365 marathoners take off across the Verrazano-Narrows Bridge, Mr. Sansone will be at one with his favorite cocoa-colored Naugahyde recliner, watching it all on television.

Even watching runners for a prolonged period makes him weary, so he will hit the remote-control switch soon after the dramatic start of the race to view professional football. From time to time, he will reach down into a small polystyrene cooler to the left of his chair for a can of cold beer, then to his right, where pretzels will be positioned. The man has personal comfort down to a science.

"I honestly don't think running would be good for Ralph," Mrs. Sansone said. "People die running. And dogs bite them."

Another customer at the shop, Rita Hastings, commented that she sometimes has problems extricating her husband from his recliner at mealtime and bedtime. Indeed, La-Z-Boy has manufactured models with food trays attached, as well as with side pockets suitable for keeping copies of *TV Guide* and other reading materials.

"When I get the urge to jog," said Bernie Berger, a salesman, "I climb into one of these chairs until it passes. We had one of the marathon runners in here looking at chairs the other day. He needs one. Running makes him awfully tired. Personally, I think the man is wacky.

"All these exercise books people are writing do more harm than good," Mr. Berger continued. "There is no supervision, and people hurt themselves. Orthopedics has become the greatest business in the world. Instead of all this running around, more people should sit down."

A lot of them have. Employees and customers at the store cited tendinitis, shinsplints, heel spurs, knee surgery, tedium and their inability to get out of bed early enough to jog before work as reasons they gave up on physical fitness.

Such injuries and unpleasantries are rare in sport sitting. A sitter noted that expensive equipment is not required for this inactivity.

Although most sitters believe that runners are addicts and that they never smile until they stop, the sitters acknowledge that running is no doubt beneficial to cardiovascular and overall fitness. But Mr. Sansone pointed out that although running may reduce the heart rate, sometimes it reduces the rate to zero. Also, he said that a man in his neighborhood had been hit by a car while running and that another was on crutches with a severely sprained ankle.

"Our chairs aid circulation," contended Stan Lozinski, the store manager, throwing the lever and putting himself in the supine position. "See, my feet are higher than my head now. The chairs also support your back. Doctors recommend them," he claimed.

Lillian Fontane, a store employee, is one who can attest to the chairs' ability to reduce heart and breathing rates, having fallen asleep the day before in a recliner on the showroom floor, an occupational hazard at the Showcase Shoppe.

Joe Hastings, who came in to buy a $435 orange and gold Herculon tweed La-Z-Boy of early American design, bore witness to the chair's health benefits: "When I sit in mine at home with a highball, there is no need for my blood-pressure pills."

He said that as wonderful as it is, however, "you do have to take breaks from the sitting."

Mr. Lozinski said that a series of exercises to be done while sitting in a La-Z-Boy was once designed but had failed to gain popularity.

For all the differences between those who run and those who sit, the sitters do see some similarities. Like the runners, Mr. Sansone practices regular "carbo-loading," often eating spaghetti while he watches television. He also drinks a lot of beer, something that many runners do to replace fluids and potassium in their bodies.

He knows that sitting does not burn as many calories an hour as running, and he has switched to Lite beer. He has been unable, however, to cut down his consumption of nacho cheese chips, but how else to get the nacho his body needs? He remains athletically inclined, watching as many as five or six televised football games each week, and has watched an aerobics class on television.

"Our customers are your traditional-type people," said Mr. Lozinski, people who aren't going to lie around in a sensory-deprivation tank or run marathons to relieve stress.

"You can buy a chair," he said, "for the cost of a couple pairs of these fancy running shoes. I'll take a recliner and a good movie on the videocassette recorder any time."

"Admittedly," said Mrs. Fontane, who has given up on her walking exercise, "there isn't the feeling of accomplishment in sitting. And sitting doesn't make you feel invigorated."

Yet Mrs. Sansone alluded to her husband's achieving a Zen-like state when he nestled in front of the television in his recliner, a blanket over his legs, a Jets game on, his remote control in one hand and a beer in the other.

No euphoria-producing beta-endorphin is released, as happens during running, but Mr. Sansone testifies to regularly experiencing a "sitter's high."

THE MAYOR
DISCOVERS BASEBALL

Baseball, HOT DOGS and apple pie are three things every American — and certainly every politician — is supposed to love.

"Two out of three ain't bad," Mayor Ed Koch said yesterday in his office, referring to the hot dogs and the apple pie — although, frankly, he said he would prefer a little schnecken, a kosher pastry, to the apple pie.

Mayor Koch knows next to nothing about baseball. This has not been a major problem in recent years, when New York baseball always turns into something of a sore subject anyhow. But with the entire city — save for the rabid Yankee fans — now excited about the Mets, the mayor is being asked to comment on baseball wherever he turns, and he is quietly boning up on the subject.

Until now, Mayor Koch has known full well what a strawberry, a darling and a knight were but had no idea who they might be, namely Darryl, Ron and Ray.

The mayor seemed fully conscious yesterday, however, that the Mets are in the World Series, noting that someone had interrupted his dinner party Wednesday night to tell him. Rude.

Mr. Koch, who said he had been the type of youngster "you would choose last" in a sandlot game, said that as part of his intensive baseball education program, he has begun looking at the pictures — said to be worth a thousand words — that appear in the sports pages. And, yes, he is even reading some of the captions.

◆ ◆

He was casually tossing around such terms yesterday as "pitcher's mound" and "home plate," pausing a moment after each term, perhaps reflecting on what he had just said or waiting to stand corrected.

He used to spend one inning, or less, at his obligatory ball-park appearances, but he boasted yesterday that he spent three innings at his last game — "An increase of fully three hundred percent," he noted. He said that Darryl Strawberry had hit a home run, tying the game, while he was there, and characteristically, Mr. Koch felt he deserved some credit for that.

He even went into the Mets dressing room after they won the divisional title and was sprayed with champagne. "It was California champagne," he said, "not fit to drink."

Mr. Koch seems most proud to say that he now knows the name Strawberry.

"And Mookie, who could forget that one?" he said. "And, of course, old Ray. Sure. Ray what's-his-name."

An aide reminded him that he had met Gary Carter and Keith Hernandez the other day, and the mayor said, "Them, too!"

"Still," he said, "when reporters ask me about baseball, I think to myself, 'You dog, you,' except I use a different word than dog."

Mr. Koch said he would forgo his great love of eating Chinese food and attending a movie tomorrow night to attend the opening game of the World Series at Shea Stadium. Moreover, he said, he intends "to stay the full, um, nine innings." Correct.

The mayor has not been asked to throw out the first ball, perhaps because of how much air time it might take to find it. He denied that he would take along a book — *Mayor* is still his favorite — or his Walkman radio to entertain himself.

"I will eat hot dogs, which I love," he said, "and I will cheer."

When?

"When the other people cheer," he answered.

Although many politicians have traded on their being fans of successful baseball teams, some local politicians avoid ballparks because of the New York custom of the fans' saluting them with a chorus of boos. Mr. Koch recalled a trip to a ballpark with former Governor Hugh L. Carey, when they were roundly booed. Mr.

Koch learned then to smile, tip his hat and wave as if he were receiving a hero's welcome.

"My mother told me," he said, "that my brother, Harold, was going to be the athlete in the family and that I was to go in the corner and practice being mayor. If I ever actually played baseball, I can't remember it." The mayor is tall and was urged to try basketball. "I was absolutely terrible," he said.

But he did not give up on sports. He became a hard-nosed philatelist and was captain of the debate team.

Yesterday, amid his meetings, swearings-in and dedications, he wrestled with the question of what to bet the mayor of Boston on the Series. "It looks like flags," Mr. Koch said, "rather humdrum."

Mr. Koch was also making arrangements for a ticker-tape parade if the Mets win the Series — and only if they win. He explained that his game was politics — "rough, cruel and with no rules of play" — and that it matters most if one wins or loses and not so much how one plays the game.

"I'm learning to love baseball," he said. "I like the crowds and the cheering," he added, agreeing that most people were proba- bly already aware of this.

He said that he positively could not wait for tomorrow night, when he will head out to Shea Stadium in his new Mets cap.

The bill goes in front.

THE COLUMBIA LIONS' FOOTBALL FAITHFUL

The Columbia Lions football team faces hapless Colgate, 0-6 on the season, Saturday at Columbia's Baker Field. Odds-makers have made Colgate a 30-point favorite.

ELIZABETH ARMSTRONG BEGAN regularly attending Columbia football games in 1928. This white-haired woman in a Columbia cap can still be seen in the crowd – at virtually every game, home and away.

Oh, sure, the Lions haven't won a game for three years and haven't had a winning season in the last fifteen, but Ms. Armstrong notes that sometimes they beat the spread and also that these things do change. Why, it seems to her like only yesterday when Columbia won the 1934 Rose Bowl. Her father, a devout Columbia fan who had played football in the class of '01, didn't go to the bowl game, figuring he'd catch the next one.

Being a fan means remaining loyal through thick and thin, said Ms. Armstrong, who was scornful of those Mets fans who were grumbling yesterday after losing the first two games of the World Series. Besides, she enjoys the conviviality of the Columbia games, the tailgate cocktails and the nice boys on the team.

She would dearly love to bring some nice homemade cookies to these fine young football players but worries that "the NCAA would nail me on some technicality."

After fifty-six seasons observing the team, Ms. Armstrong has noticed that astrophysicists and English majors – especially the shortish, bony ones with eyeglasses – do not make the best running backs. As the Lions' twenty-six consecutive losses near the collegiate record (thirty-four by Northwestern), she wonders if she should mention something to the coach.

Nah. No need to panic. Columbia could still win a game this season, although it is unclear which one that might be. "I've learned a lot about football," she said, "certainly more than these stupid referees."

She and her friend, Marion Lang, who both live in New Jersey, and a fan named D. Keith Mano, class of '63, are sometimes the only ones rooting for Columbia at away games. The three often attend scrimmages and freshman games and have even shown up at Columbia summer football training camp near the New Jersey–Pennsylvania border. Why go to scrimmages? "Because sometimes we win," Mr. Mano, a writer, explained.

"He has the disease worse than I do," Ms. Armstrong said of Mr. Mano, who has attended 145 consecutive Columbia football games, home and away, since 1970, when he missed the Brown game because his then-but-no-longer wife began to deliver their child on the way to the game. "I dropped her off within easy walking distance of the hospital," he said, "and drove to the field, but the game was over." Otherwise his consecutive streak would be 176 games.

He shows no remorse about having raised his children as Columbia fans, even though sometimes they cry with frustration. He had Columbia games written into his divorce agreement; he gets the kids on game days.

He said he has watched games through swarms of bees, "ark-launching rains" and "liquid-oxygen cold. On the nice Indian summer afternoons, we know we'll lose fifty-six to zero." He recalled sitting in a sleet storm at Colgate, the only Columbia fan, watching the Lions being slaughtered and asking himself: "Why? Why?"

He recommends plenty of alcoholic beverages for the Columbia fan, advising that such illicit liquid refreshments be brought in Donald Duck or Garfield the Cat thermos bottles, which stadium security personnel are too embarrassed to search, he said.

Ms. Armstrong, who missed one game this year and another one about six years ago, really likes Mr. Mano, the kind of guy who doesn't just throw in the towel after a couple of (hundred) losses.

"He's the cheerleader," she said. He has been known to read appropriate passages from *Henry V* in the stands. Mr. Mano is a man who has — he has to have — a wonderful sense of humor, yet he is deadly serious about his religion: Columbia football.

"I find most Columbia fans to be cynical and negative," he said, "reflecting Columbia's intellectual history and liberal tradition." Mr. Mano writes a column for *The National Review*.

"Liberals see anybody in uniform as vaguely fascist," he said, "and those who beat up on somebody, so much the worse." He thinks that setting aside this liberal tradition would help win some games — not to mention letting a few fleet, if dumb, running backs and some hulking linemen slip through the admissions office.

Mr. Mano, who lives on the Upper West Side of Manhattan, recalled the Lafayette game this year when Columbia was ready to score the winning touchdown when time ran out. "The athletic director said he'd heard I was offering one thousand dollars to tear down the goalposts if we won," Mr. Mano said, "and he didn't approve. I said he had heard wrong, that I'd wanted the goalposts and the light towers torn down."

"In fact," he said, "tearing down the whole stadium wouldn't be such a bad idea."

That's just the kind of feisty talk that is music to Ms. Armstrong's aging ears. "If you start losing gracefully," she said, "you'll never be worth a damn! Roar, Lions, roar!"

Postscript: The Lions entered the 1987 football season with a thirty-one-game losing streak, closing in on Northwestern's all-time major college record of thirty-four straight losses.

OF WRESTLERS, POLITICIANS AND SHOWMANSHIP

"**A**ND IS IT not true," the witness was asked solemnly, "that the woman in question was stir-frying vegetables at the time?"

The witness, who sat before television lights and a bouquet of microphones in the vast New York State Hearing Room on the forty-fourth floor of the World Trade Center, answered: "She was. Someone could have been seriously injured."

The Senate Task Force on Professional Wrestling held a hearing yesterday on a bill introduced by State Senator Abraham Bernstein, a Bronx Democrat, to ban professional wrestling in the state.

The witness, Judge Daniel D. Leddy, Jr., of Family Court on Staten Island, was telling the panel of senators about an incident in which a teenaged boy became crazed from watching professional wrestling and slapped a sleeper hold on his mother while she stir-fried. The sign in the hallway read SENATE HEARING ON PROFESSIONAL WRESTLING, and passersby kept sticking their heads in the doorway and saying, "Is this for real?"

Indeed, it was. There were all the trappings of real hearings: an august panel of senators, television cameras, reporters, aides scurrying about, a few uncooperative witnesses and a few others anxious to spill the beans.

"But shouldn't they be talking about something else – like hunger or deficits?" asked Vincent Fasano, who works for Shearson Lehman/American Express in the building and dropped in during his lunch hour. "There's a lot of money in wrestling now. Maybe they could help with the deficit by holding wrestling matches in the Capitol Building."

Senator Bernstein, who served as chairman of the proceedings, said wrestling required a suspension of disbelief, and several of the spectators, who watched a stream of wrestlers, promoters and others testify, said the same could be said of his hearing.

Sheik Ali Abdulia of Saudi Arabia (known to his neighbors on East Second Street as Al Greco) came to testify dressed in full regalia: robe, burnoose and aviator sunglasses. He is a wrestling manager, and he denied all suggestions by Senator Bernstein and previous witnesses that the outcome of wrestling matches was predetermined.

Dr. Robert E. Gould, a psychiatrist, testified that his studies showed illegal tactics outnumbered legal tactics in wrestling by three to one and that children who watched wrestling were more violent than those who watched swimming. Then he stated flatly, "Mr. Chairman, wrestling is absolutely fixed!"

Marge Montgomery, a member of the audience, covered her ears, smiled and said: "I don't want to hear this." Irvin Muchnick, who is writing a book about wrestling, said, "It's like the lawyer in *Miracle on 34th Street* trying to prove there's no Santa Claus."

Another witness, Burt Randolph Sugar, who writes books about wrestling, testified: "Fixed? I know the outome when I go to see *Hamlet*, too, but I go to see Olivier."

Linda Franks, another member of the audience, said the hearing reminded her of the furor a couple of years ago over what video games were doing to the nation's youth. "Generations of adults have wanted kids to all be in the library reading Shakespeare, and they just won't do it," she said.

Senator Bernstein bemoaned that only a couple of the two hundred wrestlers he had invited had shown up.

Captain Lou Albano, manager of André the Giant and other wrestlers of the World Wrestling Federation, said by telephone that he didn't attend because "some of these politicians have brains the size of dehydrated peas.

"I am well aware of the bill," he said. "I keep abreast of the issues. My favorite TV show is *Face the Nation*."

A wrestler who looked in for a few minutes and who insisted his legal name was Manfred the Maniac said he would not testify, because he might become angered by the line of questioning and decide to body-slam some senators and put Senator Bernstein in a hold called the double-arm bar. "Maybe a figure-four leg lock, too," said Mr. Maniac.

Another wrestler who showed up was the diminutive Kessler Raymond, the Haiti Kid, who said: "Certainly this bill can't pertain to midget wrestling! There's never been any criticism of that."

Two former wrestlers testified that wrestling was fixed. "I was on the ten-most-hated-wrestlers list at one time," said Eddy Mansfield, the Continental Lover, "so I know what I'm talking about."

Two members of the building-maintenance staff, Joe Pennissi and Daniel Velez, standing in the back of the room, said they doubted his word. "Got to be real," said Mr. Pennissi. A former wrestler, Ron Pope, took some of the employees in the hall and treated them to a demonstration.

Sheik Ali Abdulia, who said he "has roots in Saudi Arabia," said that if the state banned wrestling, it would next have to ban John Wayne war movies.

Senator Bernstein put his hand over the microphone and chatted with an aide — accepted practice in Senate hearings but new to the sheik, who said: "Are you listening to me? I listened to you. I find this rude."

"I am listening attentively, chief, er, sheik," Senator Bernstein said.

Senator Anthony Masiello, Democrat of Buffalo, said he did not quite believe the sheik's testimony that wrestling matches were not predetermined, and the sheik said he did not quite believe Senator Masiello's prepared statement that "this task force has not predetermined anything."

Senator Bernstein said the foul tactics wrestling teaches youngsters and the anti-Americanism of such wrestlers as the Iron Sheik of Iran and Nikolai Volkoff of the Soviet Union "disgust me." He said, "I used to think Bruno Sammartino was fair, and then I saw even him grind a peanut into another wrestler's eye."

Senator Bernstein said that seeing wrestling fans cheer eye-gouging reminded him of when a crowd yelled, "Jump! Jump!" when a man threatened to jump off the top of the DeWitt Clinton Hotel in Albany. "Why would people do that?" he asked, and someone responded, "Was the jumper a state legislator?"

"Wrestling is not legitimate," Senator Bernstein concluded. "It is just showmanship to attract attention."

"There is some showmanship in everything," said the sheik, surveying the rows of reporters and the television cameras, "even politics."

CENTRAL PARK SOFTBALL

THE BASEBALL SEASON has begun, and the men on the benches in Central Park are at it again, holding lively discussions – peppered with hot arguments – about the legendary players of old and the promising players of today.

"I thought Jack Lemmon played a good solid second base last year," Joe D'Antone was saying.

"Good fielder," Red Twohie agreed. "But just fair at the plate, I'd say."

"Phil Donahue was competent at third base," said Vic Quintana.

"Nothing like Al Pacino played the position," said the man next to him on the bench.

All agreed that Peter Falk's hustle made him a first-rate outfielder and that in her day Geraldine Page could hold her own in the infield with the best of them.

"I remember the day Judd Hirsch pitched a no-hitter," said Frank Hammond.

"Yeah," said Mr. Twohie, who has been watching games in Central Park for more than half a century, "but George C. Scott was actually a better pitcher. He won the league's MVP, and he accepted it, too" – not like the Oscar he turned down.

This week, the Central Park softball leagues are getting into full swing again. The Broadway Show League opens tomorrow, with Parks and Recreation Commissioner Henry J. Stern scheduled to throw out the first ball at noon, joined by a group of

Broadway stars to include James Earl Jones (*Fences*) and Robert Lindsay (*Me and My Girl*).

The Restaurant League is already under way, and these Central Park bench sitters were out in full force to take in a game between the Sporting Club and the Hard Rock Cafe. As you might expect, the Sporting Club won (17–9).

"When they interview for waiters and dishwashers, they definitely ask about lifetime batting averages," said the commissioner of the Central Park Softball League, Marty Mann. "That's how serious this is."

"I was actually fired at the China Club," said one Eric Nalven. "But I still play on the team." Likewise, some of the Broadway show teams outlast the shows.

There is also a Show Business League, as well as a Press League, Corporate League, Real Estate League, Engineers and Architects League and so on, Mr. Mann said.

"The teams tend to reflect their businesses," Mr. Twohie, a faithful bench sitter, said. "The Wall Streeters come in with their spikes up."

"And," Mr. Mann added, "the Park Avenue Lawyers League argues the most with the umpires, protesting and filing appeals. No kidding."

For the bench sitters, most of them getting on in years, this is old-home week. They greeted one another yesterday after another long winter, embracing and never failing to tease one another about having put on some pounds.

They traded gossip, the good along with the bad, such as news that one of the bench sitters, Mario Jolly, died over the winter. "You expect that sort of thing at our age," said Mr. D'Antone, sixty-four years old and younger, by far, than many of the others.

Mr. D'Antone was once named Fan of the Year by the softball leagues. He has come to be known as "the Mayor of Heckscher Park," which is the area of the park, at latitude 65th Street, comprising six ball fields.

He goes to the park by subway from his home in Bensonhurst virtually every day of the year, except during blizzards and torrential rainstorms, and leaves at dusk. This has been his routine for fifteen years. Mr. Twohie, sixty-eight, said he has been going to games in the park since 1934.

Mr. D'Antone arrives about 9:00 A.M., first visiting Sal Napolitano, who runs the carousel adjacent to the ball fields and who always has the coffeepot going.

"This is a little piece of heaven here," Mr. D'Antone said. "Yes sir. In summer, you've got your warm sunshine, breathtaking skyline, beautiful trees and flowers, peace and quiet, a ball game, a card table, good friends, girls in bikinis, a guy selling cold beer out of a gym bag. I'm telling you, this is heaven on earth!" The man left little room for argument.

"What's really pathetic," Mr. D'Antone said, "is that a lot of people living right here on Central Park West don't realize heaven is right out their front door, and they waste their money going out to the Hamptons."

The bench sitters are sometimes called the Red Onions, because that has been the name on their ball-field permit for more than forty years. They have procured a picnic table, where they play cards, some of the games lasting so long that they move the table from under the shade trees to under a lamppost.

Although some of the Red Onions are in their seventies, eighties and even nineties, three days a week they stand up and play ball for two hours. "We have nicknames for everybody," Mr. D'Antone said, "like 'Dressed-Up Tony,' who has four suits and always wears one to the park, in case his apartment is robbed while he's away."

The men returned to discussing the relative abilities of such ballplayers as Woody Allen, Lily Tomlin and Neil Simon. They laughed recalling the incident in which Gregory Hines made an error last year, was booed by the crowd and mooned them in return.

"Rod Steiger was a good ballplayer," Mr. Twohie said. "They say the guy could act, too."

AT YANKEE STADIUM, A WISTFUL SEPTEMBER SONG

THE CRACK OF a bat sounded amplified in cavernous Yankee Stadium, sprinkled lightly with fans on a cool September evening. Calvin Adams was off like a shot to catch the ball, looking back now and again to follow its flight, then making a neat grab after it crashed foul in the blue-plastic seats. He held up his prize to the crowd's applause.

The eighteen-year-old is a veteran ball hawk, whose sport is the competitive fetching of foul balls and home runs. "You've got to have the quickness," he explained after the game this week.

September is his favorite month, a time when the Yankees are either in an exciting race for first place or are also-rans, and small crowds such as this one make for good ball-hawking in the vast blue ocean of empty seats.

Fans said that it was a favorite time for them as well, a time for true baseball aficionados rather than the "We're number one!" rowdies. It is a time when Stan's Sports Bar across the street takes on the look of a ski lodge, with patrons in sweaters, and a time of eerie empty corridors in the stadium.

An idle refreshment-stand clerk caught up on her reading during a game this week, and ushers felt free to look the other way as general-admission customers trickled down into the reserved seats. Out on the fading green field, some of the veterans push themselves in September to keep up their fair-market values, and nervous young players invited up from the minors try to prove they have what it takes for the big leagues.

It is a time of hope among the fans, the most ardent of whom sit in the bleachers. Millie Lackey, who is thirty-five years old and lives in the neighborhood, has been to every home game this year, and she is not about to give up on her team now, despite the dreaded "mathematical elimination" of the Yankees from the division title race.

"It doesn't matter when you're a true fan," she said, dressed coat-over-sweater for an Orioles game this week. "It's very pleasant. There are no lines for hot dogs."

Craig Van Steenbergen, a vendor, has been bumped by senior vendors from beer and hot dogs to the less-lucrative popcorn. It could be worse. It could be peanuts. Fewer vendors, ushers and security people work the games now. Mr. Van Steenbergen said that per-capita sales of hot dogs increase in the cool weather, with no noticeable drop in beer consumption.

A woman working at a small souvenir stand had sold only a dozen hats, compared with ninety or one hundred on a good night. "If they would stop trading the Goose Gossages," she said, "these hats would fly out of here." She has been selling souvenirs for many years, and she recalled the glory of bygone Septembers at Yankee Stadium, when day-to-day dramas played to full houses.

Charles Gregg is a uniformed security officer whose job is "crowd control." He estimated that nineteen thousand of the twenty thousand seats in his jurisdiction, the upper deck, were empty this night. His mission now is to keep fans out of vast sections of the stadium that are roped off so that they will not have to be cleaned.

But he takes a more relaxed approach these days, and when three ball hawks raced past him chasing a foul, he let them go about their business. He also allowed someone past who said that he wanted "to play Bob Uecker" for a moment, sitting in an empty, remote area of the upper deck just as Mr. Uecker, a former player and now a baseball announcer, does in a beer commercial. Mr. Gregg gave him a puzzled look.

Even though it means more work, Mr. Gregg prefers to see the Yankees battling for the title. "It picks up the morale of everyone at the park," he said, "and in the whole city. An Orioles–Yankees September game always meant something when the place was rocking and Reggie Jackson – long live the king – was here."

The Orioles, who have been described as "September's Team" because of a long history of fast finishes to clinch pennants, looked listless during batting practice. World champions last year, they are in fourth place now, and one of their veterans commented that this September seems interminable.

By contrast, the Yankees were a spirited lot, catching balls behind their backs during warm-ups and engaging in snappy repartee. They are winning consistently and have high hopes for next season. Five eager young players called up from the Columbus, Ohio, minor-league team were in the starting lineup.

Archie Kirkland, an old codger in the stands wearing a blue Yankee cap faded purple and drinking hot chocolate, wasn't quite sure just who all these young whippersnappers were – Cowley, Meacham, Bradley, Pagliarulo and Hudler – but he was anxious to find out. He recalled the days of Ruth, Gehrig and DiMaggio but said that some of his favorite times as a fan have been Septembers like this one, when cool refreshing breezes blow and promising young players in pinstripes offer fresh hope.

"You never know, this Pagliarulo might just turn out like that other Yankee with the Italian name," he said, referring to Joe DiMaggio. Mike Pagliarulo hit a home run this night, bringing Mr. Kirkland out of his seat.

In the locker room after the game reporters clustered around the twenty-four-year-old, pressing him for a colorful quote, something to put a little snap in a September story about a third-place team.

They asked how he was able to hit home runs on consecutive nights, and he said softly that he really didn't know what to say. He appeared shy and was unaccustomed to having five microphones just millimeters from his chin. Finally, he shrugged and said: "I don't know. Maybe it's all the carrots I've been eating."

The reporters laughed loudly at that, and he smiled, realizing he had given them what they wanted. Other reporters came across the room, clamoring: "What'd he say? What'd he say?"

"Carrots," someone answered, and the reporters scribbled it down.

HUSTLERS

SPEED
MERCHANTS

IT WAS RAY.

"Ray!" shouted a dozen young men, eager to call him by name. "Ray," yelled Mike Nelson, popping the question of the day at the Early Bird messenger service, "how many'd you do today?" Without looking up, Ray Williamson answered quietly, "Forty-one."

"Ray," Mr. Nelson said, shaking his head, "is my idol. Ray can fly."

In a city where speed is of the essence, Early Bird sells the stuff, and Ray Williamson delivers: stocks and bonds, artwork, alimony checks, legal briefs, fashion models' photograph albums, goldfish, you name it.

He is among the fastest of the thousands of bicycle messengers in the impatient city and something of a hero in this frenetic office on West 49th Street, an office that is wall to wall in ringing telephones and battle-scarred bicycles, the fastest known way through the morass of Manhattan traffic.

"You have to ride offensively," Mr. Williamson explained, mounting a ten-speed and darting in front of an accelerating yellow wall of taxis on Seventh Avenue. He made straight for the center lane. To ride timidly near the curb, the twenty-five-year-old rider said, is to invite collisions with pedestrians, with opening cab doors and with turning cars.

"Avoid collisions," he said. "They slow you down." Mr. Williamson picked up a parcel at Steve Burnett Graphic Communications, 330 West 42nd Street, and, in a display of instancy, delivered it seven minutes later to Major Printing, 135 West 20th Street.

As traffic thickened and slowed in the Garment District, the rider bolted ahead — zigzagging neatly between car bumpers to change lanes; racing on the eighth and final flash of the DON'T WALK signals (before the green light turns yellow); swerving instinctively for bumps and potholes not yet in view; slipping through chasms formed by buses and trucks, spaces so narrow he had to shrug his shoulders; ducking his head to avoid the side mirrors that smack many messengers off their bikes.

He did not know or care what he was delivering. His is the pursuit of the $100 day — take home — and he had just earned $3.60, 60 percent of the delivery charge.

Veterans of the trade recall messengers carrying everything from live ducks for television commercials to Yogi Berra's uniform from a tailor shop to Yankee Stadium. This day, an Early Bird messenger delivered a slice of pizza, a costly slice.

Mr. Williamson next barreled up the Avenue of the Americas to 57th Street, slowing only at Herald Square to look for a police officer known to ticket cyclists who run red lights. To save time, Mr. Williamson uses a quick-action lock and carries tools and tire patches to keep the bike rolling. While obtaining a signature from a receptionist, he sends the elevator up a couple of floors so he can catch it on the way down. There is no lunch break.

"Speed," said Kenneth Peyser, vice-president of Early Bird, "is the name of the game in New York." The messengers, nearly all of them men, work on commission and, he said, "make as much as they dare."

There are about two hundred messenger services in the city, sporting such names as Atomic, Fireball, Jiminy-Split, Supersonic and Zoom. Some, like Bullet Messenger, have found bicycles too dangerous and now use vans and foot messengers instead.

"We don't want kamikazes," said Mr. Peyser, "but we do hire risk takers. There is macho involved."

"You can't be wimpy," Mr. Williamson said. "You ride scared, you get hurt." He has grown a beard to look a little more intimidating, and he tries to look stern. Helmets? They would sooner wear petticoats.

Mr. Williamson is on his seventh bike in less than two years. After one was stolen, he began wrapping his bicycle in black tape and leaving the seat torn to make it less appealing. The five others were destroyed in action, one crunched in a collision that propelled him over the car in front. He needed surgery to remove bone chips from his ankle. Another high-speed accident involved what cyclists call "eating the back of the bus."

Few riders last more than a few years in the job. Geza Fekete retired to an inside job at Choice Courier after suffering a broken collarbone. He does not miss sucking in the exhaust fumes or having his ears ring from the roar of traffic.

"The good side," he said, "is the exhilaration of flitting in and out of trafic like a dragonfly."

Mr. Nelson, nineteen, is just beginning. Sitting in the Early Bird office, having recently recovered from a work-related concussion that kept him in the hospital for several days, he spoke about his experiences.

"Eight hours of riding," he said, "drains you physically and mentally. It takes intense concentration. You learn that taxis don't like you, because you make better time than they do and maybe more money. Pedestrians are unpredictable, our worst problem."

Pedestrians, many of whom are injured each year in collisions with bicycle messengers, complain about the cyclists, particularly about those who run red lights — "a necessity to make any money," Mr. Williamson said — and ride on the sidewalks.

A biting wind kicked up as Mr. Williamson called the dispatcher from a pay telephone on 57th Street. He does not mind that winter is coming on; it means many messengers will quit, leaving more work for him.

He hung up and said, "Time to ride," all the way to the Battery. He said he could be there in about seventeen minutes, faster than anything or perhaps anybody else in the city could. He would ride on reflex. With the speeds at which he weaves through the hurtling steel of Manhattan traffic, he cannot reasonably expect to ask the brain a question and receive an answer in time for it to do him any good.

He pumped away, effortlessly it seemed, disappearing into

traffic down Second Avenue. When the traffic lights on the avenue turned red and everything else stopped, Ray Williamson re-
appeared, a speck in the distance, darting and moving at thirty-
five miles an hour, over a rise and out of sight, in hot pursuit of a
$100 day.

A-MARRIAGE-
A-MINUTE

THE BRIDE WORE leotards. The bridegroom was resplendent in a LET'S GO METS T-shirt. The couple was bound in matrimony in 58.5 seconds, a respectable time indeed for the city's Marriage License Bureau, considering it is so early in the June wedding season and the bureau hasn't really hit its stride.

"I know," the bridegroom said with a smile as he stepped out the door marked ROOM 257 MARRIAGE CHAPEL, "I should have on a suit, or a tuxedo. But we love each other. That's what counts, isn't it?"

The young couple walked down the hallway in the Municipal Building at 1 Centre Street with their arms around each other, then down the steps, stopping on the stairwell for a kiss and a moment alone before going out into the world.

Herbert Ryan, the first deputy city clerk who was marrying people this day, pushed the buzzer on the podium in the chapel, signaling the clerk in the packed waiting room to send in the next couple. On busy days like this one, his technique is to hit the buzzer for the next couple as he heads into the closing: "I do by the authority vested in me . . . ."

The Marriage License Bureau was jammed as the traditional June rush began. Marriage may be more popular in the city now than at any time since the boom after World War II. The number of marriage licenses issued this year is expected to surpass that of last year — 76,343 — which was an increase of 5,000 from the previous year's total and among the highest since the postwar period. The number of licenses issued by the city has been climbing rapidly each year since a record low in 1977.

And never has the city performed so many marriages. About half of the couples obtaining licenses from the city are choosing the $5 marriage service offered across the hall — "that's over in Solemnization," one of the clerks told a bride-to-be.

By comparison, about one in seven couples receiving licenses were married by the city twenty years ago, and only about one in ten during the record marriage license year of 1946.

"We couldn't afford a big wedding," said Bo Elfving, a twenty-two-year-old man dressed in a white suit and posing for a photograph in the hallway with his bride of sixty seconds, Janis, who wore a simple white dress adorned with a red rose.

"This was so New York," said one of the Elfvings' bridesmaids, Krissy Carlisto, of Gloversville, New York. "It was so fast, like an assembly line."

The bride, Janis, who seemed uncertain of just what her last name was at that point, said Mr. Ryan had directed the bridegroom to "kiss the bride" as if it were part of the state statute.

Mr. Ryan concedes it is sometimes difficult under these siege conditions to give couples the personal attention they deserve.

"We try to accommodate," he said. "When someone beats on the door after you close and they have airline tickets for tomorrow's flight to Rio for a honeymoon, you can't just turn them away."

About to retire after twenty-five years in the clerk's office — the last nine performing marriages — he has married about 80,000 couples, 140 on his busiest day.

He has just about seen it all. One couple took off their coats in the chapel and were nude. He married them, although his concentration was broken, and he recalled saying: "to live together in the state of Massachusetts" instead of "the state of matrimony."

He has married celebrities and a couple on roller skates. He has waited through many prolonged silences after asking the big "Will you take" question. And he has heard them finally answer, "No!" and "What am I doing?" before running out.

So many languages are spoken here that understanding is often a problem. Mr. Ryan speaks French and Spanish, which is particularly useful for the many marriages between immigrants from Haiti and Spanish-speaking countries.

He has also learned a few key phrases — "join hands," for example — in Chinese and Russian. In one case he asked the all-important question and there was silence before the bride impatiently coached her Pakistani bridegroom: "Say 'I do,' stupid." And that is exactly what he said.

Sometimes marriages get off to rough starts. "One time the groom forgot the ring," he said, "and the bride slapped him. He slapped her." They yelled at each other for a while as Mr. Ryan stood impatiently, looking at his watch. When they finished, he married them.

Mary Odom, the clerk at the window in the license-applications department, issues licenses at such a furious pace these days that her hand aches from stamping all the forms. She looks over the forms and tells people to raise their right hand to swear that all they have filled in is true. "I can't hear you, Thomas!" she said to one man who may have mumbled "Yes" or "No" — and took their $10.

Daniel and Alice ran in late, after the 4:30 P.M. closing, and pleaded with Mrs. Odom, weary after a busy day, to take their application. The typists yelled at Mary that they were not about to type late again this day. The supervisor said it was simply not possible.

"I'll do it," Lucy Clark, one of the typists, said meekly. The others looked at her as if she were a little crazy.

"What can I do," Mrs. Clark said. "This is a very special day for them. I remember my own wedding day."

The fluorescent ceiling lights began going out around the office as Mrs. Clark typed ever faster.

"That's nice of you, Lucy," said Mrs. Odom, who had stayed around to stamp the form. She handed it to the couple, who thanked them and ran out gleefully.

"Best wishes!" Mrs. Odom yelled. "God bless you both!" yelled Mrs. Clark.

THE ESPRESSO
EMERGENCY SQUAD

Luis MARTINEZ WAS working through the lunch hour on a First Avenue pizzeria job when his electronic paging device started to beep. He immediately called the office.

There was serious trouble, you could see it in his face, this time at the corner of Seventh Avenue and 16th Street. "Espresso emergency?" he was asked. He nodded his head, grabbed a slice of pizza and said, "Let's roll."

Mr. Martinez, dressed in a blue uniform, wheeled his red emergency espresso-machine repair van through heavy traffic toward Sarducci's Ristorante, where the espresso-cappuccino machine had broken and the crowd was getting ugly.

"People are walking out," said Joseph DiCarlo, the restaurant's owner, greeting Mr. Martinez, who jumped from his van with a briefcase of tools and began resuscitation of the machine. "Real indignation," said Mr. DiCarlo, shaking his head. "They say, 'What do you mean there is no cappuccino?'"

Mr. Martinez restored the flow of the thick, bittersweet espresso and the milky, espresso-based cappuccino that come from the same machine. Without pausing to accept thanks, he was on his way to the next emergency, and the next, and next, well into the night. For Luis Martinez and the other four or five men and women of the Expresso Machine Repair Company, there is no rest in this day and age.

The machines now number in the thousands in New York, according to the repair company. Many restaurant owners say that offering the coffee drinks is a symbol of a fashionable restaurant and that it is a requisite for any restaurant wanting to sport at least a veneer of sophistication.

Jerry Abromowski, manager of Ruppert's Restaurant, at Third Avenue and 93rd Street, another of Mr. Martinez's stops, said that – in this way – the two beverages are what Perrier was a few years ago.

Explanations for the trend vary. "Americans have been drinking this dishwater coffee for years," Mr. Martinez's boss, Rudy Barth, said at his storefront on West 44th Street. "Espresso is good. They love it."

"People order it because it's European and sophisticated," said Susan Plump, a good name for a waitress who works as she does at the Hungarian Pastry Shop, at 111th Street and Amsterdam Avenue, where Mr. Martinez made a call.

"They order it even if they hate it," Elise Mankes, a waitress at Ruppert's, said. "It is, like, suddenly cool to drink espresso."

"All I know," Mr. Abromowski said, "is that they have to have it."

Chris Binioris, manager of the pastry shop, described "the young, professional type" as those who have recently discovered espresso and said, "They are people used to getting what they want when they want it."

While Mr. Martinez worked on the shop's machine, a customer snapped, "Just how long is somebody supposed to wait for espresso?"

Mr. Martinez is a twenty-six-year-old who emigrated from El Salvador eleven years ago. Mr. Barth met him in a neighborhood supermarket a few years ago, recruited him for the anticipated boom in espresso-machine sales and repair and sent him to Milan to study the machines. Although somewhat mystified by the hysteria attendant to American trends, Mr. Martinez said he felt a responsibility to the people who want the espresso and to the restaurant owners.

He hears the desperation in the voices of the restaurateurs,

many of whom try to stay on his good side by giving him gratuities and Christmas presents. When their machines break
down, they not only call the repair company, they also call Mr.
Martinez at home, sometimes rousing him from sleep on
weekends.

Mr. Martinez has taken an unlisted telephone number, but
he said he must give it to those who ask. One of those is Yosi
Ohayon, owner of Café Orlin, on St. Mark's Place.

"When our machine breaks," Mr. Ohayon said, "we're out of
business. Luis saves our lives." Some of the restaurant owners said
they were considering the purchase of backup espresso equipment, even though their machines cost between $3,000 and $5,000.

"I try to help everybody," said Mr. Martinez, heading from a
job on the Upper West Side across to Ruppert's on the northern
edge of the Upper East Side, "Cappuccino country." Here, business men and women dressed in pin-striped suits ordered cappuccino after lunches of cold chicken tarragon and "Quiche of the
Day" as Mr. Martinez worked feverishly over a Rancilio Z9/RE
espresso machine, with beads of perspiration forming on his
brow.

Next, he worked on an espresso coffee grinder at the Yaffa
Café in the East Village among people with maroon hair. "Everybody wants espresso and cappuccino," he said undiscriminatingly.

Traffic and parking problems hinder Mr. Martinez in his efforts to bring help to all those who need it. Sometimes when he
parks in a no-parking zone, however, the police are sympathetic
to the emergency nature of the call. Special license plates for
espresso-machine repair vehicles would be helpful, Mr. Barth's
wife, Lina, suggested.

"There is a real shortage of espresso-machine service in this
city," Mr. Binioris said. "The situation could become critical." He
said his pastry shop has sold espresso for twenty-two years, but
"for a lot of these restaurants, espresso is just the latest gimmick."

As Mr. Martinez was restoring espresso service to anxious
patrons at the pastry shop, an Emergency Medical Service ambu-
lance pulled up next to his red van. One of the paramedics, Owen
Traynor, purchased some coffee and cookies and lingered for a

moment on the sidewalk in the warm spring sunshine.

Would that Mr. Martinez could do that. He whisked out of the shop past the paramedic and sped off in his red emergency vehicle.

"People in New York like espresso," Mr. Traynor said. "I like espresso. In New York you could consider this an emergency."

NEW YORK'S ONE PATIENT MAN

LENNY DIBARI LIKES to wait. "I really don't mind at all," he said cheerfully, standing in a line that horrified, disgusted and maddened others who arrived at the Department of Motor Vehicles bureau yesterday. "I kind of enjoy it."

Those in line with him at 141 Worth Street said they figured him for a "nut" or perhaps a disciple of "some kind of Eastern religion." It was a customarily angry crowd, with those in line frequently mentioning that they were spending perhaps the finest day of the year, weatherwise, inside the motor vehicles bureau.

The captive audience listened as Mr. Dibari told his life story, a tale of an uncommonly patient child who grew up to wait in line professionally. He is an employee of Services Unlimited, a Manhattan company specializing in waiting in lines for its customers.

Mr. Dibari will wait for you. He will wait without complaining in awful lines for passport renewals (lines that can be six hours long), for license plates, for copies of birth certificates, to pay for parking tickets, to obtain traffic-court continuances, even to plead traffic-court cases that can be proven with documents and, on occasion, for theater tickets.

He sort of figures that fortune smiled the day he was born in New York.

"New York has the worst lines," said David Alwadish, founder of Services Unlimited. "Bank lines, ticket lines, post-office lines, money-machine lines, restaurant lines, subway-token lines, pizza lines, grocery-store lines, airport lines. I don't have to tell you. They are everywhere you look. Waiting on line is a way of life here. People hate it; so we have been very, very successful."

Mr. Alwadish's mother wanted him to be a doctor, he said, but he gets tremendous satisfaction from relieving human suffering in this line of work. "Standing on line," he explained, "is a great, great pain." He said he helped his father, who operated a driver-training school, with driver's-license paperwork. "I loved keeping people away from the motor vehicles bureau," he said.

Bruno Klang, one of his customers, said he would "happily pay ten times" the $7.50 he is paying Services Unlimited to obtain his driver's-license renewal "just to stay out of the motor vehicles bureau."

The charges go up to $22.50 for, say, a complicated transfer of vehicle ownership. "For a $7.50 fee," said Mr. Alwadish, "we will stand in line and get Mr. Klang's driver's license renewed, and he can retain his dignity."

Standing in front of Mr. Alwadish at the Traffic Violations Bureau, 50 Fourth Avenue, yesterday was David Kwait. He had received a ticket for making an illegal turn and was yelling while he waited in line: "My time is more valuable than it is for these creeps! I can't stand here all day! They try to wear you down!"

When his turn came, a clerk informed him that the police officer was unavailable and that he would have to return another day. "Oh, the cop is better than I am?" he said loudly. "This is going all the way up to the mayor, who happens to be a personal friend of mine!

"This whole thing is a racket," Mr. Kwait shouted, turning his attention to Mr. Alwadish, "so guys like you can make money standing in line for people."

Mr. Alwadish bristled. "I do not make my living from the suffering of others," he said. "I help people.

"These places we work in," said Mr. Alwadish, "are not exactly places you would go to make friends. We are still mammals. We get crazy in lines when we are all crammed together. The New York mentality is to keep moving, and waiting even for five minutes can drive someone nuts. My business would not be so successful anywhere else in the world."

The twenty-nine-year-old Mr. Alwadish started the business seven years ago with a $1,900 investment, and he has seen it grow to three offices, in Rockefeller Center, at Penn Plaza and on East 47th Street.

"I only wish I could open offices behind the Iron Curtain," he said. "Do you see pictures of the lines there?"

As the service becomes more and more popular, lines have actually been observed at Services Unlimited. "Everyone comes at lunchtime," Mr. Alwadish said defensively. "What am I supposed to do? They wait five minutes maximum. OK, maybe eight minutes. Ten at the absolute most."

As Lenny Dibari stood in line at the motor vehicles bureau, people around him were reading books, listening to cassette tapes, knitting sweaters and learning a variety of foreign languages. Sharon Upchurch had a book titled *Learning French*, and she said that thanks to the motor vehicles bureau, she has.

Several people listened curiously as Mr. Dibari talked about how he finds standing in line relaxing and about having met many of his friends in lines, including a young woman he is still seeing. He did admit to occasionally becoming bored and to not liking to stand in line on his own time. "Aha!" said a colleague in line, Laura Miles.

Mr. Dibari told exciting tales of fistfights he had seen when people tried to jump in line. He let others in this line in on some tricks of the trade, such as having someone hold his place while he runs across the street to get a copy of a death certificate, as he had just done. He had used the excuse of having to make a telephone call.

After listening to Mr. Dibari, one woman in the line concluded, "I still think that you have the worst job in the world."

But then, she did not know about a new job Mr. Alwadish is creating at Services Unlimited. The job is to take documents to Albany every day on the bus.

TOURISTS WHO
STOP AT NOTHING

Leading his family on a forced march through Manhattan, Tom Sparacio of Snohomish, Washington, looked over his shoulder to announce that the next stop on their sightseeing tour was the New York Stock Exchange. His six-year-old son, Jeff, could not wait to see the cows and pigs.

This is tourist season in New York, a time when an inordinate number of pedestrians seem to be looking up and walking into things, when people with cameras around their necks can be seen greeting total strangers on the subways, when New Yorkers are asked to open their couches to visitors and when even hot-dog vendors and pigeons are expected to pose for family albums.

The first man in Budweiser logo shorts has been sighted in Times Square. "We're going to the Empire State Building," said the man, Earl Williams of Kansas City, Missouri, who also wore an Atlantic City T-shirt. "Then my wife wants to go to '21' for lunch." Mr. Williams said he had no reservation. "21" might.

With maps unfurled and two cameras at the ready, the Sparacio family scampered through New York, having allotted one day to see the city on their trip East. Mr. Sparacio, his wife, Rozaine, their sixteen-year-old daughter, Trish, and their two sons, Ted, fourteen, and Jeff, rose at 6:00 A.M. in Philadelphia and arrived in Pennsylvania Station on an early train. Mrs. Sparacio observed the hordes of commuters and uttered, "Oh, God."

"It's just so big and foreign to us," Mr. Sparacio said. "It's like if a New Yorker came out to climb Mount Pilchuck." The Sparacios were not about to travel by subway, not yet. They observed others catching yellow taxis, much as New Yorkers might watch Snohomish residents angling for brown trout, before hooking a taxi themselves to Battery Park to see Mr. Sparacio's top priority of the trip, the Statue of Liberty.

He bounded ashore on Liberty Island, climbing the steps of the statue's 142-foot pedestal, then the steep, narrow, 168-step steel staircase to the crown. Halfway up, Trish announced that the statue was not *her* first priority; Macy's was. Mr. Sparacio, who is in the sheet-metal business, marveled at the statue's construction. His wife said her legs hurt. Mr. Sparacio looked over at Ellis Island and said his grandfather had arrived there from Sicily in 1899.

Arriving at the World-Trade Center, the Sparacios did what they were supposed to do: They stood outside and gawked for a few minutes, and after reaching the top, they remarked that the people 110 stories below looked "like ants."

Much to their mother's dismay, the children made a beeline for the souvenir shop, perusing everything from the phosphorescent NEW YORK CITY pillowcases that looked like they would make sleeping impossible, to T-shirts exclaiming I RODE ON A NEW YORK CITY SUBWAY . . . AND SURVIVED!

On their way to the stock exchange, they happened upon a convenient display of New York street life assembled in a tiny park. They saw street musicians and vendors selling tube socks and strawberry incense. They passed up an opportunity to get rich quick playing three-card monte.

From a large assortment of pushcart foods – from papaya drink to Tofu-zert – the Sparacios chose traditional hot dogs for lunch, devouring them while continuing their quick pace. "Alexander Hamilton is buried there," Mr. Sparacio shouted, never breaking stride while passing the Trinity Church cemetery.

The sidewalks of Wall Street were packed and nearly impassable. "Does everyone in New York just walk around all day?" asked Mrs. Sparacio. "Why aren't they working?"

Having seen a recent television show about the Brooklyn Bridge, Mrs. Sparacio was able to explain to Trish on their walk across it what exactly was "so hot about it, anyway," as Trish had wanted to know. But the children most appreciated the man roller-skating across while listening to a Walkman radio and juggling several balls.

"New York is expensive," another tourist, Dorothy Sholeen of Ithaca, New York, commented to them, "but the best part is looking at people and buildings." Indeed, Jeff's favorite sight was "that man with the neat Mohawk haircut." Trish liked "the strange clothes people wear and all the limousines." On a ten-day vacation, the family expected to spend about $3,500, but they would spend less than $50 in New York.

"This is where representatives of all nations come together to insure peace," Mrs. Sparacio told the children as their taxi sped past the United Nations. "It doesn't work."

Bloomingdale's was next, where they went up seven flights of escalators, back down and out the door. Trish checked the price tag on a blouse marked $178 and exclaimed, "Wait till I tell my friends." A woman tried to squirt "an exciting new fragrance" on Mrs. Sparacio, who recoiled in the nick of time.

"There's nothing where we live," said Trish. But her excitement at detecting the scent of horses as she neared Central Park betrayed her. She has a horse at home named Cinnamon. The children petted the carriage horses and tried to grab bullfrogs, which they were surprised to find in a pond one hundred yards from Fifth Avenue.

"Seen enough?" asked Mr. Sparacio, and they were off, swerving into Tiffany's to ogle a $21,000 diamond necklace.

Joining a group of jaywalkers, Mr. Sparacio said, "They arrest people for this in Seattle," and added with a touch of pride, "we're catching on fast."

He thought they were ready for the subway now, and Mrs. Sparacio nearly squeezed the blood from Jeff's hand as they descended into the strange and pungent world below. Asking directions, they caught an E train back to Penn Station.

"People are less rude and more helpful than I expected," said Mr. Sparacio. Samuel Silverman, a New Yorker, explained: "This is a big city. We're all tourists to some extent."

"This is New York, Jeff," said Mrs. Sparacio, riding the rush-hour subway train. "Squished." Noting an advertising message

headlined IS RIDING THE SUBWAYS THE ONLY ADVENTURE IN
YOUR LIFE? Mr. Sparacio, who was trying to keep his feet, commented, "This is adventure enough for us.

"It's regrettable," said Mr. Sparacio, arriving at Penn Station,
"that we don't have more time."

"At least we can say we've been here," said Mrs. Sparacio,
who had the Instamatic snapshots to prove it. All admitted to
exhaustion after their sightseeing steeplechase, except Jeff. He
announced that he might stay up until 3:00 A.M., then fell over
sideways in his Amtrak seat, to sleep, to dream, to wake up in
Philadelphia.

LITTERERS, COMPLAINERS, THE VERY RUDE . . .

THE LITTERATI

PEOPLE EVERYWHERE LITTER, of course, but there are those in New York who seem to regard it as an inalienable right.

"It's a free country," said Reginald Stuart after tossing his coffee cup into the gutter yesterday, delivering his proclamation in Times Square as resoundingly as a founding father at the Constitutional Convention.

Other New Yorkers practice littering as a civic duty: "New York has always been dirty," said a young man tossing a crumpled paper bag onto Seventh Avenue, a young man belonging to a new generation of litterers to whom the torch has been passed.

Still other New Yorkers regard littering as a moral responsibility: "It gives them a job," said another Times Square litterer, Dick Jamieson, referring to city sanitation workers.

At 11:00 A.M. George Baskins and Louis Pepe, enforcement agents with the city's Department of Sanitation, showed up in Times Square to issue summonses that carry $50 fines for littering as part of the city's latest offensive in the unending war on litter. They had their work cut out for them.

"I hate you! I hate you! I hate you!" Maria Bershad shouted at Mr. Baskins as he issued her a summons for throwing down one of those handbills that are always being shoved into pedestrians' hands.

"It's getting hot now," said Mr. Baskins, who had just finished ticketing Michael Ramsay for the same offense. Mr. Ramsay also did not view the summons with equanimity, showering Mr. Baskins with curses.

"I won't pay," said Mr. Ramsay. "No way. They're going to have to build jails the size of this city if you start giving tickets to litterers." He crossed Seventh Avenue, ripped up the pink ticket and deposited the pieces in a trash receptacle.

Some people will fight for their right to litter. Mr. Baskins said he has been assaulted in the line of duty. This day, he works one corner of 42nd Street and Seventh Avenue, and Mr. Pepe works another, while Officer Michael Roberts, a sanitation policeman armed with a pistol and nightstick and wearing a bullet-proof vest, looks on. He came running when Mr. Ramsay protested vociferously.

On a day of light and scattered litter, only thirteen summonses were issued at four locations in Manhattan to people Mayor Koch is calling "litterpigs" in his antilitter offensive.

The agents said they had heard a wide range of excuses for litter falling to the ground, from holes in pockets to sudden attacks of arthritis. There were wide-ranging stylistic differences. Some New Yorkers crumple their litter and drop it stealthily, others do it as an act of defiance, while still others toss it as innocently as a flower girl tosses rose petals at a wedding.

"Everybody throws stuff on the ground," complained a thirteen-year-old boy when Mr. Baskins told him he could have been fined.

Not everybody, actually. "Standing here gives me great faith in New Yorkers," said Mr. Baskins. "For every one who litters, a thousand go by here who don't." Mr. Baskins said he has seen, in Montreal and Toronto, just how clean a city can be. "It hurts me," said the Queens resident, "to think visitors are going home and telling people how dirty my city is."

"New York is a uniquely dirty city," said Donald Rechtenwald, a passerby. "People here have developed a tolerance for it and accept it."

Mr. Baskins is not so sure. He doesn't know why New York has so much litter, but he noted that there were more people at the moment in Times Square than attend the Super Bowl and recalled what a stadium looks like after a sporting event.

"A hundred people wait at the corner," said Mr. Pepe, "and when the light changes, they go and there are gum and candy and cigarette wrappers. Who dropped them? Who can say?"

Officer Roberts came running again when Isaac Folder took umbrage at Mr. Pepe's issuing him a summons for throwing down the leg bone of a Kentucky Fried Chicken and an empty bottle wrapped in a brown bag.

"A chicken leg," argued Mr. Folder, "is not litter."

"I agree," said a passerby, one of those New Yorkers who don't mind taking a little time out to join a fray, any fray.

"I have no respect for that man," commented another passerby, in reference to Mr. Folder. "Dropping litter in front of a cop is as stupid as robbing a bank next to a police station."

E. Crawford, accompanying Mr. Folder and serving as a second in his duel of words, pointed out to the litter agent that no trash receptacle was available nearby.

There were fifty-six thousand wire-mesh trash receptacles in New York in 1968, and there are about ninety-five hundred now. They are crunched in garbage trucks, and they are stolen by the thousands every year and used in the most creative ways, city officials say: as lobster traps, clam bakers, three-card-monte tables, basketball hoops and leaf burners.

Different solutions to the problem have been tried, including receptacles with 470-pound concrete bases that proved extremely difficult to empty.

"A chicken bone is not litter," Mr. Folder said again. "Certainly not. We shall see you in court."

"Is this New York?" said another passerby. "People getting tickets for littering? Excuse me, I have to pinch myself." He did and was on his way.

FETED
WITH TRASH

AFTER BEING CHEERED by the multitudes in the Los Angeles Coliseum, praised by the President in a personal audience and treated to ceremonial exaltation in our nation's capital, America's Olympic medalists are to be honored by the City of New York today with the traditional tossing of tons of trash on their heads from high buildings.

"Odd custom," said Richard Gaines, a tourist from London visiting Wall Street yesterday. Maybe so, but New York has so honored its conquering heroes since the first ticker tape was tossed out a window in the financial district and landed on Theodore Roosevelt during a parade honoring him in 1910.

"It's the least we can do to show our appreciation," said Roseanna Nuciforo, an employee of E. F. Hutton, who was collecting all manner of scrap paper yesterday to throw out the window at the 221 Olympic stars marching in a ticker-tape parade at noon today up Broadway from Battery Park to City Hall.

A coworker, Carolyn Roskoski, a veteran of many ticker-tape parades, was showing others in the office the proper technique for heaving a heavy pile of computer printouts so that they unfurl. "You have to kind of whip it, like this," she said.

"The athletes are heroes and deserve our recognition," said Louis Mammolito, a Sanitation Department employee who will help clean up the garbage of glory. "Naturally, I think there must be some other way."

He and other Sanitation Department employees reminisced yesterday about great moments in ticker-tape parade cleanup.

"The Mets parade in 1969 was the worst," Mr. Mammolito contended, referring to the parade after the team won the World Series. "The stuff was a foot deep."

The Department of Sanitation keeps records ("for planning purposes?" one department official guessed) on the amount of trash thrown during ticker-tape parades that date back to Charles Lindbergh's parade on June 13, 1927. Records show that 1,254.6 tons of debris were thrown at the '69 Mets, an all-time sports-team record.

Purists might argue, however, that the Mets' trash was "wetted trash" — damp trash — and that 30 percent of the weight should have been deducted, making it roughly equivalent to the 971 tons of trash heaped upon America's former hostages (held in Iran) during the city's last ticker-tape parade on January 30, 1981.

So, others might argue, why didn't the wetness factor help Pope John Paul II, for example, who compiled a paltry forty-three tons in a driving rain on October 3, 1979? Not to mention Van Cliburn, who drew a measly half ton of trash in 1958 and — perhaps not incidentally — was the last pianist honored with a parade. Apologists for classical music point out that 1958 was a bad year for trash, noting that leaders of West Germany and the Philippines also only recorded but a half ton each that year.

In 1962, with President John F. Kennedy whipping up enthusiasm for the space program, John Glenn, Jr., set the all-time trash mark with 3,474 tons, and Gordon Cooper followed that with 2,900 tons in 1963. Some aficionados of trash argue that Mr. Glenn's record is tainted by the infamous "long route" controversy, similar to the "long count" controversy in the Dempsey–Tunney fight, because Mr. Glenn's parade route was longer than that followed by many other heroes.

A two-day celebration of V-J Day resulted in a cleanup on August 14, 1945, of 5,438 tons of trash, transcending all previous notions of litter.

"It is difficult to compare records," said Vito Turso, a spokesman for the Sanitation Department, "because of factors such as the length of route, weather conditions, the disappearance of ticker tape and modern buildings with windows that don't open. In the old days, 1938, even Wrong-Way Corrigan compiled ninteen hundred tons."

Indeed, because computers have made ticker tape obsolete on Wall Street, 250 miles of donated ticker tape is being trucked in from the Trans-Lux Corporation, in Norwalk, Connecticut, which manufactures the tape. The mayor's office distributed 145 thirty-gallon bags of tape, confetti and other donated paper debris to forty office buildings on Lower Broadway yesterday. "It is somewhat embarrassing when enough debris is not thrown," said Tom Kelly, a City Hall spokesman.

Midtown boasts ample trash for a parade, and it seems that only tradition and the proximity to City Hall keep the parades on the stretch of Broadway that has come to be known as "The Canyon of Heroes." Here, thirty-five ticker-tape parades have been held for such returning heroes as Lindbergh, Eisenhower, Neil Armstrong, the 1969 Mets and the 1978 Yankees.

In addition to windows that don't open and a lack of ticker tape, rising cleanup costs have threatened ticker-tape parades. To cut costs, none were held from the Mets' parade in 1969 until the Yankees' World Series parade in 1978, although officials patently endorsed the throwing of trash at the queen of England on a 1976 visit.

During recent ticker-tape parades, workers in modern buildings with windows that don't open have crowded on rooftops to throw rolls of toilet paper and computer printouts and cards. "They throw a lot of other stuff, too," said Mr. Turso.

After the parade for the hostages, sanitation workers noted that quite a number of hats had been exuberantly thrown, as well as many shoes, flags, jackets and several bag lunches. Some wastebaskets were emptied, and Mr. Turso said that there was evidence to suggest that building-maintenance people tossed their garbage off a few buildings so that they would not have to pay private carting concerns to pick it up.

The Olympians are not expected to set any new records today. "But don't count them out," said Angelo Bruno, another Sanitation Department worker. "There has been a great upsurge in patriotism in this country that should result in a tremendous outpouring of trash."

THE NEW YORK CITY
COMPLAINT DEPARTMENT

SOME PEOPLE COMING into the office are so mad they can barely speak; others casually drop by just to mention what a dirty, crowded, dangerous and dehumanizing city New York is. "Thanks for listening," one complainant chirped yesterday on his way out.

This is New York City's complaint department, if one can imagine the magnitude of the concept.

The office, at 61 Chambers Street, is formally known as the Mayor's Action Center, where about five hundred complaints are lodged every day — more on cold, rainy Mondays, when people are in foul moods, and fewer on warm, sunny spring days such as yesterday. The full moon makes for a stranger brand of complaints, the office employees say.

It is a matter of policy, the office director, Kate H. Klein, said during yesterday's relative lull, that no sharp objects — indeed, no objects of any kind, including letter openers, paperweights or staplers — are to be placed on the countertop, where they might be used against employees of the City of New York.

Sometimes, of course, complainants bring their own weapons, such as the tepid chicken noodle soup that one malcontent poured over Mrs. Klein's head. She has an emergency button to push that alerts the police to trouble.

Complaints range from callers saying they just cannot put up with life in New York any longer and are about to commit suicide to those who want to let the mayor know that actors in a play on

Broadway are saying bad words. A lot of the complainers add for good measure that the civil servants listening to their complaints are probably corrupt, like everybody else in city government.

"But when we solve a problem," Mrs. Klein said, "people are grateful. Some even send flowers. Now, I have to call the Board of Ethics, to see if I can keep them."

She told of one grateful man who had demanded to treat her to dinner. "I told him the guidelines would only permit me to accept a five-dollar dinner," she said, "and that, frankly, I wouldn't want to eat such a thing."

Those answering the incessantly ringing telephones often receive complaints they can do nothing about. If there is a complaint about roaches at a restaurant, for example, the agency immediately notifies the Health Department. But people call to complain about their children not doing their homework and also about dropping too many bombs on Libya, or not enough. New Yorkers can be very provincial sometimes, and there are apparently those who believe it was the New York City Air Force that did the bombing.

"When you can't promise to stop the bombing," Mrs. Klein said, "that's usually when they say, 'Oh well, you're all on the take.'

"They'll call," she added, "and say that the neighbor's dog is barking or the neighbor is playing the stereo too loudly, and they want the mayor to do something about it. I ask if they've tried talking nicely to the neighbor about the problem, and they say, 'Hmmm, that's an interesting idea.'"

"The mayor is seen as a father figure in New York," the deputy director of the office, Jane Huntley, said. "People want Koch to speak to a son or daughter about being tardy at school."

Trying to talk to the mayor, they say: "Is Ed in? He asked me to call," or, "This the mayor's sister," or, "This is Mrs. Koch, his wife."

Ms. Huntley said people have called complaining of bills they have received for elevator inspections in their one-story homes; about their cars having been towed, in contradiction to all notions of justice, in their opinions; about cabdrivers who have charged $60 a person for a ride from the airport and about the light bulb in the hallway having burned out.

"The longer I'm here," an office employee, Kim Andrews, said, "the more I come to realize that people have got to do more for themselves. They want government to take responsibility for every aspect of their lives."

People call complaining that Mayor Koch dresses too casually or call to correct his grammar. "One woman who loves him," Mrs. Andrews said, "calls to complain that he looks too heavy or too thin and to remind him to exercise."

Mrs. Klein insists on courtesy and compassion from her employees but does not mind an infusion of common sense once in a while. When a mother asked Mrs. Andrews, who has three children and lives in the East Flatbush section of Brooklyn, to have the city intervene in the case of her eleven-year-old son, who would not go to school, Mrs. Andrews told the woman that she is the boy's mother and that it is darned well up to her to see that he goes to school.

Another caller complained day after day about the landlord, and finally Mrs. Andrews told the caller, "It's time you got off your rusty dusty and took your landlord to court!"

Judging from the volume of complaints, Mrs. Klein believes that the biggest problem facing New York is affordable housing. "We hear from the woman and her three kids living for months and months in one room at a welfare hotel," she said. "We have to tell people in need that there are 170,000 eligible applicants on the public-housing waiting list.

"There are the homeless people that we call the 'undomiciled,'" she said. "There are the elderly people on fixed incomes who get evicted."

Although she described the complaint flow yesterday as "light to moderate," Mrs. Klein's telephone console was a blaze of flashing lights. She answered one line, and the caller had this to say: "You are an idiot." Click. That would be a miscellaneous complaint on the tally sheets Mrs. Klein keeps, with categories reading lead poisoning, hot water, food stamps, litter, playground repairs, illegal parking, abandoned cars, potholes, subways, cave-ins, burned-out street lights, rude cabdrivers, dogs, prostitutes, drug addicts and so on down the litany of urban problems.

Some of the complaints, according to one employee, are not really legitimate complaints. She said newcomers, in particular, often mistake some intolerable condition in New York for something out of the ordinary that needs correcting.

COURTESY – A
SIGN OF WEAKNESS

"**I** HAVE ALWAYS CONSIDERED courtesy a sign of weakness," said Buford Davis, a former cabdriver who now sells hot dogs from a cart outside the New York Hilton.

The Association for a Better New York (ABNY) is starting a campaign to teach cabdrivers, bellhops, waiters, street vendors, bank tellers and other service employees to be polite – not rude – to visitors.

This seems clearly to be one of the greatest mass thought-modification efforts since Mao took power in China.

One of Mr. Davis's customers on the Avenue of the Americas made this comment about the program: "Lots of luck on that one." Another asked if electroshock treatments would be used in the program, adding: "That's a tough breed to train."

This "New York Loves You" campaign is part of a larger effort promoting tourism – a $7 billion industry – in New York, a city that has, as some of those running the campaign recognized, "an image problem" when it comes to courtesy. One of them said a survey showed that residents of the city were perceived by outsiders as "unfriendly, rude and downright nasty."

Alphonse Salomone, the chairman of the courtesy committee for the overall tourism effort, acknowledged how huge the task was. "We are lighting candles," he said. An executive of one hotel chain said, however, that the image of New York is already better than it was ten years ago: "Japanese executives told me," he said, "that [then] they were given send-offs to New York by weeping relatives similar to those given to kamikaze pilots."

"It's stunning," said Mary Holloway of ABNY. "The first few days you are out of New York on a trip you notice people are so polite and friendly that you are downright suspicious of them. Even in France they seem friendly compared to New York."

The owners of Morgans, a recently opened hotel in midtown, said they hired an entirely middle-western staff to insure a polite and courteous staff.

"We come by our rudeness naturally," remarked a street-corner falafel salesman. "We live in a city that is rude to us — the noise, the dirt, the subways."

Other New Yorkers agreed that to make New Yorkers behave courteously, the environment must be changed, that it is the fast pace and the crush of the masses that make New Yorkers brusque.

Marcia Skyers, a chipper, young information-booth clerk in a midtown hotel, said politeness is more difficult in a city where one can experience rush-hour battle fatigue by the time one arrives at work. Mrs. Holloway noted that against all these odds, one can be a hero by being polite. She recalled applause for a courteous bus driver and items on the 11:00 news about cabdrivers returning purses.

Some New Yorkers described the campaign to make New Yorkers polite as so much tilting at windmills, and others said that New Yorkers' rudeness was "overrated." A cabdriver in front of the New York Hilton said that people were not rude to him, that he was not rude to them and that at the slightest hint of rudeness, he would sock them in the nose. Another cabby in line suggested that he would throttle anyone who tried to give him manners lessons.

Service employees throughout the city said out-of-towners are forever expressing their shock and surprise at the courtesy given them.

"You can't be from New York." Bo Fritz, who works on the observation deck at the Empire State Building, said that is what visitors to New York always tell him when he is nice. He has to admit that his hometown is Valley Forge, Pennsylvania.

Doris Scadron, a cashier in a midtown hotel, has to admit to them that although she was born here, she was raised in California. John Sim, a bell captain, answers: "You're right. I'm not a New Yorker. I'm from Brooklyn."

Murray Albin, the Hilton doorman for twenty-two years, said he had recently traveled to Chicago, San Francisco and Los Angeles, and he seemed pleased to report that people there were rude, too.

Mr. Fritz recently completed the first of the courtesy seminars, which includes a training film and workshops. The training film touches on the nobility of courtesy, but the theme is that courtesy pays financial rewards.

"Please let us know if we can be of further assistance," says the film's bellhop after receiving his tip, and the guest says, "Wait a minute," and hands him more bills.

After the film, seminar participants turn to their workbooks, entitled "Skills That Show Visitors New York Loves You." One of the skills involves greeting visitors – with a smile, good grooming and a good attitude. "They really ask a lot," remarked one bellhop. Another skill is personalizing the approach. "You've chosen a wonderful show," says the woman who is a ticket agent in the workbook. "You'll be humming the music when I see you tomorrow."

"Frankly, I think people would wonder what is wrong with this woman," commented the veteran bellhop.

... AND OTHER
NEW YORK
INSTITUTIONS

ABANDONED CARS AND A MIRACLE ON 104TH STREET: A CAR GOES UNSTOLEN

A LATE-MODEL Volkswagen Rabbit — No Rust, Runs Good! — is parked on Broadway at 104th Street with the keys in it, if you'd like one. It has been sitting there, unlocked, for eight days.

"Amazing!" said Kay Demetriou, a barber, looking at the car outside his Broadway Barber Shop.

"Unprecedented," a customer said very carefully, as Mr. Demetriou shaved him with a straight razor.

"Cars are routinely stolen here," Mr. Demetriou said. "Some men went by here with a shopping cart the other day, stealing one car battery after another."

The continued presence of this car, which by all New York laws of antisocial behavior should have been stolen *days* ago, has astonished many in this neighborhood and has left many residents searching for answers.

"I think leaving the keys in the ignition has thrown them off," said Ronnie Douglas, a twentyish neighborhood resident, referring to some apparent confusion and consternation on the part of local car thieves and vandals.

He stood on the corner Monday night about 10:00 P.M. as two young men slowly circled the car, kicking the tires and running their hands over the upholstery as if they were on a used car lot.

Many others have stopped to examine the car, looking under the hood, sitting behind the wheel and coming into the shop to ask Mr. Demetriou about it, as if he were a used car salesman. He can sound like one, too, noting that the car would cost $12,000 new, and adding: "It's in good condition. There is no reason not to steal it."

It is young Mr. Douglas's understanding that the car has been taken for at least one "test drive" by teenagers, after which it was returned, undamaged. The car was also moved by the driver of a vegetable truck, who found the car in the way of his deliveries. The keys were in the ignition for several days, then were missing for a few days, but were back yesterday.

A police officer stopped by last week to ask Mr. Demetriou what he knew about the car, which is parked in a bus zone, but the officer seems to have dropped the case.

"The owner parked it there last Tuesday," Mr. Demetriou explained. When he came back Wednesday there were tickets on the car. He put the tickets into a bag, put the license plates in the bag and scraped off the registration and inspection stickers. Then he put the keys in the ignition and announced, "Anyone who wants it can have it."

Mr. Douglas's companion said he had heard that the owner of the car was fed up with trying to keep a car in New York and had complained that there was nowhere affordable to park, no way to keep a radio in a car and no way to get through all the traffic. "He'd just had enough," the boy said.

There are already folktales about the car. According to another youth on the corner, there are rumors the car was left with the keys in it by the police as a setup for car thieves. Another is that the car was used by the Mafia in some awful crime — maybe even a rubout.

"There has to be some explanation why this car has been left alone," Mr. Douglas said.

Others theorize that maybe if the owner had locked the car and not left the keys in it, then somebody would have stolen it. That's the way most people get their cars stolen.

And if the owner wanted to just abandon the car, they said he should have taken it to the shoulder of an expressway, stripped it and set it on fire, in accordance with traditional car abandonment customs and guidelines.

The consensus in the barbershop is that the man should at least have left the car on the other side of the street, the east side of Broadway, if he truly wanted it stolen or disassembled. "This is the nice side of the street," said Mr. Demetriou, who has been cutting hair here since World War II and is considered an expert on the neighborhood's social dynamics.

Dressed in his working whites and carrying his clippers, Mr. Demetriou walked out of the store, pushed the button on the trunk and said: "Can you imagine that the spare tire is still here!"

Not even minor signs of vandalism showed up until Monday. The door on the driver's side appears now to have been forced open, probably by some veteran New York car thief who would never have thought to see if the door was simply unlocked.

Some graffiti has been written on the side of the car in grease pencil by the Department of Transportation, indicating that the car may be towed away someday.

If not, barbershop patrons speculate that some homeless street person may soon take up residence in the vehicle.

The troubled patrons wonder about the meaning of all this. Is this an isolated oversight on the part of some neighborhood criminals, or does it signal some significant change in the New York crime scene, a change in the social fabric of the neighborhood or even a profound change in our nation's youth?

The consensus in the venerable barbershop seems to be that it is just one of those freaks of nature, like a five-legged cow: A car was left unlocked in New York for eight days in 1987 with the keys in it and nobody stole it. Seriously.

POTHOLE PRIDE

DONALD MAXWELL, LIKE a lot of other New Yorkers, believes that the city offers the very best and the very worst of everything.

He takes a perverse pride in New York's potholes, for example, and said he was upset this week by Mayor Ed Koch's announcement that Operation Asphalt, the city's latest offensive against potholes, had been "a tremendous success" and was ending.

Had all New York potholes been eradicated? Mr. Maxwell wondered. Could he never again match pothole stories with his brother-in-law in Pittsburgh? Mr. Maxwell would say such things to his brother-in-law as "That's nothing; a garbage truck fell into a pothole on the FDR Drive." And his brother-in-law would reply, "I didn't know New York had garbage trucks."

Well, Mr. Maxwell said his mother always told him not to worry, and sure enough, two days after the mayor's announcement this week, Mr. Maxwell's car hit a huge pothole, blowing out the tire, bending the wheel rim and throwing the front end out of line. He said that he felt better now, no longer worried about a pothole shortfall in New York.

Mr. Maxwell, who was out getting a few estimates at the cavalcade of auto repair shops on Queens Boulevard, considers New York to be the Bordeaux region, the Château Lafite-Rothschild of potholes. He said that he has lived in Boston, Dallas and

Philadelphia and that "New York's potholes are the biggest and the best."

"They are something special," said Eldan Avner, a cabdriver. Mr. Avner pointed out that New York has registered potholes, referring to the 750,000 potholes cataloged and reported to the city by the Big Apple Pothole and Sidewalk Protection Corporation, a private enterprise that sprang from a law stating that the city is liable for damages caused only by registered potholes.

New York potholes have been exported to foreign countries. Plaster casts of New York potholes were made by the manufacturer of Jaguar automobiles to be exported and re-created on test tracks in England. "The feeling is," said Michael Cook, a spokesman for Jaguar Cars, Inc., "that New York has the finest in the world."

New York's potholes are scientifically measured and studied. The Automobile Club of New York developed a "joltmeter" to measure the bumpiness of city streets. The needle moves on graph paper through these categories: smooth, uncomfortable, bumpy, jarring, teeth rattling and impossible. Then, there are the *really* big potholes that are measured by the breakdown of the equipment.

A spokesman for the auto club said this week that the condition of New York's sixty-two hundred miles of streets is improved. But Mr. Avner said that his measuring device is his head and that the frequency with which it hits the top of the cab indicates that New York's roads are "painful."

"Some streets have holes," he said. "Others look like hot lava has poured down in many levels. Others are wavy and almost make you seasick. Women try to put on lipstick and mascara in my cab," Mr. Avner said. "They get out looking like some kind of Indian.

"Just by saying that the streets are better," he added, "the mayor cannot make them so." Another cabdriver asserted that potholes are good for the economy, something that proprietors of automobile-repair shops along Queens Boulevard would not deny.

"You don't watch for potholes around here," said Raza

Manji, assistant manager of East Coast Auto Repair. "You watch for a little roadway between them."

Tony Blasi, who was having his tank filled with gas at Al's Tire on Queens Boulevard, looked at a young boy bringing in three shiny hubcaps and said, "Mmmm, looks like you got some nice ones there."

The boy, Richard Davis, said he does not have to steal hubcaps. He picks up the ones knocked off by potholes, brings them in and sells them to Al Unger, who in turn sells them to people with cars that lost their hubcaps when they hit potholes.

Mr. Blasi said he knows a man who is about to become engaged to a woman he met at a pothole on the West Side of Manhattan. The man stopped to help the woman when she had a flat tire. Still, Mr. Blasi and others stopped short of accepting the idea that New York's potholes are inherently romantic.

"When you aren't hitting potholes," said Bill Amalfitano, checking the rate for a front-end alignment at East Coast Auto Repair, "you're sitting in a traffic jam caused by the repair crews."

The city crews that fill potholes say motorists curse them for holding up traffic, and they recall incidents of workers being punched.

"New Yorkers are very impatient," said Rosario LaMalfa, a foreman with the Bureau of Highway Operations. As he said that, two men walked past cones set up around a work area and straight across asphalt that his crew was spreading on a pothole at First Avenue and 15th Street. "And when we block a whole street so we can work," he said, "they drive on the sidewalks."

Mr. LaMalfa, a thirty-two-year veteran, held the attention of the younger men when he spoke of a pothole back about twenty-five years ago at 42nd Street and Third Avenue, where "half the street fell in – it was something to see."

"Technically, that was a cave-in, not a pothole," said a spokesman for the Department of Transportation, charged with filling the city's potholes.

"There aren't many unfilled potholes," he asserted. "Potholes can only be caused by freezing and thawing. The rest of these things are actually what we call 'cylindrical depressions,' and sinkholes, cutholes, washboards, push-ups, cave-ins and so on."

ROACHES

I<small>F</small> N<small>EW</small> Y<small>ORKERS</small> happen to awake tonight to some high-pitched snickering out in the kitchen, they needn't bother getting up. It's probably just the cockroaches reading the first edition of the morning paper.

A tactical public-relations squadron, spearheaded by "a top, eminent entomologist" virtually surrounded by publicity agents, swept into New York yesterday, carrying the good word to city residents, via radio, television and newspapers, that their worries are finally over, cockroach-wise, that finally there is an insect-control device to completely eradicate the little . . . . devils, shall we say.

People do this – come to New York and announce the ultimate victory over roaches – from time to time. The roaches have earned the right to chuckle. Now celebrating their 350 millionth year on earth, despite man's best efforts to kill them off or at least make them an endangered species, they occupy a preeminent position as unofficial mascot of the City of New York.

"I have to admit they are rather amazing," said Dr. Austin Frishman, the respected entomologist heading yesterday's publicity mission and a professor who taught entomology at the State University Agricultural and Technical College in Farmingdale, Long Island, for seventeen years.

Dr. Frishman pointed out that the little critters can taste poison without ingesting it and, by sending warning signals directly to their six legs, bypassing the brain, they can be off and running in 0.054 second.

He is impressed with their ability not only to develop immunity rapidly to new wonder pesticides but also to alter their behavior to elude humans. Dr. Frishman visited a few office buildings before hitting the news-conference trail yesterday and found that the roaches of today are moving into computers, smoke alarms, microwave ovens and Mr. Coffee machines — places that haven't been sprayed.

"Humans suffer from the Baseboard Syndrome," he explained. "We spray the baseboards, and the roaches move to the clocks, lamps and ceilings."

He admires their ability to go weeks without food or water, to collapse their wings and hide in tiny spaces. Cockroaches are accustomed to being bugged by humans, from the time of sharing caves to today's sharing of condominiums. The tempestuous relationship between the German cockroach and the American people continues.

The people in the white lab coats are bombarding them with radiation these days and putting them on treadmills, giving them hormones to induce attacks in their little hearts, hacking off their legs and heads to see what that might do and dangling them before predatory lizards.

Scientists have tried tampering with their reproductive and respiratory systems — and even with their sex lives. We can't really nuke them, because it turns out they're rather impervious to radiation.

Although the Geneva Convention did not address the issue, some of the scientists' methods seem a bit out of bounds, such as feeding them hydroprene, which causes homosexuality among the adult males.

Yale University has produced synthetic cockroach aphrodisiac-periplanone-B — which causes male roaches to go into a sexual frenzy, standing on their hind legs and beating their wings wildly for several minutes until their antennas break and their wings are tattered. That may be fun to watch, but it only works on American cockroaches, while the German cockroaches — the most prevalent variety in New York – are cleaning out the cupboards.

The new product Dr. Frishman was here to endorse is called Combat, invented by American Cyanamid in Princeton, New Jersey. It is a small feeding station, shaped like a pinwheel, that looks like fun, where the cockroaches nibble on a snack made of oatmeal, corn syrup and a dash of amidinohydrazone. Field tests show that roaches, like humans, just don't bother reading product labels.

"New Yorkers must not give up!" Dr. Frishman said, although acknowledging that New York – where the smell of roach spray in April, the opening of roach season, hangs as heavily in the air as the honeysuckle (and the paper processing plants) in Savannah – may well be the roach capital of America.

He recalled being on a flight when a woman told a man that a cockroach was crawling on his seat. The man questioned whether it was really a cockroach, and the woman replied smugly, "Look, I'm from New York."

New Yorkers tend to accept a certain number of roaches in their lives, Dr. Frishman said, but need not. He said that he has actually seen a New Yorker hit an exterminator over the head for trying to kill a cockroach the person considered a pet. Some have given their roaches names and others have said they have rather enjoyed meeting their little friends in the kitchen for late-night snacks.

Dr. Frishman isn't laughing. "I have devoted my life to the household pest," he explained. He doesn't look like a man to trifle with. He wears a string tie with a scorpion tie clasp and a belt buckle adorned with a scorpion and crossed pistols.

Roaches have bedeviled him all his life. He said that in one case someone gave up on the roach problem and burned down his home. Others have used flamethrowers to rid their homes of roaches, he said, and still others leave the lights on all night. He knows New Yorkers who buy lizards to eat the roaches and others who keep rubber mallets in the kitchen.

He grows silent for a moment, shaking his head, then mutters, "We'll never, never get rid of them all, of course."

But he brightened a moment later as he told of watching roaches being killed off by Combat. "With every other product they flip over on their backs," he said enthusiastically, a demonic smile creeping over his face and his hands gesturing. "But with this one they go straight down on their noses, like this. There is a thrill, a joy. . . ." Easy, professor, easy.

FUNNY
SMELLS . . .

YOU CAN HELP Annette, or you can turn the page.

Annette Green is hyperosmic. There are times when it seems a measure of fate's cruelty that she must live in New York. Hyperosmia, you see, is a somewhat heightened sense of smell. New York, she says, is the nation's most pungent city.

Ms. Green, who is executive director of the Fragrance Foundation and author of *The Forgotten Nose*, is concerned, as one might expect, about the aroma of New York and is forever urging others to do what they can to improve it.

She looks forward to the upcoming Fragrance Week, which was her idea, to be observed here by mayoral proclamation from June 4 to 9. It is designed, she said, "to increase odor awareness" and is not just coincidentally scheduled at the beginning of what Ms. Green calls "New York's smelly season": summer.

Activities this year will include free testing of sense of smell at several locations and the hanging of floral wreaths around the necks of the lions at the New York Public Library on Fifth Avenue. There will also be a panel discussion of the psychological impact of fragrances. She admits that this is tantamount to arresting a jaywalker to solve New York's crime problem.

Ms. Green discussed all this while walking to work yesterday morning along Third Avenue in a cloud of perfume that she described as "multifloral with spicy top notes." For her, perfume seems to be the olfactory equivalent of the Walkman portable stereo headphones, blocking out undesired fragrances.

She said she will use the occasion of Fragrance Week to urge all New Yorkers to plant fragrant flowers on windowsills and to talk about regularly washing and deodorizing city garbage trucks.

She recalled several proposals for making New York smell better over the years, from putting perfume in the fountain in front of Bergdorf Goodman to piping pleasant-smelling perfumes into the subway system. She said she kind of liked the idea of fragrances in the city's fountains and will urge that this be done during Fragrance Week.

She also likes the idea of blowing a little fragrance through the subway and bus stations: "They could use a new ozone fragrance that doesn't smell at all. It would just make everyone think they were standing on top of a mountain.

"Bad smells," she said, "have a powerful psychological influence. They depress people and can even make them aggressive. Margaret Mead said that whole tribes went to war because they didn't like each other's smells.

"Maybe we need a new government agency to deal with quality-of-life things like this," she said.

In her book — which includes such information as "The Burmese phrase for 'Give me a kiss' is 'Give me a smell'" — she writes: "Of all our bodily functions, few of us give much, if any, conscious thought to the act of inhalation."

Except, of course, in New York, where she agrees that it is probably best to give each inhalation a little thought.

Ms. Green believes that many New Yorkers hold their breath or breathe through their mouth several times each day: while stepping onto a subway platform; reviewing a cavalcade of garbage bags while walking down a sidewalk; disappearing into a cloud of bus exhaust; pressing into a crowd of the great unwashed on an afternoon rush-hour bus or occupying an elevator with a man who buys his after-shave in fifty-five-gallon drums.

"However, being the most pungent city," she added, "isn't all bad by any means. Some of New York's strong odors are bad, and some are quite nice indeed. But we must be vigilant."

Her walk to work began at the Gramercy Park Florist, at

21st Street and Third Avenue, to pick up some flowers to take to the office, where fresh roses now adorn her desk. The offices of the Fragrance Foundation, which serves the fragrance industry, are permeated this day with a fresh garden scent. She has an Aroma Disk machine with cassettes labeled Country Garden, Fireplace and Mountain Air.

Passing the Gramercy Pastry Shop, she smiled and said, "The smell of this place always gives me a lift." The pizza place she regards with ambivalence, aromatically speaking, but has great admiration for an ice-cream parlor where, she said, "The lady has cookies that smell great clear out into the street. And she smells good, too.

"Overall, New York is a much better smelling city now," she said confidently, crediting tougher dog-cleanup ordinances and whoever invented the plastic trash bag. She also said that for some reason storekeepers now are paying more attention to cleanliness outside their stores.

It is an unseasonably cool morning with a nice breeze tempering street smells. The sense of smell is weakest in the morning, she explained, but still she recoiled and pinched her nose between thumb and forefinger while passing a pile of malodorous bags of garbage.

Rhim's fish market, as odoriferous as could be, she liked. She stopped to smell the cantaloupes and apples outside Rhim's fruit and vegetable market next door and to issue a statement: "The proliferation of these outdoor markets is an extremely positive step in bettering the aroma of this city."

She was displeased with some of the "greasy smelling" restaurants on Third Avenue and with the sight of several people walking their dogs on East 30th Street, not far from the Fragrance Foundation offices.

Some people on the street had set geraniums out on their windowsills.

"That's the spirit," she said. A street sweeper went by, and her heart was glad.

...AND FUNNY
ACCENTS

"**J**EET?"

"Nah. Oi could shuwah usea slice-a-pizzer anna soder."

"Theh-sa staw ovah theyah."

"Soopa."

It is 7:00 P.M., and it is New York. Students up on East 76th Street are taking a ten-minute break from the first meeting of their adult evening course, "How to Lose Your Noo Yawk Accent."

Marilyn Rubinek, the instructor, is in the business of curing New York accents, a real-life Professor Henry Higgins, who refashioned Eliza Doolittle in *Pygmalion* and *My Fair Lady*. Mrs. Rubinek, who describes herself as a speech consultant, can pull the drawl out of a southerner like a cork out of moonshine and can as easily exorcise a rural midwestern twang.

She helps immigrants overcome their accents, too, but mostly Mrs. Rubinek exterminates New York accents — pests of proper speech. The afflicted come in droves, from Brooklyn, of course, and Queens — as well as Staten Oi-land, da Bronx, Joisey, Long-Giland and Uppuh Manhattan. None yet from Toidy-toid and Toid.

Each wants to shed a New York dialect, which they say makes them sound dumb and holds them back professionally and socially. These accented Americans say they are victims of discrimination, passed over for promotions, passed by in singles bars and told they sound like taxi drivers or members of the *Saturday Night Fever* cast.

"People today," says Mrs. Rubinek, "want to sound like they are from nowhere in particular."

"People cringe when I say, 'Hello,'" says Howard Belasco, a class member from the Bronx. "That is not good."

"I don't want to sound like the Lords of Flatbush anymore," says Gale Cantor, a student from Brooklyn. "I want my speech to reflect my education. That's just good packaging."

Stuart Jacobs, one of Mrs. Rubinek's clients, talks too fast and grew tired of people saying, "What? What?" to him all the time. "New Yorkers," Mrs. Rubinek says, "speak too quickly. Life is so fast paced, we feel we have to get out the information quickly or we are holding things up."

Other New Yorkers come to her with such problems as pronouncing *oi* for *i*, as in "Froiday"; removing their *r*'s and putting them back in the strangest places, as in "lawryuh" (lawyer); substituting *d*'s and *t*'s for *th*, as in "Let me tink about dat," and mispronouncing such other vowel sounds as "bawss" for boss.

Consultants acknowledge that even if the accent is eradicated, a New Yorker's vocabulary remains to be dealt with: standing "on line" rather than "in line," schlepping, schmoozing, ordering a schmear and all the rest.

Implied in all this corrective therapy is the notion that something is suddenly wrong with being from New York. "No," says Dorothy Sarnoff, who performs extraction of New York accents and other "speech cosmetics" at her company, Speech Dynamics, in Manhattan. "It's just like singing out of tune." The speech consultants describe a New York accent as being monotone, nasal and staccato.

Laura Darius, who runs the Center for Speech Arts on 57th Street and claims to have originated therapy for New York accents four years ago, says her success would never have been possible a generation ago. "New York is changing," she says, "becoming more 'upscale,' and the people want to sound that way." She suggests the old dialect is being replaced throughout the city, just as boutiques are replacing older stores.

"This is the age of image," says Ms. Darius, "and also a time when television is moving us toward a standard general American speech."

Students and clients acknowledge that with the loss of their accents, so too goes some of the flavor of this polyglot city, where the mixture of immigrant dialects combined to form the accent in question. "We don't have to talk like clones," says John Girollomo, a client of Mrs. Rubinek's from East Harlem. "But speech reflects your background, and I don't want mine reflected."

Mrs. Rubinek works with the class, which meets at the Robert F. Wagner Junior High School, using mirrors, tape recorders and mouth and throat diagrams.

"It's not fair," says one student. "A guy from England can order a pastrami sandwich and sound like Shakespeare."

"My tongue," says Maribeth Murphy, "is apparently too short."

"How," asks Mr. Belasco, "can we tell we are doing something wrong if it sounds right to us?" That is: Can a course in New York on how not to speak like a New Yorker be any more effective than a class for fish on how to breathe on dry land?

"It's so easy to slip back," says Elizabeth Alpert, a Brooklyn client of Mrs. Rubinek's, "when you're with family and friends. It's a touchy subject with them. You're saying that the way they speak isn't good enough. I feel like an alien when I go home, afraid to speak properly."

Indeed, Mrs. Alpert speaks now like a generic American from Nowhere in Particular. "I was on the train platform with a friend of my sister's," she says, "and she said: 'What are you talking that way for? You don't say the word "bawss" "boss." You're all wrong.'

"I looked at her, and I said, 'No, Rose, believe me, you are.'"

NOON SCHMOOZERS

Q UICK THINKING BY a patron of Hershey's restaurant recently saved Herman Aronowitz from an afternoon of embarrassment.

Mr. Aronowitz had the misfortune to spill some lunch on his necktie and yelled to a waiter for seltzer to remove the spot. Hearing the distress call, Alex Weinig, a nearby diner, whipped out a pair of scissors and cut Mr. Aronowitz's tie in half, instantly removing the spot.

No thanks were necessary. That's just the kind of place Hershey's is, the kind of place where you might order a Norwegian sardine sandwich only to get some cheese blintzes, because the waiter thinks they're better. Menus are often incidental.

Hershey's, at 167 West 29th Street, is an old-fashioned kosher dairy restaurant, one of the few surviving. This restaurant that serves gefilte fish and fried kreplach — "like your grandmother's, but better" — serves also as the heart and soul of one of the city's many specialty commercial areas, the Fur District.

It is strategically situated near Seventh Avenue at the epi-center of a world of fur manufacturing and marketing, complete with a Fur Center Synagogue, a Fur District American Legion Post, twenty-story buildings filled with large fur companies and storefront specialty shops selling fur hats, fur tails and lotions that enhance luster. Deliverymen, some of them wearing headphones and T-shirts sporting names of rock groups, scurry along the sidewalks with strings of mink pelts, giving the impression that young America is turning to trapping.

Over bagels and bialys every morning of the week and chopped herring and kasha varnishkes every lunch hour, the people in the fur business come to Hershey's to schmooze, discussing such things as the price of Russian sable pelts and the birth of children and grandchildren.

"It is really more like a club," said Sol Goldstein, one of the regulars.

Now, with Labor Day past, these customers are flocking back to Hershey's, comparing suntans, waistlines and degrees of baldness. They greet one another with vigorous handshakes, embraces and offensive insults that only the worst of enemies or best of friends could allow. Laughter reverberates off the woodlike Formica walls; the camaraderie as thick as the apple strudel.

"I haven't had ptomaine poisoning in a month," one returning regular said by way of greeting the owner, Roy Herschenfeld.

Mr. Weinig, who owns a fur-manufacturing concern in a high-rise around the corner, comes down out of the clouds of coyote, mink, fitch, stone marten, fox and other furs to sit in the same seat twice a day, as do most of the regulars in the 128-seat restaurant.

The white-haired Mr. Weinig, namesake of the "Alex Weinig Special" blintz, spouts the latest jokes and gibes, regularly infuriating Harry Kisselofsky, another patron, to such a degree that Mr. Kisselofsky storms out of the place vowing never to return.

The waiters and waitresses are also subjected to disparagement in the hailstorm of repartee. One waiter, Jack Weinblatt, strikes back by dangling his thumb in the split-pea soup while serving. Customers also set aside time for resolution of world problems, as well as for free psychiatric and legal counseling and diagnosis of health problems that have stumped medical science.

For thirty-five years Murray Lenkofsky has been complaining about the food and lowering the prices on his checks to "more reasonable" levels. "I come here," he said, "only because Mr. Weinblatt will argue with you about anything, and he gets my blood flowing in the morning."

After breakfast and lunch, games of poker, played not with

cards but with the serial numbers on dollar bills, break out. Mr. Weinig skims money from the winners for the Hershey's Breakfast Club, whose more than three hundred members are listed on the wall.

The club discreetly gives money to members who may have fallen on hard times. "We know each other so well," said Mr. Weinig. "When someone is in trouble it's written all over his kisser."

The club also buys flowers for club members in the hospital and wedding gifts for members or their children. When the Fur Center Synagogue badly needed money, the club sold seats in Hershey's to the regular customers for $50 each and brass name-plates were affixed to the backs.

Champagne-and-scrambled-egg parties are sometimes held to celebrate the birth of a grandchild or the fact that it is Friday or some other blessed event. Occasionally a wedding-anniversary party will be held, with the man's family invited to Hershey's to meet the characters with whom their husbands and fathers spend most of their days.

"We get to know each other so well," said Mr. Weinig, "like brothers. Better than brothers. We might spend more time here together in the course of a week than we do with our families.

"Occasionally one of the fellas will die or retire, and those are sad, sad occasions after spending years at Hershey's together."

Those who retire – even to distant climes – seem to return frequently. Mr. Aronowitz retired to Florida recently but was back for a visit this week. He made it a point to settle in Florida near several people he had known from the fur business.

There they get together and talk of their cravings for the gefilte fish at Hershey's and of their years spent at these tables.

DREAMERS (TO INCLUDE HOPELESS ROMANTICS AND THE TERRIBLY NAIVE) . . .

THE PARK
AVENUE DELI

KYU-SUNG CHOI thinks that a twenty-four-hour delicatessen selling some fruits, vegetables and other foods is just what Park Avenue needs. He has not been in this country long.

As remodeling progressed in recent days at his store on the northeast corner of Park Avenue and 75th Street, stop-work orders were issued by the City Buildings Department and the Landmarks Preservation Commission. The local community board has filed a complaint against him with the city. Inspectors, police officers and irate neighbors have visited.

Monitors from the Friends of the Upper East Side Historic Districts have stopped by to oversee the remodeling. Engineers, architects and lawyers are poring over zoning laws and even Mr. Choi's plumbing diagrams, seeking technicalities on which to run Mr. Choi's delicatessen aground.

Borough President Andrew J. Stein of Manhattan is opposing the delicatessen, as is State Assemblyman Mark Alan Siegel, Democrat of the East Side. A spokesman said Assemblyman Siegel is "considering legislation to insure that this can never happen again."

Mr. Choi is shell-shocked. He thought his twenty-four-hour deli would be welcomed. After all, there is hardly a food store to be found anywhere on the famous residential stretch of Park Avenue from the Sixties to the Nineties.

"Do the residents of Park Avenue want to look out the window at vegetables?" Shirley Bernstein asked rhetorically. "They most certainly do not."

Mrs. Bernstein, who leads the opposition to the delicatessen's "despoiling" of the neighborhood, was sitting in the library of her apartment across Park Avenue. "A delicatessen," she said, "is simply inappropriate. It belongs on Lexington or Madison, not here."

For the first time in her life, Mrs. Bernstein is actively protesting something. "My daughter thinks it's hysterical," she said. Mrs. Bernstein, who has lived in her building since 1950, has taken to the streets – clean streets here, streets of limousines and snap-to doormen, of budding trees and sprouting flower bulbs – to peek through holes in the paper on the delicatessen's windows to make note of the work in progress and to distribute 750 fliers in the neighborhood.

The fliers urge residents to protest against the delicatessen to city offices, and those offices have been busy in recent days handling the calls and letters. "The people here on Park Avenue are just wonderful," Mrs. Bernstein said. "And so are the people downtown; people like Mr. Stein have been very, very helpful. His parents live in our building."

As Mrs. Bernstein spoke, the telephone interrupted her continually, and she would tell concerned callers that Mr. Choi's delicatessen would ruin the character of the neighborhood, lower property values, disturb their sleep with lights and noise at all hours, generate litter and attract criminals to the neighborhood, along with "a generally undesirable type of person that we are not accustomed to," not to mention rats.

One of the calls was from Mr. Choi himself, and Mrs. Bernstein erupted. "Oh, absolutely not!" she said. "Your being Korean has nothing to do with this. I am not prejudiced. I *employ* Chinese people." A Chinese maid, in uniform, appeared in the doorway, holding a silver tray filled with canapés.

Mr. Choi explained that his fruits and vegetables would be displayed inside the store, not outside, and he asked what kind of food store would be acceptable to her.

"We do not want a food store of any kind," she replied. "Flowers might be all right," she said, noting that the site had previously been occupied by Flowers by Cort, whose sign is still hanging. "Or chocolates. Yes, Swiss or Belgian chocolates."

Flowers by Cort closed in June 1982 after the owners pleaded guilty to selling heroin in the store and to arranging to have bombs set off at a competing florist's shop five blocks away.

Mr. Choi is getting the message. He has surveyed Zabar's and the DDL Foodshow to find out what this unfamiliar upper-class species he has come up against on Park Avenue eats. He has hung a small canopy reading GOURMET FOODS.

But it would appear that no amount of Grey Poupon Mustard or Fauchon Herb Vinegar is going to get Mr. Choi out of the jam he is in. At a recent meeting residents of several buildings agreed they wanted no food store of any kind on the premises, and they approved funds to retain a lawyer to fight Mr. Choi at city hearings and in the courts, if necessary. "It takes money to fight something like this." Mrs. Bernstein said.

The considerable forces marshaled against the delicatessen have discovered some fine print that was added to the zoning laws after the Great Chinese Restaurant Imbroglio on Park Avenue nine years ago, wording that can be used against Mr. Choi. Upset about double parking at the carry-out restaurant, neighbors were able to obtain an amendment to the zoning code to say no food could be prepared on Park Avenue for takeout.

The issue of the wide variety of prepared foods sold by virtually all grocery stores on the avenue, as well as the conundrum of restaurants on Park Avenue giving people doggie bags, has yet to be addressed.

At any rate, Mr. Choi has been ordered to remove his coffee urn forthwith, and Assemblyman Siegel is vowing to have the zoning code amended to prevent any more such delicatessen controversies on Park Avenue.

The landmarks commission ordered that work be stopped because he was using the basement of the building for storage, and the basement is not covered by a zoning exemption that allows the premises to be used for commercial purposes — although the florist used it.

All the forces marshaled against Mr. Choi, who has been in this country for five years and formerly operated a Carvel ice-cream store in Brooklyn, seem to agree with the City Planning Commission that a delicatessen is a permitted use of the store under the zoning law. But the opponents hope to show that it should be disallowed, because it "increases the degree of non-compliance" with the strictly residential zoning of the neighborhood.

Rezoning in 1961 made Park Avenue strictly residential between 60th and 96th streets. A few stores, such as the one that is now Mr. Choi's, were allowed to remain because they were there before the rezoning.

A woman writing to Mrs. Bernstein to proclaim her protest of the deli described the beloved neighborhood as "an oasis of peace and safety in a crazy world." Through vigilance, neighbors plan to keep it that way. The Friends of the Upper East Side Historic Districts has 120 monitors watching for the slightest change.

In closing her telephone conversation with Mr. Choi, Mrs. Bernstein said: "Our lawyer will call your lawyer. I am sorry about all this, but you must understand that you have your ways and that we have ours."

Postscript: An uproar ensued after publication of this article, with Mr. Stein and others retracting their anti-deli positions while pro-deli politicians held press conferences inside the deli, and Mr. Choi eventually opened for business.

THE MATING GAME AND OTHER EXERCISES AT THE VERTICAL CLUB

A YOUNG WOMAN in a leotard stood at the juice bar in an East Side health club, enjoying some low-fat dutch apple yogurt, when a remarkably handsome, sweaty stranger with really good deltoid definition sidled up and ordered carob peanuts and freshly squeezed grapefruit juice (the large). He turned slowly, looked her in the eyes and spoke.

"Yogurt is mucus forming," he said softly.

"My name is Sharon," she replied.

They repaired to their respective locker rooms to use many grooming products before departing healthily into the night from the Vertical Club, a glamorous, celebrity-studded health club that has become so much more — serving not only the physical-conditioning needs but also the social, psychological, occasionally professional and even spiritual needs of the Upper East Side.

"We have no fat people here," said Tom DiNatale, the manager. That is his pledge. "People join other health clubs to get in shape before they join here," explained Heidi Halliday, a supervisor at the club.

"The Vertical Club is today's Studio 54," said High Voltage, a person and a bizarre hybrid of the show-business and physical-conditioning industries, with glitter in her hair and sequined leg warmers. "Same people, same scene," she said. "Only positive instead of destructive. People are getting up when they used to go to bed — five A.M. I was there."

As an aerobics instructor to the stars here, this little nerve

ganglion of a woman has become a celebrity in her own right.
She always gets the best table at Elaine's, regardless. She has the
disconcerting habit of constantly doing stretching exercises, even
in restaurants, and she sometimes rises from her desk during a
conversation and flies into the splits.

Michael Rodriguez, an assistant manager at the club, sat
calmly cutting up important little white slips of paper in the center of the vast, open, teeming room that was all aflutter with
hundreds of exercise disciples. "Pure Fellini," remarked Ron
Haase, a program director. The gleaming room of mirrored walls
and wraparound neon is filled with energizing rock music. "You
might as well JUMP!" prodded a Van Halen recording.

The club membership was grunting, discreetly, on more
than 250 of the very latest chrome exercise machines, kept glis-
tening by a squad of uniformed cleaning personnel. The members
jogged on a bouncy track that seemed almost to run for them.
They furiously pedaled exercise bicycles, with digital calorie
burn-rate readouts, on their way to where they were going. An
already anatomically correct club member, Leslie Arden, pedaled
wildly toward her goal of looking great in her swimming suit on
Memorial Day at Southampton.

Mr. Rodriguez is a gregarious, twenty-year-old conditioning
expert, who is attending to the important task of replenishing the
little white slips of paper. He said the exercisers keep coming over
and grabbing them in their sweaty hands and scribbling down the
names and telephone numbers of people they have just met who
can be useful to them — socially or professionally or perhaps to
provide the name of a good plumber.

"People see someone they like," said Mr. Rodriguez, "and
they ask me things like the person's name, telephone number,
job, marital status, sexual preference, whether they rent or own in
the Hamptons, things like that. Two couples I introduced are
married."

Although there are hundreds of members, Mr. Rodriguez
happens to know the correct answers. Through his orientation
sessions at the club, he gets to know all of the members, who he
said range from professional models and athletes serious about
exercise to socialites and dirty old men whose attitude during

orientation is one of cardio-schmardio, where are the dancing aerobics girls?

Some club members say health clubs are replacing the networking function of the old men-only clubs. Jack Krenek, a professional model, attested to this, saying he met his accountant here, as well as his insurance man and an advertising executive who gave him a modeling job.

Theresa Echeverry, an admirer of Mr. Krenek, is a twenty-five-year-old restaurant hostess, who comes to the club during the day. "That," said Mr. Rodriguez, "is when I advise women looking for rich men to come." He told of several members who scrimped and saved for the $1,150 to join so that they might meet well-to-do mates here. Several members remarked that the cloakroom at the club looks like a fur vault in the winter.

Ms. Echeverry wears gold necklaces and bracelets while exercising. She and other female members say space at makeup mirrors in the women's locker room is often strongly contested by women about to take the exercise floor. "Sport perfumes" and "sport jewelry" are also applied. A $1,500 gold Cartier bracelet is a current favorite. Reebok sport shoes and Ellesse sportswear – a sweat suit selling for $325 – are the vogue.

Ms. Echeverry said she is weighing several offers from fellow exercisers for lunch this day. Putting her arms around the owner of two restaurants, she said, "Everyone around here owns something." Phil Suarez, co-owner of Bob Giraldi Productions, quipped, "Guys can't get on the elevator with her unless they make seven figures."

"People come to see and be seen," Mr. DiNatale said of his club, where even the sauna has glass walls. There is also a communal spa, a bar and restaurant, and a rooftop sunning area for socializing.

"It is better socially than a singles bar, because it's not so obvious," said Ms. Arden. "You also don't meet as many low-life creeps and insistent drunks. It's safer. The only problem here is that a lot of these people would rather go home and look at themselves than somebody else."

THE PRIDE
OF BUSHWICK

SOME OF THE neighbors leaning out windows on this warm afternoon clapped as Joselyn Estevez walked by in her crisp, white cap and gown.

In the summer breeze the slight young woman held tightly to her cap with one hand and to her speech with the other. Scratch and rap music blared from open windows. A few small children ran to her as she stepped gingerly on the gritty, broken sidewalk in her new high heels. As she passed the corner delicatessen, a man drinking a beer from a brown bag tipped his cap to her and said, "The pride of Bushwick."

Ms. Estevez had spent the day having one cousin trim her hair and having others sit on the couch and listen while she practiced her speech, the valedictory address at Bushwick High School in Brooklyn. The cousins counseled more calmness. A friend from upstairs, Rosina Herrera, brought her a bouquet of pink carnations.

The address she delivered to her cousins – and later to a standing-room-only audience in the hot auditorium – was a message of hope, a common theme for a graduation address, but something not much heard in the neighborhood surrounding Bushwick High.

This is a week of graduations for students in New York's public high schools, and nowhere does it seem a grander occasion than in Bushwick, one of those neighborhoods where grasping a diploma seems most difficult.

Louis Santiago, the principal, commended the students last evening for overcoming the obstacles, which he had enumerated privately as pregnancy, drugs, having to hold jobs to help support their families, parental indifference to education and language problems, to name a few.

The dropout rate at Bushwick is one of the highest in the city, and yesterday the seniors could not help thinking about those who didn't make it.

"It's sad," said Belkys Tejada. "I think about a friend who was very smart and wanted to be a lawyer. My mother always told me to be more like him. But his father left home, and he became the man of the house, the breadwinner."

Mr. Santiago noted that single-parent households were probably the rule rather than the exception among Bushwick's students.

Comments by the seniors beneath their yearbook photographs most frequently expressed thanks to mothers:

"Being in this school was rough, but thanks Mom for your support" – Radames Torellas.

"Phase one completed, Mom" – Norbert Gutzmore.

"Thanks Mom. I made it!" – Mira Rodriguez.

Ms. Tejada, who lives with her mother, said that in addition to several of her relatives, many residents of her building attended the commencement. "They are crazy about me," she said. "I'm one of the few who made it."

She said that when she was in Catholic school, she was kept in line by "raps on the knuckles with rulers and nuns who pulled my ears." In public school she was able to avert the pitfalls, "because if I had turned to drugs or something, I would have let down my mother, who loves me, and teachers, who showed they cared."

Both the Bushwick neighborhood and the high school are regularly treated to doses of unfavorable publicity. One of the teachers recalled a student coming to her with a newspaper and saying: "It says here that Bushwick is a ghetto. We aren't ghetto kids, are we?" The teacher said that the students were "terribly hurt" by such descriptions.

Crime statistics for the school are high, mainly because of

assaults, which both students and school officials said were usually fistfights between two students. "We have a lot of fighters here," said Mr. Santiago. "Our mascot is the fighting tiger."

Ms. Estevez is a fighter, too. She lives in a small apartment one block from the school with her aunt, Otille Lawrence, who supports them with her job, running a knitting machine in a factory. Ms. Estevez moved to New York from the Dominican Republic four years ago, alone, without her parents and brothers and sisters. She had visited New York and wanted to go to school here. She tutors to earn money for such things as school expenses and doctors' bills.

This fall Ms. Estevez plans to attend Wellesley College in Massachusetts — "a long, long, long way from Bushwick." She hopes to become an architect, "to build things."

Some students said they couldn't wait to take their diplomas and flee Bushwick, but most were thinking sentimental thoughts about their neighborhood.

Ms. Tejada told of having yelled and screamed at her mother for years, pleading for them to move out, off their corner where drugs were sold and fights were commonplace, off the corner and out of the neighborhood, to the dream worlds of Long Island or New Jersey.

"Now that I am working part-time," she said, "I realize that we couldn't afford it, that my mother would have moved us to a nicer place if she could afford it, that she tried to give us what we needed."

After a moment's pause, she said, "I think she did."

Many of those who made it through are off to college, "where we will have to prove again that Bushwick kids are not second class," as one put it. Alma Flores, the salutatorian, is going to Smith College, in Northampton, Massachusetts. "I will be in pre-med," she said, "and I'm wishing now that our laboratory classes were a little better, that I had dissected a few more frogs."

In the last line of her speech Ms. Estevez exhorted her classmates, "Let's go out there and show them that we can do it better" — by which she meant better than people out there think that Bushwick people can do.

The ceremony continued in the hot auditorium. "Pomp

and Circumstance" was played. The Medal for Excellence in managerial-level data processing was bestowed. The New York State Declaration of Loyalty was pledged. A few fathers and babies cried. Multitudes of mothers sobbed. Pocket cameras flashed on the pride of Bushwick.

ACTING LIKE WAITERS, DREAMING OF BROADWAY

Sonia glides gracefully across the restaurant floor, carrying two orders of chicken salad and her dreams of dancing on Broadway.

Mary delivers a Miller Lite, wishing she were playing just down the block at Carnegie Hall.

Nancy recites the specials of the day, hoping someday to utter immortal lines on some great stage.

Lory seats customers and writes lyrics for his songs in the reservation book.

To pay the rent, these aspiring artists work at the Magic Pan Restaurant, on the Avenue of the Americas at 57th Street, one of the many restaurants in New York where virtually all of the waiters and waitresses are struggling actors and actresses, dancers, singers and playwrights.

They come to New York from throughout the country to hit it big on stage, screen or television, paying the price with grueling days that become weeks and years of serving steaks and chops, auditioning, attending classes, sending out résumés to agents and hoping to break out of the pack of young aspirants arriving daily in New York with the same dreams.

Some are making it, by degrees, while others say they have nightmares about waiting on tables for the rest of their lives.

Sonia Cedeno, a waitress, is a twenty-four-year-old dancer who has performed in revues, in summer stock and in productions as far away as Venezuela, taking leaves of absence from the Magic Pan, where managers seem to understand such things.

"It is tough," said Ms. Cedeno, who also models shoes to make ends meet. "It seems like I'm too short at one audition, have too dark of a complexion at the next and too short hair at the next one."

She works five days a week at the restaurant to pay for rent, food and classes. She takes dance classes seven days a week — ballet in the morning, jazz dance in the evening — voice lessons, lessons in acting for commercials. She is about to begin lessons in voice for dancers. At night, she sends out her photographs and résumés.

When there are lulls at the restaurant, Ms. Cedeno and the others scour *Variety* and *Back Stage*, looking for announcements of casting calls and for tidbits about possible future productions that might mean jobs that are right for them. They discuss acting, offer one another encouragement and consolation, and trade information about the latest auditions for plays, musicals, commercials and soap operas.

"Everyone here is great about filling in if you have an audition," said Nancy Abraham, an actress-waitress.

Dana Keeler, another actress-waitress, agreed, adding, "And when one of us is performing, the rest show up and cheer loudly." Mary Wooten, a musician from Greenwood, Mississippi, said, "We always go out after work and celebrate if someone has had some success."

They refer to the restaurant's bar as "the mental-health center." They place the drink orders of their customers, and Hilda Gutierrez, the veteran bartender, serves them up, along with free psychological counseling and philosophy.

"I tell them that not getting a certain part is not the end of the world," said Mrs. Gutierrez, who attends their performances, "and that something even better will come along."

"I came from Milwaukee in 1977 to become rich and famous," said Lory Lazarus, a playwright who, like the others, has experienced disappointments and who has branched out into songwriting, as well as putting together a "rock-vaudeville" band in which he plays guitar.

"Things keep falling through," he said. "You keep going on, keep seating people, keep thinking about committing hara-kiri with the cocktail swords."

"I came wide-eyed from Norristown, Pennsylvania," said Sidney Myer, an aspiring singer who is manager of the restaurant's cabaret. "The frustration is that there doesn't seem to be any logic to who makes it."

Ms. Abraham, who came from Cheyenne, Wyoming, to be an actress "a long time ago," said she was ready to settle for jobs in regional theater and voice-overs for commercials. "We all dream of the day we can say, 'Take that man his salad with blue cheese, I'm off to Hollywood,'" she said, "but it never happened."

Once in a blue moon, it does happen here.

Sam Shepard was a busboy at the Village Gate and Jessica Lange was a waitress at the Lion's Head, for example. The manager of the Lion's Head said that Ms. Lange "was the second prettiest waitress on her shift."

Magic Pan alumni include several actors playing major parts in television series, stage productions and films.

Many of the current employees were there a few years ago when one of the waitresses, Mary Steenburgen, called from Hollywood to say she probably wouldn't be coming in to work lunch on Monday because Jack Nicholson had picked her to play opposite him in the film *Going South*.

Mr. Myer recalled that Diane Keaton, Faye Dunaway, Dolly Parton, Barbra Streisand and Jane Fonda had all been mentioned as contenders for the part, "not our Mary, who was doing improvisation in church basements."

Belkys Ulloa, a cook, said of Ms. Steenburgen, who has since won an Academy Award: "One day I was holding back Mary's orders when I got mad at her. The next day, she's out there with Nicholson!"

Mrs. Ulloa said she and the others in the kitchen often found it amusing working with actors and actresses.

"They are so dramatic — 'Where are my cheese fritters?'" she said, mocking them in a theatrical voice. "They whisk away the orders like they were onstage, which I suppose they wish they were."

A dishwasher declined to be interviewed, explaining that his mother thought he was a master chef. Some of the actors and actresses laughed long and hard at that.

"And my mother thinks I'm the next Greta Garbo," one said. "I used to think so myself."

SHOPPING FOR ROMANCE
AT BLOOMINGDALE'S

"WE'RE GOING IN," said Martin Gallatin to the fifteen apprehensive men and women under his command, one of whom confessed that he would just as soon be parachuting into combat.

Mr. Gallatin had seen his people freeze at this door, but this day the brave charged ahead and the timid swallowed hard and followed, popping into the revolving door at Bloomingdale's one after another. This was the culmination of their training in Mr. Gallatin's class, "Finding a Mate in Bloomingdale's," a $25 seminar for single people seeking to meet members of the opposite sex.

At a briefing before entering the store, Mr. Gallatin had denounced singles bars, computer dating services and the like as largely ineffective ways to meet people for New York's estimated two million singles. Rather, Mr. Gallatin teaches tactics for meeting "mates" naturally, in such places as museums, Laundromats, food stores, buses and Bloomingdale's. Explained Mr. Gallatin, "You avoid the 'If-you're-so-great-why-are-you-here?' question."

Mr. Gallatin – a bearded, bespectacled sociologist – likes Bloomingdale's, "because it is a kind of Disneyland, with interesting displays and gadgets to aid conversation. The sixty thousand people in the store on a busy day mean a lot of prospects, and the demographics are right." A class member, Howard Kaplan, said with a moan, "And I've been going to Syms all these years."

The class entered the fray, ever mindful of Mr. Gallatin's

philosophy: "This is highly competitive. You must use sales and marketing skills to sell yourself."

They took mental and written notes from the lecture with them: opening lines, such as "What do you think of this tie?"; and store geography, such as the best departments in which to find mates.

They fanned out quickly to the electronics department, the men's department, household goods and the card shop – all recommended by Mr. Gallatin – but not to the first floor, crowded with tourists, and certainly not to cosmetics, where Mr. Gallatin said "very serious business is being conducted."

The instructor was available for consultation during this practical exercise. A twenty-seven-year-old class member cornered Mr. Gallatin behind a pile of designer handbags for some quick advice. He had struck up a conversation with a married woman, and Mr. Gallatin reminded him that this had been covered under "Special Problems: Married/Attached."

Richard Smith, a class member, stooped to read a greeting card, remarking to a young woman that the cards were impractically displayed.

"You need binoculars to see them," he said. "Yeah," she replied without looking up. But he somehow continued the conversation for a few seconds before she stopped responding, and Mr. Gallatin said enthusiastically, "See, they will talk to you."

Other members of the class were self-consciously unbuttoning their coats to give a more casual appearance, body language that Mr. Gallatin had recommended, as well as making obvious attempts to gauge distance between themselves and their prospects, a recommended twenty-five inches.

To warm up, some could be seen talking to demonstrators of perfume or cooking utensils, as Mr. Gallatin had also instructed. "They have to talk to you," he explained.

A few class members quoted Mr. Gallatin's opening lines verbatim: "How do you like this tie?" one woman asked a male customer. "I don't," he replied, turning away.

Bob Howard came to Mr. Gallatin and said he had gone all the way to the sixth floor "and couldn't think of anything to say about pots and pans." Mr. Gallatin suggested he pick out some sort of utensil and ask someone what it was used for.

"I keep seeing prospects," complained one man, "who are with other women. Women are like cops, always in pairs."

Most in the class had carried conversations through the Greeting, Response and Main Body stages, as discussed in class, but were unable to make the transition to the critical Closing stage — "that's the hard part," explained one class member, "where you go 'from nice Mixmaster' to 'how about a date.'"

The twenty-seven-year-old class member, who said he had just returned from a Club Med trip to Martinique, thought that next time he would try "the women's lingerie department, because the conversation transition from product to personal would be easier."

Michael Posner seemed to be doing well, having given out three cards with his name and telephone number on them, after animated conversations in the electronics department. "Everyone is interested in the new gadgets," he said, "and no one understands them."

The group gathered in the back of the store for the scheduled departure. When some members of the class failed to show up, Mr. Gallatin worried: "These sessions are hard. Some never come out." As it turned out, three had gone to the Alexander's store down the street by mistake.

The group went to a nearby delicatessen to discuss the class exercise. "Don't worry about rejection," Mr. Gallatin told them. "Success is the ability to talk to people, so that one rejection won't mean so much."

The group lingered, most saying they had no plans on this weekend evening, and the discussion turned again to the problem of meeting members of the opposite sex in New York.

"If you are friendly in New York," said Helen Keating Lopez, a forty-two-year-old widow, "people are suspicious. But subtlety doesn't seem to be getting anybody anywhere."

Mr. Gallatin had told them to "show interest, not need" in meeting prospects at Bloomingdale's, something class members said was easier said than done.

"I've tried everything," said Mr. Kaplan, staring into a coffee cup. "I feel like giving up sometimes."

Said another man: "I've been having this discussion about not having anyone to date for fifteen years, since high school. My relatives always ask if I've met somebody. It's like a disease that won't go away.

"It's tiresome," he said. He left the table, walked through the door of the delicatessen and pulled his collar up against the blustery chill of an autumn Saturday night.

TAXI DANCING AND ROMANCING AT ROSELAND

Out of a heavy fog of maroon-lit darkness swept two dancers in tuxedo and taffeta, gliding high on their toes through smooth spins and smart turns that quickly carried them back out across the vast dance floor, where they disappeared among the shadowy figures of other dancers like ghosts that had not been seen in many years.

Johnny Mulay's Orchestra completed the number, and some of the dancers took a break. Robin Strick sat down hard at a table with a sign in the center reading HOSTS AND HOSTESSES — $1 A DANCE. TICKETS AVAILABLE AT SODA FOUNTAIN. Ms. Strick is a hostess, a taxi dancer, at the Roseland Ballroom on West 52nd Street.

"For a dollar," she said, "anyone can take me out for a spin."

She poured a glass of ice water from one of several large pitchers on the table. After she took two sips, an elderly man came up and reserved her for two tangos and a rumba at 8:00 P.M.

A debonair man — maybe the last in America — approached, wearing a brilliant red ascot, his jet black hair slicked straight back. He handed her a ticket, she tucked it down the front of her dress and the two waltzed off to "My Funny Valentine."

Another hostess asked what time it was. The time was 5:00 P.M., but the answer came back, "Oh, I'd say about 1935."

With the changing times six men have joined the ten women taxi dancers, and it now costs $1 to rent one of the partners celebrated in the 1930 Rodgers and Hart song: "Ten cents a dance

– that's what they pay me, / Gosh how they weigh me down!/ Pansies and rough guys, / Tough guys who tear my gown!"

Occupational hazards persist. "I got kicked good during that Viennese waltz," said Christopher Daniels, a taxi dancer, as he returned to the table. Clods crush their toes.

"We're supposed to smile through the pain," said Shirley Ann Steffee, another dancer. Penny Prucha said that sometimes she goes home limping. Most of the taxi dancers own electric foot massagers.

Waxy buildup on the soles of their shoes causes the dancers to slip and fall. Suzanne Huyot, another dancer, said that old codgers try to lift her and dip her, sometimes with excruciating results.

Another hazard is the occasional masher. "A guy holds me too close," Ms. Prucha said, "and I say, 'Hey, no rub-a-dub-dub, buddy.'"

"We need to take a caring, personal approach," said Ms. Strick, thirty years old, who gave up her job as a registered nurse to become a taxi dancer and dance instructor, "but this can be misunderstood."

Ms. Huyot said that she was recently grabbed by the shoulders and kissed. "Only a fool would wonder why," commented a man who had danced with her.

"In the old days at other dance halls," recalled Ramon Argueso, whose orchestra alternates on the bandstand with Johnny Mulay's, "the taxi dancers used to do more than dance."

Not here, where Florence Forder is chaperone of hostesses and insists on dresses cut no lower in front than the top of the sternum and the uppermost lumbar vertebra in back. Still, taxi dancers are forbidden such things as drinking, gum chewing and falling in love with customers.

"People think I have a crazy job," said Ms. Strick, echoing the comments of the others, "but I just love to dance."

The taxi dancers are at Roseland every Thursday, and when they are not here, they hold a variety of occupations, including housewife, model, dance instructor and actress. Dwight Carter is a real-estate salesman who aspires to the stage. The group had a cake and balloons at the dancers' table in January when Ms.

Steffee, an associate professor at New York University, received her Ph.D. in psychology.

They reported their earnings variously, from about $20 to $65 for the 4:00 P.M. to 10:00 P.M. period that they dance. They keep the dollars they receive. The male taxi dancers wear tuxedos; the women wear dresses or slacks.

Mr. Daniels rarely has a chance to sit down. Reaching for the water pitcher, he said: "We've got to talk to the band about playing shorter numbers. Those mambos are killers, and some of these women buy ten tickets at a time." One woman after another comes to the table to ask him to dance. "They tell me," he said, "that I am their Prince Charming."

The quarter-acre dance floor, which will accommodate two thousand dancers, is nearly half full this afternoon, a popular time for many retired people.

The rose motif carries throughout, from the rose-colored light bathing the dancers to the cabbage roses, three feet in diameter, in the carpeting pattern. In the lobby a Wall of Fame contains the shoes of famous dancers, including those of Betty Grable, June Taylor, Ruby Keeler and Ray Bolger. And there is a scroll of several hundred married couples who first met at Roseland.

Mr. Argueso has been playing at Roseland since 1948, when the taxi dancers cost thirty-five cents. The two bandleaders recalled the old days, when a dance marathon was held, and before the police came to break it up, the dancing couples were trucked to a pier and sent out on a boat to complete the contest. Female prizefights were also held to bring in extra money, much as Roseland today hosts rock concerts and has regular disco nights.

"This place is really still the same," Mr. Argueso said. "People still love to dance for all the same reasons."

George Fizer of Perth Amboy, New Jersey, who recalled coming to Roseland in 1938, said, "I come to dance with the hostesses and remember." Irene Fletcher of Queens was recently divorced and said she comes to dance with the hosts and forget.

THE MELTING POT
BUBBLES IN REGO PARK

ROLL CALL, THE teachers agree, is the most difficult part of the day: Ho Suk Ping He, Yana Katzap, Tkkun Amongi, Azaria Badebr, Rotcheild Boruhov, Eduardo Yun.

Eduardo Yun? Sure, the Portuguese-speaking Korean boy who immigrated from Brazil. His adjustment to America has been eased by the presence of other Portuguese-speaking Koreans from Brazil – one of whom also speaks Hebrew – who are enrolled at Stephen A. Halsey Junior High School, a polyglot school in Rego Park, Queens.

"Even when you get their names right," the principal, Domenick Uzzi, said, "some are from countries where they put first names last, last name first. It's impossible."

Nicknames are popular. Chin Sheng Chu said, "Call me George." Some students pick an American name they like and then, to add to the confusion, switch names when they tire of the old ones.

"We've got everything imaginable, and unimaginable, here," said Mr. Uzzi, who said his job was simpler when the neighborhood and the school were pretty much made up of middle- or upper-middle-class Jewish students. That was before a Chinese man bought the luncheonette and learned how to make egg creams and before waves of immigrants from throughout the world began settling in the neighborhood.

This is not a testing ground, nor is Halsey a special project like the United Nations School. This is real life in New York, once again a city of immigrants. There are more foreign-born city residents now than at any time since 1930, with almost one in three being foreign born.

"New kids walk in every day," Mr. Uzzi said. "We had a couple of kids from Haiti register yesterday, which may have something to do with Duvalier's overthrow. We always know when and where there's trouble in the world. We have Nicaraguans coming in now. We expect to see some Libyan kids soon."

"The diversity can be annoying," Mr. Uzzi said. "We pair Chinese kids, and one turns out to be Mandarin and the other Cantonese, or two Russians, and one is Georgian and the other Ukrainian."

Recently, the school counted thirty-four different languages and dialects — Persian, Hindi, Gujurati, Spanish, Portuguese, Cantonese, Mandarin, Greek, Japanese, Korean and Russian, to name a few — spoken at Halsey. The number of countries represented at the school? Don't ask.

The language survey did not include those languages contrived by students to communicate. An Indian student, Chettan Patel, said he spoke five languages, two of them of his own invention. One student is proud to say that he knows one four-letter profanity in twenty-five languages.

"Cultural exchange," Mr. Uzzi commented, "it's great."

"You can discuss the Vietnam War and have kids whose fathers fought on opposite sides," said Jim Perine, a teacher.

Teachers believe the students learn tolerance. "Kids this age call each other 'fatso,' 'retard' and 'pizza face,'" Mr. Uzzi said, "I admit. But we never have fights over remarks about nationalities."

"Never a dull moment," said Irene Clarke, a teacher. New students, according to teachers, arrive asking if the school has a jai alai team, if there is a place in the school band for a sitar player or if poori bread and envueltos de maiz could be added to the school lunch menu.

Mr. Uzzi finally won a protracted battle with city dietitians and federal officials in Washington for dispensation from the rule that there must be a meat course in every cafeteria lunch. Some of the Indian students were not eating anything, because there was meat on the plates.

For all the diversity, the school, at 102nd Street and 64th Avenue, does not appear any different from other schools, except maybe a bit cleaner and more orderly.

There is not a sari or sarong among them. "I think they issue these kids designer sweatshirts and jeans and expensive sneakers at Kennedy Airport," a teacher, Carol Davidson, said. "They are all in a mad rush to be totally American."

Her students said they had come from schools where teachers meted out stern punishment, usually with a rod or stick. Some of the Halsey teachers concede they are slow to tell students they cannot hit them with sticks here.

"Our principal cut our hair if it was below our ears," a girl from Korea said.

"You couldn't even wear a watch in Russia," a girl from the Soviet Union said.

"Gross!" commented a girl from Queens.

Teachers said they were amazed at how quickly most of the students learned English and how quickly they adjusted. "Eileen Chang came in from Taiwan as a seventh grader and couldn't speak a word of English," one teacher said, "and graduated as valedictorian from ninth grade."

The word is out among students that the Asians catch on quickly, and one student from Guyana described them as "death" in math. "When you look around and see a lot of them in your math class," she said, "all you can do is try to transfer."

Mrs. Davidson said that Halsey students could be picked out by translation dictionaries in their hip pockets and by the new trend to electronic vest-pocket translators.

"It's nice sometimes," a student from Yugoslavia said, "being in a country where your parents can't read your report card."

Teachers said they found the mix stimulating and energizing, if sometimes confusing. "It offers teachers great rewards," Ms. Clarke said. "The students want to learn, and you can watch their progress."

She said the teachers had recently discussed an enticing help-wanted advertisement for teaching jobs in a wealthy suburb. "We agreed we could never go to a place that dull," she said.

"It's true that these students try very hard," said Sara Tsinberg, a counselor and recent immigrant. But, she added, there is a tendency to stereotype them as a quaint group of happy toilers.

"We have students ranging from the children of ambassadors to children of the unemployable," she said. "They all struggle, but not all succeed."

The final bell rang, and the students filled the hallways, yelling and laughing, before pouring out the front door past an old wood desk. On it were names carved in the traditional fashion: Takiyaki, Carlos, Trikona, Shreeti.

... AND SCHEMERS

PLOTTING TO SELL
OUTER SPACE
BURIAL PLOTS

IT USED TO be that everybody was just buried over in Queens.

"This, gentlemen, is the Space Age," Rafael Ross announced to an audience. "There are thousands of machines in space, and now it is time to put a person up there. Not a machine, but a real person. A dead person."

From his World Trade Center office, up in the clouds, Mr. Ross is selling the idea of alternative interment in outer space. "No kidding," he told a caller, he was selling what he described as the latest in luxuries offered for wealthy New Yorkers.

Mr. Ross, a fifty-two-year-old psychotherapist, already has some "cremains" – cremated remains – right there at the office, awaiting the first lift-off, including those of an Italian woman and her cat, which will go up together as one payload. Each launch will carry about seven hundred individual containers of cremains, Mr. Ross explained.

All "passengers" – as he calls them, in the grand tradition of funerary euphemisms – will be sterilized with gamma rays, then, hermetically sealed and vacuum-packed in ultralight, ultrastrong Torlon containers.

"The containers for whole bodies," he said, "look just like King Tut, and you can paint anything on the cover you want." When? "Beforehand," he said.

He anticipates very few uncremated passengers, explaining, "We charge by the pound" – about $10,000 a pound. The payload of the average cremated passenger will be about four pounds, although the bereaved has the option of discount-orbiting as little as one pound of the loved one's ashes.

"We offer a choice of three trajectories," said Mr. Ross. He leafed through a promotional brochure headlined SEND YOUR LOVED ONES TO SPACE, ignoring for the moment the calls and letters from potential customers, as well as from people who think he is crazy, people who think he is irreverently tampering with the heavens and those who believe he is cluttering up the universe.

"I don't want junk up there either," he said to one caller, "especially war machines."

But there are also those callers who absolutely cannot wait to blast off. "They're excited about it," said Mr. Ross, "even though they will be dead."

Some tell him that they want to be in the heavens "closer to God" or "back where we all came from." Others say they are simply too claustrophobic to be in a closed coffin, and still others can't stand the thought of worms.

"We have the 1,900-mile-altitude polar orbit," explained Mr. Ross, who formed his space company, Lad, Inc., two years ago, "the 22,300-mile geosynchronic orbit and then our deluxe trajectory into deep space."

He had to hop up and hurry out the door to continue spreading the word. Hurtling through the Lincoln Tunnel and out across New Jersey in his Oldsmobile 88 to address a meeting of the Eastern Pennsylvania Funeral Directors Association in Easton, Pennsylvania, he explained that he was marketing his idea throughout the country and in nineteen foreign countries, as well as in New York.

"Physicists project that the capsules orbiting at nineteen hundred miles will remain unchanged for sixty-three million years," he said. "Space is the perfect resting place, absolutely peaceful and cold enough to preserve things forever." He said this permanence was a big selling point.

"Our deep-space shots will follow Pioneer 10 out beyond our solar system," he said in reverential tones. "Can you fathom that?"

He admitted it was difficult, lost as he was at the moment in New Jersey.

After listening to Mr. Ross's pitch, one of the Pennsylvania undertakers said: "This may fly in New York, but people out here are different. You offer the bereaved out here a space shot and you might quite possibly get punched in the mouth."

But some others were hesitant about writing off the idea. "I would consider offering it to someone pre-need," said Jeffrey Naugle, another undertaker, "but it would seem inappropriate to bring it up in an at-need situation.

"If the price came down, some people might be interested," said Mr. Naugle, noting that it is not as if they don't get some unusual requests as it is. "One of my families asked that cremains be scattered over town," he recalled. "I didn't think much of that idea. You know, people hang out their wash."

Mr. Ross explained to them that just four weeks ago, the Reagan administration approved a proposal to send human remains into space, lauding the idea as "a creative response to the President's initiative to encourage the commercial use of space." Mr. Ross hopes to be the first to launch. "The first person buried in space will go down in history, like Neil Armstrong," he predicted.

Mr. Ross explained that to guarantee the loved one is actually launched, he has opened an escrow account. The entire price of services will be deposited there until ground control confirms the orbit specified in the cargo manifest.

The undertakers asked about the legal and religious ramifications. One of them said, "Catholics are only to be cremated for good reason." Another undertaker hollered out, "Ten thousand dollars a pound is a heckuva good reason!"

"We never even thought cremation would catch on," Mr. Naugle noted, "and now it's the fad."

Mr. Ross said that because it was inexpensive, cremation caught on during the last decade, when no-frills goods and services were popular.

"We are now in a time of luxury," he said. "The funeral industry should stop worrying about charging too much for funerals and offer something outrageously expensive that we can all make money on!"

With that, the undertakers repaired to the bar, where a local casket company was sponsoring a cocktail hour.

"People have come out here from New York with the darnedest notions," said one of the dark-suited funeral directors, who spoke softly, solemnly, gravely, with his hands folded at the belt buckle in the finest funeral director style. "But in this day and age you never know. Best not to laugh at anything." And he looked as though he never had.

Mr. Ross slipped out the back way with his briefcase on this cold, clear, moonless night, to speed homeward in his Olds Rocket 88 beneath the star-filled heavens.

THE BOLD
MEAT LOAF
INITIATIVE

THE $486 MILLION Jacob K. Javits Convention Center opens tomorrow, and Charlie Hristidis, owner of the River Diner across the street, has seized the moment, adding not one but two meat loaf items to the one already on the menu.

"You must reach for the stars," Mr. Hristidis said philosophically of this bold menu change that has startled some in the 11th Avenue dining community. "How could there be three kinds?" asked one patron, Bud Demler.

Mr. Demler will find out today, when the new menus arrive, with meat loaf prices slightly higher. As crews at the convention center work feverishly to complete the heralded all-glass structure in time for the grand opening, Mr. Hristidis works overtime across the street, making improvements to cash in on what he views as a miracle — "a wondrous crystal palace that has set down like magic in my grimy neighborhood."

"Opportunity knocks but once," said Mina, his wife, divulging for the first time anywhere the names of the new meat loaves to be added to the American Meat Loaf already on the menu: Greek Meat Loaf and Rumanian Meat Loaf. "Keep them under your hat," she said.

Mr. Hristidis said that winds of change were blowing through the diner — you could feel them yesterday with the kitchen door propped open — and that the meat loaf was just the tip of the iceberg. He expects to extend his hours, add more seats and make more dramatic menu changes.

The new menu, he said, will cater to "the new higher class of people" – such as the furriers in convention across the street this week and art dealers next week – than his former clientele, which before construction of the center, he said, included those involved in New York's drive-through prostitution industry.

Yesterday, Leon Kassman, a furrier setting up a booth in the center for the International Fur Fair, sipped a cup of coffee at the counter and offered Mr. Hristidis $1 million for eight years on his lease. Mr. Kassman envisions turning the diner into "a classy bar" and adding a second-floor "executive dining room."

Mr. Hristidis, perspiring over a grill full of hamburgers, said he did not see it that way and turned him down. This was not the first offer he has received.

"He has a golden opportunity here," Mr. Kassman said, "if only he can step out from behind the burners and realize it. He can stop flipping flapjacks and smell the flowers."

"I don't want to sell out, and I don't want to make this something other than a diner," Mr. Hristidis said. He recalled a preview party at the convention center last week for three thousand guests, after which a few of them found their way to the diner.

"Some of them started telling me that I had to change the place and make it fancy," he recalled. "When I said I wouldn't do it, the other customers cheered."

"We like it here because it's real," said Harriett Mason, who lives in a new high-rise nearby. "The old diners are disappearing, and the one over on Tenth has a piano player."

Mr. Hristidis's stance has made him something of a folk hero to people like Ms. Mason. His diner is a stainless-steel classic, where scenes for such films as *After Hours*, *Tattoo* and a new work featuring Mia Farrow were filmed.

Some of the construction workers at the center, however, shook their heads in disbelief when told that Mr. Hristidis was turning down windfall offers.

"If he wants to keep it a diner, he should at least make it a forty-story diner," one workman suggested.

Mrs. Hristidis said that sometimes their two children, who

will be called upon to work at the diner now with the extended hours, think "he is a little nuts, too," for not taking the money.

She looks forward, however, to the new challenges of expanded hours, such as dinner, when steaks, chops and shrimp can be served: "I am so sick of hearing 'buttered corn muffin – buttered corn muffin – buttered corn muffin' I could kill them, you know?"

Mr. Hristidis said he will paint the outside, shine the stainless steel and fix the neon signs. The decor inside is laminated plastic and stainless – give or take a few stains – steel, dressed up with a BUD ON TAP neon sign, and framed Heimlich-maneuver instructions and drawings showing what to do when someone is choking to death on a meal.

"Lately," the waitress, Anne Grey, said, "Mr. Hristidis has been making changes little by little. There are a couple of plants and curtains now instead of the venetian blinds."

She noted that Heineken and Michelob have been added to the Budweiser and said Mr. Hristidis had once mentioned something about fettuccine Alfredo. Brunch has even been discussed. "He drew the line," she said, "when I mentioned quiche."

The current menu is cemented on a firm foundation of mashed potatoes, meat loaf, moussaka and Charlie's French toast served with butter, syrup and two scoops of ice cream. He swears the French toast has never induced insulin shock.

Samples of the dishes are helpfully splattered on the menu. It has been suggested that the menus and Charlie's apron be donated to a local food bank.

"I am very excited," Mrs. Grey said, "excited but nervous. Life was simple before, and now it is more confused and tense."

Mrs. Grey said that another waitress would be working alongside her and that Mr. Hristidis had established waitress stations in the small diner.

Mr. Hristidis said he was thinking of expanding the seating but would not build a second-story dining room, as several people have suggested. Nor will he rename the diner, as has also been suggested, either the Convention Center Diner or the Jacob K. Javits Memorial Diner.

"All my life has led up to this moment," said Mr. Hristidis, a balding fifty-four-year-old, who emigrated from Piraeus, Greece, in 1968. He worked his way up in a Manhattan restaurant from dishwasher to chef, where he learned to prepare some of the fancier dishes he now wants to add to the menu.

He leased the diner, and five days a week for twelve years he has been rising at his home in Hampton Bays, Long Island, at 3:00 A.M. so he can arrive at the diner at 5:30 A.M. He now wants to stay open seven days a week.

"I have seen it through the bad," he said, "and now I want to enjoy the good. I've built something. People come in and yell: 'Good morning, Charlie. What are the specials?' And it is like music to my ears."

THE POLITICS OF
WHAT'S-FOR-DINNER

"**M**ADAM CHAIRPERSON, WE know you for what you are," charged Moe Doctrow, a member of the powerful Food Committee at the Hebrew Home for the Aged at Riverdale. "You are part of the fanatical anti-fish faction. Because of your prejudice, the stuffed flounder before us for consideration does not have a prayer."

Estelle Small, the chairperson, was steamed and shot back: "How can you say that, Moe? My dearly beloved husband was a fisherman. You, Moe, have no taste at all; you just love everything!"

She turned to the others present and said: "Have you ever had a delicious glass of water? Well, he has."

Senators are elected every six years, presidents of the United States every four and food items are voted on and off of the menu every two years at the Hebrew Home in the Bronx. Senators and presidents are considered relatively inconsequential compared to what residents of the home eat.

"A bum senator we can live with," said one of the nineteen voting members making a speech at the meeting, where tasting, debating and balloting took place yesterday. "Ratatouille we cannot."

"Nothing is more important to people here than meals," Marcus Solot, a member of the Food Committee, explained to an observer. "It's just about all anyone talks about."

Members of the powerful Food Committee have been but-tonholed by their constituents for days before this meeting, but-tonholed by people who wanted to lobby for the ouster of stuffed cabbage or for the introduction of banana pudding.

There are many single-issue factions who want the ear of committee members, such as those seeking less sodium in the food, less sugar and more spices. There is the "no breakfast be-fore 8:00 A.M." group, the *al dente* spaghetti coalition and the anti-cheese factions, including a "no-Parmesan" splinter group. And there are those pushing for larger portions.

"It is an awesome responsibility," said Naomi Schwartz, re-ferring to making decisions concerning the daily meals served to nine hundred residents, eight hundred staff people in the home and the four hundred meals delivered to the elderly outside the home.

"When you're on the Food Committee," said Mrs. Small, "people pester you all the time, asking, 'Why can't we get this?' and 'Why can't we get rid of that?' When they don't like things, they take it out on us." She was reminded of her immensely un-popular zucchini vote two years ago.

"They cornered me on the consistency of the scrambled eggs," said Helen Goldenberg.

Because of the hassle, members often think about leaving the Food Committee, but they cannot bring themselves to give up the power and prestige.

Victor Williams, director of food services, wore a white lab coat with a food thermometer in the pocket as he introduced the thirteen food candidates to the committee. He told them to mark their ballots "excellent," "good," "fair" or "poor" on each dish.

"Hey, this looks like the same ballot we had two years ago," said Helen Goldenberg, bemoaning the lack of good candidates, a perennial problem in a democratic society.

Mr. Williams noted that the stuffed flounder was making a comeback, after being bumped from the menu two years ago. "I think people were skeptical about what was inside," he said.

He made a joke about his continuing search for a kosher shrimp, and he enthusiastically introduced ratatouille as "an ad-venture in vegetables."

Samples of the items were served three and four at a time, and the tasting began. Debate ensued instantly, along with mass confusion over what was what.

"The ratatouille is delicious," said Mrs. Schwartz.

"Don't try to influence my vote," snapped a Mrs. Weinberg.

"Do they seriously expect us to take this back to our constituents?" said another member, speaking of the spinach-cheese quiche.

The open-faced tuna melt sparked controversy, as expected, with many of the committee members considering it to be overly casual. One member criticized the fish-stew creole as "a triumph of image over substance" – another problem with candidates in this country – and he was in turn criticized as being a "reactionary conservative" member of the Food Committee, who never seemed to like anything new.

"Please stop peeking at my ballot," said someone at another table.

It was discovered that Mrs. Goldenberg was putting checks in the "poor" column that she intended for the "excellent" column. Mr. Williams told her to erase the marks and initial them so he would not be accused of vote fraud.

Arguments broke out over portions, with Mr. Doctrow saying residents are "overfed," and others saying they were being starved.

Mr. Solot argued that there is a gender gap on the portion issue, with the minority male population of the home being unable to sway women to vote for larger portions or, for that matter, red-meat dishes.

"Some dishes just didn't seem to have the charisma to be elected," said Mr. Williams, the bland fettuccine Alfredo chief among them.

The ratatouille failed to pick up support, with one committee member announcing that it made her sick to look at the stuff. She was criticized for unfair electioneering practices.

It was the second time ratatouille had failed with the voters, and the consensus was that ratatouille is through in politics.

Receiving the highest rating – 100 percent "excellent" or

"good" ratings — was the stuffed flounder, which pundits said seemed to be riding the wave of "overall fish popularity" in this country.

"Some candidates win election just because they are something new," said Mr. Williams, explaining the high vote tallies garnered by the baked ziti, which will replace the similar baked lasagna on the menu.

"There is an initial honeymoon period for any newly elected dish," said Mr. Williams.

"But some don't make it to the next election," said one committee member, who recalled, "We had a dessert that was impeached," but he said it was not melba.

To make room for the newly elected dishes, some old ones will be knocked off the menu. The pineapple-cheese-raisin casserole has come under wide criticism recently, and insiders said it will probably be run out of the home soon, with no one expected to offer asylum.

Sources also said that the egg cutlet's days are numbered. Mr. Williams said that certain dishes lose their constituency. One member of the committee explained that most of the people who had liked the egg cutlet have passed on.

Another committee member, who had been sharply critical of the cutlet, said she was not surprised.

STOPLIGHT ENTREPRENEURS

THE OUT-OF-TOWNERS drove in through the Lincoln Tunnel and had probably been in New York no more than thirty seconds when they came to the first stoplight on 42nd Street and — it's been a good life, Martha — their car was set upon by a band of young men wielding sticks of some kind.

Passengers in the car with Pennsylvania plates hastily locked the doors and rolled up the windows as one of the young men slapped his stick — a long-handled squeegee, actually — on the windshield and said, "We won't bite."

He stroked the windshield clean in six swipes, asking first for a dollar, then fifty cents and finally a quarter, the usual tip. The out-of-towners stared straight ahead in silence until the light changed and they sped off.

"Pennsylvania, man," said the disparaging windshield washer, James O.G., twenty years old, who is called by the first two letters of his last name. "One of them asked me once if this was a hobby."

Spring is a time for clean windows in New York, sometimes whether you want them or not. "Be a sin not to have a clean windshield on a day like this," said O.G., basking, during a green light, in the bounteous sunshine and all sixty-seven degrees at Ninth Avenue and 42nd Street. Just a few days ago, he had been forced to warm his hands with bus exhaust. "I use all-temperature Cheer," he said, pointing to the bucket of soapy water he uses to wash the windshields.

The perennial appearance of flocks of windshield washers on the street corners has become a harbinger of spring in New York. Some urbanites say they have lost touch with nature and count on such signs as the windshield washers and the color of the plastic leaves in Macy's window displays to give them an idea of just what season it might be.

During the windshield-washing season, which coincides closely with that of the Yankees and Mets, O.G. plunges his squeegee down into the bucket, and just as he withdraws it, the light at Ninth Avenue turns red. Every time. The heavy traffic of 42nd Street backs up like some swollen, raging river suddenly dammed, and O.G. and his colleagues jump in, squeegees flying.

For Sergeant Kenneth McCann of the 10th Precinct, the windshield-washing season means calls from angry motorists and neighbors, some of whom regard the washers as "pests" or even "little extortionists." It means that the police will be chasing O.G. and the others off the corner of Ninth Avenue and 42nd Street for several months. "We hear," said Sergeant McCann, "of some of them tearing off windshield wipers when they don't get tips."

The returning washers are greeted variously. "Where you guys been?" said Phil McNicols, a motorist, as O.G. wiped his windshield clean. "I can't see without you," he said, handing over a dollar. Some drivers said they think the washers provide a service no longer offered at gas stations, that it provides jobs for the young men and even that "they are part of New York's great street theater."

Others side with Linda Brockmeier, who shouted: "Get away! I hate you guys!" She pulled over to amplify: "If they want to offer a service, why don't they ask first? This is a form of mugging, definitely."

Over the years, New Yorkers have developed evasive tactics to thwart the washers, such as yelling obscenities, said by Sergeant McCann to be a common solution to problems of urban life; turning on the windshield wipers; honking the horn; ignoring the young men when they ask for money and slowing down a half block from the corner and never allowing the car to come to a complete stop.

"You have to be a salesman," said Patrick Green, another washer. "You smile, you dress nice, you act nice. We get a lot of repeat customers." O.G. stated proudly that he has been in the business since he was ten years old and "here in the same location for more than four years." As for criticism of the windshield washers, O.G. said there are "bad actors" in every business.

He credited "horrible traffic" with the growth of the industry, which feeds upon unmoving vehicles, as do the pretzel and Coke vendors at entrances to bridges and tunnels.

The amounts the washers earn vary greatly but can frequently be as much as $50 a day, they say. Mr. Green said he once received a $100 bill, and others said they occasionally receive $10 or $20 bills, which some motorists apparently view as a kind of direct welfare payment with no administrative costs.

Still, virtually all of the washers say they want out of the business, especially on Mondays, when they say commuters are broke and angry about having to come back to work, as well as on rainy days and on those days when "The Dime," the name the washers give the 10th Precinct, is chasing them. O.G. does not want his full last name published, he said, because he would be embarrassed to have his girlfriend find out what he does for a living.

All the washers at Ninth Avenue and 42nd Street this day are between the ages of sixteen and twenty-six, and all are from the neighborhood of 125th Street and Second Avenue. Some of the young men are angry about their inability to find better jobs, particularly one who calls himself "Sam" and claims to have a high-school diploma and an honorable discharge from the Army.

"You can never be poor as long as you have this stick," proclaimed O.G., and Sam shot back sarcastically, "That's one way of looking at it."

The light went red. "Yeah, I'd love to get out of here too," said O.G., working on the car of a young woman who smiled at him through the windshield. He took the quarter from her, smiled and said, "Take me outta here, baby."

MOVERS ...

CRASH COURSE
IN CITY DRIVING

"I WOULD SUGGEST," Bob Kousoulos says calmly to his driving student, Jules, "that you do something soon with the brakes. It is a red light, Jules. *Jules, the brakes!*"

Mr. Kousoulos, who has been teaching driving for twelve years and is a veteran of thousands of driving missions on the streets of New York, chain-smokes Marlboros, chuckles nervously and tries to appear calm.

"This pedestrian in the middle of the street," Mr. Kousoulos says softly as the vehicle picks up speed after the light, "has apparently decided to end it all. I know you have the right of way, Jules, but let her go in front of you, Jules — let her go!"

"Jules," he says, as the student driver weaves his way tensely through pedestrians crossing against the lights, through fields of potholes, numerous construction projects, bicyclists, triple-parked cars and other obstacles that make up the New York motoring experience, "I am sure that this man ahead likes his car, that he would prefer you not hit it.

"Get into the next lane, Jules. Jules, please!

"This is not the Indianapolis 500, Jules," he continues, as Jules tries to squeeze between double-parked trucks on either side of the street. Mr. Kousoulos suddenly grabs the wheel and stomps on his brake pedal on the dual set of brakes.

The student is eager to try some parallel parking.

"Jules," Mr. Kousoulos says, gripping the edge of his seat,

"we may not have to worry about the parking segment of your instruction if you don't stop for – the red light!"

There are those who would compare learning to drive in Manhattan with learning to swim in the killer-shark tank at Sea World. The crew of instructors at the Model Auto Driving School on West 14th Street say that they survive by virtue of quick reflexes, constant vigilance and petitioning the Lord with prayer.

The school uses old Plymouths spray-painted red, the better to be seen, the cheaper to repair. A pile of crash helmets sits in the corner.

Herbert Williams, a student, comments that he has transferred to Model because his instructor at another school was always drunk. "I guess that's understandable in this profession," he adds.

Holt Sturgess, an instructor whose manner resembles that of test pilot Chuck Yeager, likens the job to his days as an Air Force pilot. "You have to be constantly alert," he says. "If you start picking the lint out of your navel, you're dead. You learn to live with the tension."

He teaches students who have never driven before.

"You really must start the engine," he suggests at the beginning of a lesson.

"In what sense?" was the student's reply, and minutes later they were hurtling up Eighth Avenue with taxicab drivers honking and making obscene gestures at the car – perhaps because the student was driving a meager five miles an hour above the speed limit – and with Mr. Sturgess alternately urging the student to "slow her down" and grabbing the steering wheel to avert disaster.

Mr. Sturgess does not wear a seat belt, because he must have the freedom to grab the wheel. The trade-off is an occasional smack of the head on the windshield when a student driver unexpectedly mashes down on the brakes.

Delio Valdez holds a three-hour classroom seminar at the school, having given up on street instruction after a student he was teaching froze with her foot on the accelerator and drove down a sidewalk.

He teaches students the rules of the road. Then he teaches

them that there are no rules of the road in Manhattan, where the guiding principle of driving is survival.

"New Yorkers are a people in a hurry," he tells them. "They get frustrated sitting in traffic jams, and once they get momentum, they go as fast as they can go, and sometimes they don't stop for anything, including red lights."

He gives the students detailed, practical advice.

"When you see someone hailing a cab who is leaning way out and stretching out the arm, it means the cab is on the left side of the street and will be cutting across in front of you," he said.

He discusses street hazards peculiar to New York drivers: bicycle messengers who heed no traffic laws, gridlock, horses, hot-dog carts, such distractions as pedestrians with blue hair and people who stagger in front of cars to wash windshields or beg.

Courtesy can be a problem in New York. Students are cautioned not to slow down to allow a pedestrian to cross the street, because "courtesy is not expected by New York drivers, and you will get rammed in the rear."

Mr. Valdez tells class members not to argue if they are involved in an accident. "People have been killed in arguments over 'fender benders.'" he says.

"Well, that's interesting now, isn't it?" says a class member, Phylomena Barton, who is newly arrived from London. "Driving here is altogether unruly business, isn't it? None of the rules in the book seem to apply."

"It's worse now," another class member says, "than when I was driving during the La Guardia years, and there were absolutely no laws then. La Guardia's idea was to let all the bad drivers kill themselves off."

"You would never get anywhere if you obeyed the rules," another student says. "Try keeping one car length between you and the car in front for every ten miles an hour. At fifty miles an hour, five cars would slide in between."

"In London," Ms. Barton continues in her British accent, "the system is you-go-first. It's quite different here, then, isn't it?"

"Quite," says Mr. Valdez.

MANHATTAN'S WEEKEND DRIVERS ON THE MOVE

HARVEY KAPLAN, mild-mannered Manhattan psychotherapist, leaped into a sporty black Thunderbird with red pinstripes yesterday at Budget Rent-A-Car. He flipped on the radio, gave a little wave and put the car into — "Reverse! Reverse! The car's in reverse!" shouted a frantic attendant. Mr. Kaplan shifted gears and lurched out into a blaze of brake lights for the holiday weekend.

Bill Southerland, manager of the Budget Rent-A-Car office on West 48th Street, winced now and again yesterday as his three hundred pristine automobiles left the garage for the Memorial Day weekend: Skylark after Somerset after Caravelle after Laser.

The Friday before Memorial Day weekend marks the opening of the rental-car season, expected to be one of the busiest ever because of lower gasoline prices and fear of foreign travel. Virtually all of the estimated seventy-five hundred rental cars available in Manhattan were rented yesterday, most of them to Manhattanites who don't drive very often and who will be turned loose on terribly congested highways.

"Manhattan," said George Babcock, owner of the nine Budget offices in Manhattan, "has a high percentage of, shall we say, relatively inexperienced drivers. People don't drive in the city."

"What is dull routine in the rest of the country," said Jill Reading, renting a car yesterday, "is an adventure in motoring here."

The people lining up at 7:00 A.M. yesterday to rent cars said that frequent escape is an essential part of living in New York.

"The place drives you bananas!" in Mr. Kaplan's professional opinion. Those in line yesterday carried dogs, cats, birds, water skis, charcoal grills, fishing tackle, kites and inner tubes.

Mr. Southerland planned to rent all of his cars and just close up and go fishing until late Monday, when his cars will return to the fold bearing nicks, scratches, bumps and dents. Left behind in the cars will be sand, seashells, suntan lotion, beer cans, forgotten fishing tackle and the occasional fish. A few of the Lincoln Town Cars will come back with rice from weddings, and some will have the rental-car window sticker scraped off. "Those are the ones from class reunions," Mr. Southerland said, "where they want people to think they own the Lincoln."

Employees of rental-car concerns in Manhattan said they had seen it all, including cars returned with drugs, pets and machine guns in them. Gina McIntosh, risk manager for Manhattan Budget Rent-A-Car, recalled a car returned with bullet holes in it, a car that had backed into a plane, the one reported stuck in a cave and the one they had to fish out of the Hudson River. "That," she said, "we did not appreciate."

A customer returning a car riddled with bullet holes in New York, she said, is automatically placed on the unpreferred-customers list.

"You cross your fingers that the cars come back in one piece," said Mr. Southerland, who wears ties and sweaters inscribed BUDGET and who somehow remained unruffled amid the mayhem. He knows there will be the inevitable discussions Monday evening about whether the customer hit the deer or the deer wantonly attacked the car. "New Yorkers get in all kinds of trouble when they get out of the city," he said.

Many get in trouble a lot sooner than that, ramming into poles and walls in the parking garage before they even hit the street. Mr. Southerland explains it as "Manhattan Weekend-Driver Syndrome."

He recalled the car towed out of a cornfield in New England last year. "The guy drove through the field on purpose," Mr. Southerland said. "I think he'd had too much fresh air."

"We hear some real doozies," said Linda Carter, who works behind the counter at Budget. She recalled the man who returned a Tiempo that was "totaled," with all of the windows busted out and the front end smashed in. "I don't know what could have happened," she recalled him saying. "I ran in the house for a minute, and when I came back out, this is the way it was."

"Come off it" was Ms. Carter's reply.

She said another customer that day wanted a discount, because there was no cigarette lighter in his Lincoln Town Car and he had no way to light his campfire. "You rented a Lincoln Town Car to go camping?" asked Mr. Southerland.

Some customers in line at various rental-car outlets yesterday said they have complaints, too, such as the place being out of the particular car they were promised or giving them a car that hadn't been cleaned or charging them $1.75 a gallon to refill the tank.

A good rule of thumb, Mr. Southerland said, is that the customer will want the car in the very back of the garage. When that happened yesterday, Mr. Southerland pleaded: "Please, sir, not that one. Give us some *justice* here. How about that pretty blue one up front?"

The customer laughed, in part because Mr. Southerland delivers his lines like a comedian. "You gotta be nice in New York," Mr. Southerland explained, "and keep on being nice until gradually you wear them down."

Another man returned a car, and Mr. Southerland noted there had been some damage to the car since it was rented.

"Well, I'm certainly not responsible!" the customer barked.

"I'm quite sure someone else did it," answered Mr. Southerland, as the customer turned and walked briskly out of the office.

"New Yorkers walk fast," Mr. Southerland noted, "but never quite so fast as after they turn in a rental car."

Sometimes, of course, the cars are not returned at all. Sometimes customers keep the cars or sell them, explaining to the rental firms that their sister borrowed it and never brought it back.

And then there are the situations, a rental-car executive said, when a customer might just leave New York for the weekend in a $22,000 Lincoln Town Car, and he might get out of the congested city on the open road with the windows down on a nice day and the tape player going and, after a little reflection about returning to work in the city, just keep right on going.

OARLOCK

"**W**HY DON'T YOU watch where you're going?" roared the man in the straw hat, after his red rowboat had been rammed broadside by a green one on the lake in Central Park.

The man in the green boat retorted with a snappy "Why don't you?" and was instantly cracked in the rear by a little gray rowboat. "Sorry," said a passenger in the gray boat, inspecting the beer that had slopped on his lap.

On a fine weekend day the first bend coming out of the Loeb Boathouse might be likened to the first turn at the Indianapolis 500.

New Yorkers stand in long lines at the boathouse for a chance to escape the hustle and bustle of the city, to paddle around and relax. But they wind up casting gridlock upon the waters. One can hear the thwacking and thunking of wood and aluminum hulls.

"It's OK if you like bumper boats," observed Larry Parker, a rower.

"They need the Coast Guard out here to restore order," said another, Richard Levitan.

Rearview mirrors are also advised: "You row backwards," said Marlene Levin, who had just whacked into a nice-looking family. "Of course there will be accidents."

The weekend waters bustle with the 160 to 200 rowboats that are seaworthy at any given time. On a recent day there were some teenagers trying, successfully, to capsize their boat; a woman with a parasol striking a pose with one foot dangling in the water; a mother holding a crying baby next to a boat with a sleeping man; three men dressed up like Boy George; a man playing a radio in one boat and a man playing a trumpet in another; a crabby father telling the kids to "shut up, for the last time"; a whining child claiming to be seasick; a group of girls from the High School of Fashion Industries who shrieked when they came close to rocks and a lot of people laughing through multiple collisions.

A birthday party, with cake, was being held in one boat. Michael Bilginer, assistant manager of the boathouse, said there were many such birthday and anniversary celebrations on the water. Last year, he said, a man hung a banner with a marriage proposal on the Bow Bridge and rowed his intended under it. It worked.

And now, ladies and gentlemen, coming under the beautiful cast-iron Bow Bridge is "The Boat Show," so called by a group of four actors who take it upon themselves about once a week to rent a boat and entertain — themselves, primarily — but also others in the vicinity.

The actors are roommates, and the group is led by Todd Engle. They open the show by humming the theme from Tom Snyder's old *Tomorrow* television program as they come under the bridge. They tell jokes, sing, interview people in other boats, tell them their horoscopes and hold row-off competitions through rocky shoals where many a rowboat has been hung up high and dry.

Through all of this scoots a boat with a seven-horsepower motor. Operated by the boat concessionaire, TAM Concessions, the boat serves as something of a harbor patrol to help people who have lost oars, to restore order when someone gets rowdy or perhaps to catch someone else trying to rent out an already rented rowboat. Some young men have been known to row to the other side of the lake, have someone run back with the ticket to retrieve their deposit, then rent out the boat on the other side.

They are not the only entrepreneurs. On a rock outcropping at the opposite end of the lake from the boathouse, a man sells cold cans of "beer for a buck." Another man will take a color Polaroid photograph of you and your cruisemates for a price that seems to vary depending on your appearance.

Back at the boathouse – which is on the east side of the lake, near 75th Street – TAM Concessions has set up a taco stand to serve those waiting in line for boats and a hot-dog stand to serve those waiting in line for the restrooms.

Sights along the teeming shores add to the adventure. There are the anglers casting their lures too close for comfort. Lee Johnson, fifteen years old, says he has caught a turtle, a catfish and a goldfish. There are break dancers, peddlers, salsa bands, couples grappling affectionately and painters with easels.

"During the week, it's more like a boat ride in the park is supposed to be," said Mr. Levitan.

Indeed, the birds were louder than the ten boatloads of people out on a day this week. The water, somewhat murkier than the boaters prefer, was placid, reflecting trees and distant skyscrapers. Winifred Beatty said she had seen a raccoon drinking from the water. "It's like Club Getaway for an hour," said Kevin Simons.

A number of people came from their offices for lunch on the lake, including several couples there for romance. "You can't find a more romantic place than this," said Luis Quinde, who was there with Margarita Martinez.

A man in another boat was observed kissing a woman, who turned out to be his wife. He had consumed several glasses of wine.

The natural beauty of the setting attracted several fashion models and a photographer on this day. "Sinatra, Streep, O'Toole and all the rest," said Shaun Boland, the boathouse manager. "You name it, they've been here to do a film."

Clarence Switzer rowed frenetically across the lake with Bea Richards, who said later that she had tried to slow him down but couldn't. "It wasn't a race," she said, observing that New Yorkers aren't the best relaxers in the world.

Alex Abraham, a customer in the snack bar, agreed with that assessment. He said he once spotted a man in a pin-striped suit out in the middle of the lake with an attractive woman, talking on a portable telephone.

CAR SHEPHERDS
MOVE THEIR FLOCKS

CAROLYN WELLS WAS hopping mad. She could not believe, as great a man as the Reverend Dr. Martin Luther King, Jr., was – the Nobel Prize and the whole bit – that the city would not honor his birthday with a suspension of alternate-side-of-the-street parking regulations.

It seemed to Ms. Wells that the city practically invents religious holidays, holidays she has never heard of, in order to suspend the parking regulations: not one, but two Good Fridays; Ascension Thursday; Assumption of the Blessed Virgin Mary; Succoth; Shemini Atzereth. "I mean, come on!" she said.

Her deep feelings for Dr. King seemed to have been stirred by a $35 ticket on her windshield yesterday morning for not moving her car by 8:00 A.M. from one side of the street to the other on the Upper West Side. It was just another day, like all irritating days, for New York car owners.

"Do you know what it is like," Ms. Wells asked rhetorically, "to go to bed very late and have to get up at 7:45 every morning and get in your car and drive around in your nightgown looking for a place to park on the other side of the street? Do you?"

"I have to get rid of my car," she said, finally. "Cars and New York seem to be incompatible."

As usual on West 79th Street, Johnny was up and hustling before dawn yesterday, moving one car after another to the opposite side of the street, or lining them up in the neat, double-

parked rows that can be seen throughout Manhattan and that
serve as holding patterns until parking spaces open up.

Johnny is a car shepherd, one of those distinctly New York
vocations that grow out of some distinctly New York problem.

"When you can't pay the exorbitant garage prices," one of
Johnny's clients, Len Small, said, "and you think you'll crack up if
you drive around one more block looking for a parking space,
which is like finding gold around here, then you go to Johnny."

Johnny tends to a flock of about twenty cars, keeping them
on the move from one side of the street to the other and out of
trouble for fees ranging from $25 a month for old customers to
$60 for new customers. Another car shepherd, over on West 78th
Street, claims to be making as much as $150 a month for some of
his cars.

"I don't want any more customers," said Johnny, a gray-
haired car shepherd, who is also a building superintendent and
would not give his last name for fear his employer would fire him
for spending time tending cars. "But they pay whatever I ask. The
garages around here cost more than $200 a month, and some
people are also too lazy to get up and move their cars."

"There are times," said Mr. Small, "when I don't see my car
for six weeks and have no idea where it is." Johnny knows. On
some of Johnny's streets alternate-side-of-the-street parking
regulations specify that cars must be off the street between 8:00
A.M. and 11:00 A.M.; on other streets the hours are 11:00 A.M.
to 2:00 P.M.

"I pay any parking tickets," Johnny said. "If they tow, I drop
dead. It costs me over $100."

On this cold and blustery morning Johnny had to jump-start
some of the cars and unfreeze door locks. He has been doing this
for twenty years, but he said the job has become far more difficult, with fewer and fewer parking places to be found.

He took a wayward yellow Toyota on the wrong side of the
street down a few blocks to a line of double-parked cars. He put a
note on the windshield notifying the motorist whom he was
blocking in where he could be reached to move the car.

"People who visit me from out of town," said Michelle

Daley, who was out early yesterday on 85th Street, taking part in
the daily car-moving ritual, "always marvel at the rows of double-
parked cars. They like weird stuff like that better than the Empire
State Building."

Such illegal double-parking has become a necessary illegal
practice in Manhattan that is accepted by authorities. When police sometimes do decide to ticket the double-parkers, vehement
protests are mounted by New Yorkers wanting to protect their
right to double-park illegally.

Veterans of double-parking streets tell of strange tactics to
keep from being blocked in. Notes on windshields, such as
DON'T BLOCK — WOMAN IN LABOR, seem to have no effect whatsoever, they say. "Try to get a choice end spot, so you can just
drive out or back out," one veteran advised, "and don't park next
to a tree, because that way you can't drive down the sidewalk to
get out."

Robin Warner is part of a parking *ménage à trois*, if you will,
having staked claim to a parking place on 69th Street for four
years with two other motorists. Yesterday she took the spot from
Bill at 3:00 P.M. and passed it along at 11:00 P.M. to Pat, who
would give it back to Bill at 7:00 A.M. "You have to do it," said
Ms. Warner, "or pay the parking garage fourteen dollars a day."
Some parking garages in Manhattan charge a lot more than that.

For his part, Glen Bolofsky, an accountant, has paid hundreds of dollars in parking tickets. He decided to publish a "New
York City Alternate Side of the Street Parking Calendar," listing
thirty holidays when the regulations are suspended.

Gerald Mayer was something of a folk hero to suffering motorists in his neighborhood on West 79th Street. Mr. Mayer
prided himself on always finding a parking space on the street.

"I tried to make it a game," he said. "Otherwise you go out of
your skull. You have to have the eyes of a hawk and quickness at
the wheel. You have to watch people's hands for keys and even
listen for the jingle. You have to get to know what the doctors
and dentists and shopkeepers in the neighborhood look like,
what kinds of cars they drive and what time they leave every day."

At one time, he said, there had been a funeral parlor in the neighborhood where he could park illegally and the police would think he was one of the bereaved.

Mr. Mayer recently retired and did not need his car anymore. Out of the goodness of his heart, he gave it to his son, who also lives in Manhattan. But his son quickly recognized the ploy and gave the car back.

THE ORATOR OF PENNSYLVANIA STATION

DANIEL SIMMONS DOES not, simply cannot, take requests from the audience, no matter how much his fans wave and cry out for their favorites. These people just have to understand that he cannot, for example, just belt out his ever-popular "All aboard!" unless a train is actually about to leave the station.

Mr. Simmons is the train announcer at Pennsylvania Station, and his distinctive style has made him something of a celebrity to the hundreds who work there and to many of the estimated half million travelers who move through the station each day. A few aren't even going anywhere; they just come to catch his act.

He sits alone in a darkened Plexiglas booth that juts from the wall ten feet above the floor of the main waiting room. One day this week a commuter leaned against a post and waited for Mr. Simmons to bellow his next "All aboard!" then gave him the thumbs-up sign and hustled off to work. An elderly woman waited for an "All aboard!" then blew Mr. Simmons a kiss and was on her way. A group of soldiers returning to Fort Jackson, South Carolina, listened to his lengthy list of destinations for the next train and gave him a standing ovation.

People come into the passenger-service office and ask Moira Knutson if they can meet the train announcer. Others come in offering to buy him breakfast or give him gifts that range from liquor to rosary beads. He receives fan mail, much of it from people describing how his voice carries them back to more romantic days of rail travel, and he receives calls from radio stations across the country asking him to do his "All aboard!" on the air.

Sometimes, Mrs. Knutson said, the people come in wanting autographs. Mr. Simmons always tells her that the people have got to be kidding, but he signs. "Only in New York," said Mr. Simmons, shaking his head, "could a train announcer become a celebrity. I guess it's because so many people pass through here."

Many of the people passing through shout requests. "A big favorite," said Virginia Keeler, who works in the information booth, "is The Crescent. A lot of people ask for that one." The Crescent is a train to New Orleans and Los Angeles, and the fans delight in hearing Mr. Simmons rhythmically rattle off the twenty-seven stops between New York and New Orleans — with the *p*'s popping, the *r*'s trilling and the *t*'s snapping.

You really have to be there to appreciate Mr. Simmons's snappy, syncopated "All aboard." He pauses after the train's last destination and takes a breath before leaping on the first *a* in "all," holding it for a while, then lingering on the double *l*'s. He then attacks the first *a* in "aboard," holds the *o* for the longest time and bites the word off at the end: "Haallll haaboooo-wit!" It packs a wallop and sometimes sets patrons of the adjacent Nedicks restaurant to running out with napkins flying.

There are moments when one detects traces of Walter Winchell in Mr. Simmons's voice. Or the midget in the pillbox hat on the old radio show, crying out, "Call for Phil-lip Mor-ee-s." When Mr. Simmons bellows the names of such cities as WASH!-ing-ton-a!, with his head bobbing up and down, he touches an evangelical note. And when he says Tus-ca-LOOOO-sa! and Al-TOOOON-a, it recalls Mel Blanc on the old Jack Benny show barking out, "All aboard for Anaheim, Azusa and Cuc — amonga."

"You've got to dress it up," said Mr. Simmons. "It can get boring for the people waiting for trains and for me. This way we're all happier. One day early in my career I was doing five trains in a row, and I started to sense the rhythm of the thing. I ended it up with a spirited "All aboard!" and I noticed all these people who rush around out there actually slowed down for a minute and looked up and smiled."

Mrs. Knutson came in to spell him for the lunch hour. "He is a tough act to follow," she said. "It's embarrassing. On your first announcement people look up from their newspapers like: 'Who is that?' And if you try to say 'All aboard' with any style, it just invites comparison."

Mr. Simmons has worked Penn Station for seventeen years, and he likes announcing there. One might think that the old, ornate Grand Central Terminal might be the Carnegie Hall of train announcing, but Mr. Simmons said the acoustics are better in Penn. "This place looks like an airline terminal," he said, "but you don't get the echoes in here that you do in Grand Central." He has fans there, too, one of whom is a Metro-North Commuter Railroad official, who said she "would love to steal him away."

Mr. Simmons, who is fifty-eight years old, said that he drinks a lot of fruit juice at this time of year to ward off colds. He also relies on throat lozenges and wintergreen Life Savers to keep his voice in shape. "The public expects that big 'All aboard,'" he said, "and when it's not there, they complain. I stay home when I'm sick."

"They complain then, too," said Mabel Gittens, a waitress at Nedicks. "He's a celebrity. When he walks in, everybody says: 'All Aboard's here!'"

"The man knows how to call a train," said another waitress, Vergie Stephenson. "When he calls out the Rocky Mount, North Carolina, stop, which is near my hometown, I just want to throw down my apron and hop aboard."

"Other people can call the trains efficiently," said Winston Wilson, a customer, "but with no style and no smiles."

Up in the booth Mr. Simmons barked out the last call for The Crescent. An elderly couple applauded. A young couple held each other in a last embrace. A young man crashed through the crowd, racing for the train, and several commuters charging to another train sang out the "All aboard!" in chorus with Mr. Simmons.

THE SWIM MOBILE

FLAP, FLAP, FLAP. Here comes big
Antoine McCrorey, eleven years old, flapping down the sidewalk
in Bedford-Stuyvesant, wearing a swimming suit, goggles, swim
fins – and looking for all the world like an escapee from the New
York Aquarium, or maybe some other type of institution, the way
people are looking at him.

But Antoine knew where he was going all right, as word
spread yesterday that some strange sort of truck towing a swimming pool had appeared over on Prospect Place on this scorching
day, and that scads of neighborhood kids were diving in.

Antoine admitted it seemed an unlikely occurrence but said
that he was not about to walk all the way over there and then all
the way back home to get his swimming suit if it were true.

It was no mirage. A tractor-trailer carrying a 30-foot-by-7-
foot, 4-foot deep, 800-gallon swimming pool, complete with
three lifeguards, had set down on Prospect Place between Sche-
nectady and Troy avenues.

Seeing this, children scurried home to get their swimming
suits and to spread news of the miracle, a story most of their
mothers considered to be rather lacking in credibility.

"My friend Raymond isn't here today," commented William
Ricks, twelve years old and dripping wet outside the pool, "and
he'll never, ever believe this. It's like a spaceship landing."

What seemed an apparition was actually the Swim Mobile, a
Department of Parks and Recreation vehicle, one of two that will

be making stops throughout Queens and Brooklyn this summer. It was out for its first test run yesterday.

"We came out of the Coney Island yard this morning," said Walter Gaillard, who drives the Swim Mobile, "sort of bringing the beach along with us." He said he loved having a job where he was greeted each day with such enthusiasm.

The children came running in their swimming suits, although a couple of them changed clothes behind some bushes — but barely behind. They set down their clothes in piles on the sidewalk and lined up.

Kevin Williams, a recreational specialist who is a lifeguard of the Swim Mobile, along with Mike McCune and Darryl Hamer, instructed the children before they climbed up the ladder that there was to be "no wearing of socks, no diving, no dunking and no horseplay" — but to little avail.

The children may never have seen such a thing, but they certainly knew what to do with it on this hot summer's day. They splashed about wildly and laughed as they doused each other, the lifeguards, passersby and spectators — especially one stiff in a collared shirt and tie who was taking notes.

"There is no age restriction," Mr. Hamer said, "but we find that not too many adults want to get into a small pool with fifteen kids. Think about it."

Also, the water in the pool, which comes straight from the hydrant, was quite cold. A few of the children complained they had been tricked into torture, and climbed out with their teeth chattering, then sat down on the hot sidewalk for warmth.

"Sometimes adults get thrown in," said Steve DiGiovanni, dispatcher for the Swim Mobile. "Last year in a Hasidic neighborhood people tossed in their rabbi, clothes and all."

William Castro, the city's chief of recreation, said the Parks Department also operates a Play Mobile, which is a portable playground; five Skate Mobiles, each carrying 120 pairs of roller skates; five Arts and Crafts Mobiles, a Puppet Mobile for puppet shows; five Sports Mobiles, equipped with Ping-Pong tables, Wiffle Balls and bats, a pool table and such; and a Show Wagon, carrying a portable stage, live bands, clowns, jugglers and stilt walkers.

"But the Swim Mobile is the most popular unit," said Mr. DiGiovanni. The children in the pool said they could see why, most of them living in red-brick buildings more suitable for baking loaves of bread on days like this than for human habitation.

"These mobiles are delivery of services — literally," said Henry J. Stern, commissioner of Parks and Recreation. "They were conceived in an era of more free spending. There used to be more of them, but we're trying to keep some of them on the road."

"People told me they'd seen this thing," said Marvina Ricks, mother of William, one of the swimmers, but she had regarded it as urban folklore.

"Alligator!" screamed Devon Creel, waist-deep in water, and the others turned in horror to see for themselves, but all they saw was eleven-year-old Devon with a big smile and an inflatable toy.

"That is not funny, Devon!" ten-year-old Cheryl Morgan screamed back at him. "We don't know what's in here."

She hit him with a beach ball. A lifeguard splashed her as punishment for horseplay.

At 3:00 P.M. the pool was drained, and the truck disappeared around the corner, leaving only pools of water that were quickly evaporating on the sidewalk.

William Ricks was right. Raymond would never believe it.

. . . AND SHAKERS

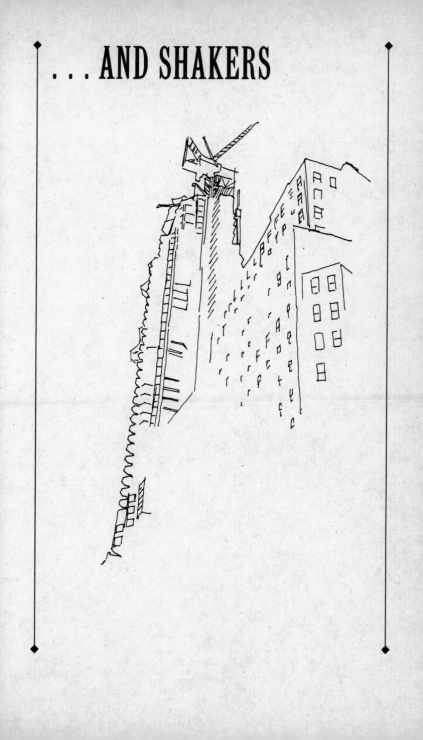

DONALD TRUMP, BIRTHDAY BILLIONAIRE

DONALD TRUMP TURNS forty today, and it's about time.

This is a difficult occasion for Mr. Trump. Not that he is terribly troubled about being forty. After all, most of the people he hobnobs with, people at the top of their fields, are two, three and four decades his senior. In his world he remains annoyingly young.

What's tough is that everyone has been asking him what he wants for his birthday. One person even asked him what he *needed* for his birthday.

And, frankly, he can't think of a darned thing. That tomorrow is Father's Day only makes matters worse.

The newspapers on the backseat of his limousine yesterday listed lots of GIFT IDEAS FOR DAD, one advertisement reading SURPRISE DAD with a $4.79 clip-on necktie. And Mr. Trump commented that he'd be surprised all right.

"I have a tough time with the whole idea of presents," Mr. Trump said yesterday, watching the world – the Park Avenue part – roll by the smoked-glass windows of his stretch limo.

He said that he still has Christmas presents he hasn't opened yet.

For many, a fortieth birthday is a time for reflection, but Mr. Trump said he didn't really have the time for that, thanks, what with dozens of appointments yesterday that began with meeting architects for Trump Park.

Don't panic. That's not a plan to develop Central Park, as his critics who see him as a rogue billionaire might imagine, but a remodeling of buildings at Central Park South and the Avenue of the Americas to make a condominium and rental complex.

Then there were meetings with lawyers on the $1.32 billion antitrust suit he and others filed against the National Football League, meetings on his proposed $5 billion Television City project (to include the world's tallest building) and a meeting with bankers who are apparently lending him money — although with Donald Trump it could be the other way around. There was brief discussion of his plans to build a domed sports stadium in Queens. He then met with a television director about a mini-series, *I'll Take Manhattan*, in which Mr. Trump is to play himself.

There was a newspaper ad on the next page for a Weedeater, one of the items pictured in an ad headlined GIFT IDEAS DAD IS SURE TO LOVE. There aren't too many weeds in the life of Donald Trump. He lives most of the time in a Trump Tower triplex penthouse that might even be worth the $10 million he says it is.

At forty he lives up there in the clouds with his three children and his striking wife, Ivana, a former fashion model — "a top model," in Trump-speak, who was married to him ten years ago by the family's minister, the Reverend Norman Vincent Peale, who is, incidentally, one of the top men of the cloth in the country.

At thirty-eight Mrs. Trump retains her model's figure and is devoid of wrinkles. She claims to work ten-hour days at the office, handles a heavy social calendar and does most of the cooking for the family. (C'mon!) Without trying to arouse further undue sentiment against her, it must also be said that she is a top-flight skier (an alternate on the 1972 Czechoslovak Olympic team) and that when she was eight months pregnant with their last child, her condition still didn't really show.

In addition to her, Mr. Trump's further holdings at forty include the Grand Hyatt Hotel — his first big project in Manhattan — the St. Moritz Hotel, waterfront condominium buildings in Palm Beach and not one but two Atlantic City hotels, with casinos that make what he describes as "ridiculous" sums. Their reported gross revenue last month happened to be $38.6 million.

He also has this professional football team, the Generals, that doesn't play games.

Shown with the Weedeater is a home suit-steaming outfit for dad, something Donald Trump could press his own suits with up in the penthouse and save wads of cash.

A birthday gift most people would be thrilled to receive is a 118-room Palm Beach mansion, but it turns out Mr. Trump already has one of these. He also has a house on the water — to include an island in the water — in Greenwich, Connecticut.

At forty Mr. Trump is trim, with no midriff bulge and no gray hair. He has abandoned the flashy haberdashery he favored on his thirtieth birthday, which included a much talked about burgundy suit and matching shoes. Now his dress is rather conservative and casual; he often wears dark suits, white shirts, subdued ties and loafers.

He doesn't drink or smoke and has almost totally given up prevarication, perhaps because he couldn't make up anything half so outrageous as what he's actually doing.

He rises at 5:00 A.M. and is often still making business calls until bedtime. "I love what I'm doing," he said. "I may just now be hitting my stride." Think of it.

"I always had confidence I could do things," he said, leaning over his desk, piled high with proposals and renderings, and adding in a hushed tone, "But you know, this is all a little preposterous." It is not completely lost on him that he, Donald Trump, of Queens, sits now in his office in his Trump Tower, adjacent to the IBM and AT&T buildings. Far be it from him to remind us that his building is taller than those two and that he is on Fifth Avenue next door to Tiffany's and that they, well, they are not.

People ask for his autograph on the street, and yesterday one pedestrian touched him for good luck.

At forty Mr. Trump seems to be in the enviable position of being able to buy stock and see its price go up simply because he bought it. And isn't that a whole lot easier than having to put on an apron and stand over a hot, dirty press printing the damned money yourself?

He is, chronologically, part of the baby-boom generation

that began turning forty this year. Magazine cover stories on this historic phenomenon tell of a generation of aggressive and idealistic youths turning into realistic middle-aged citizens. The articles say this generation works long hours, exercises a lot and consists of couples of which both partners must work outside the home to "have it all." (Of course, to achieve all that he has, Mr. Trump's wife, Ivana, has to work outside the home, as an executive for The Trump Organization.)

There are often accompanying articles on "the problems of having it all," but Mr. Trump said in his limo yesterday that he wasn't sure exactly what that meant.

EVERY FATHER WILL ENJOY THIS 8-PIECE DRILL BIT SET read another ad in the paper on the backseat, and as Mr. Trump vigorously discussed some deal or other on his limo phone, one wondered if perhaps he indeed wanted and needed this drill bit set but had just never thought of it. Or does he just call one of the major construction companies at his command when Ivana nags him about fixing the screen door or hanging a picture?

As far as presents go, he isn't really interested yet in airplanes, race cars, polo ponies, artwork, yachts and the like. He says he doesn't have time for all of that now and prefers putting his money back into deals. He fully believes that life is a game but figures, as long as he's going to suit up, why not try to win.

He believes further that New York will be totally destroyed by nuclear weapons within the next fifty years, not by Soviets but by some radical leader who gains access to nuclear arms.

He would like to negotiate arms treaties with the Soviets. Really. "Negotiation is an art," he said, "and I have a gift for it." Those who do business with Mr. Trump think the Soviets would be crazy to sit at a negotiating table with him, certain that Mr. Trump would emerge with every Soviet missile, pistol and footlocker and the Kremlin's air rights. And the Moscow Hyatt.

"It's in his genes," said Fred Trump, Donald's father, explaining his son's success in real estate and recalling his three sons growing up on construction sites and in rental offices. "We did business with Donald when he was sixteen years old," said the owner of one of New York's largest construction companies. "He was a veteran by the time he was twenty-five."

Oh, now here's something: DAD IS SURE TO LOVE THIS THREE-SPEED OSCILLATING SPRINKLER.

A surprise birthday party – "something on the order of the Statue of Liberty celebration," in the words of one of his friends – was planned for Mr. Trump, who found out about it and scuttled it. He loves nothing more than seeing one of his projects in the spotlight, but he actually seems uncomfortable when he is personally at center stage.

Mr. Trump said that he took on his most recent project, the refurbishing of the Wollman Memorial Skating Rink in Central Park, because the delay by the city of more than six years in fixing it irritated him.

Reporters now ask Mr. Trump if he'd mind doing something about the subways, the crime, the weather and so on. He is constantly asked about his interest in running for elective office. "Absolutely not," he answers. "It is too difficult to really do anything."

"I won't skate at the opening of the ice rink," said Donald Trump. "There are too many people who'd love to see me fall down."

RALPH LAUREN:
HOLIER THAN THOU

THE CHAIRMAN OF the board wore a work shirt, old jeans with holes in them and scuffed-up cowboy boots as he discussed the business of the day: what American business executives should be wearing.

"Poetic license," explained Ralph Lauren, who heads the international Polo/Ralph Lauren fashion empire.

How the chairman of the board gets holes in his jeans sitting in an office on West 55th Street in Manhattan is anybody's guess. But when Ralph Lauren is wearing old clothes with holes in them around town, and even in some of his advertisements, it can't be too long before tailors will offer HOLES IN YOUR CLOTHES WHILE-U-WAIT and shoe repair shops will advertise X-PERT BOOT SCUFF-ING — ASK ABOUT OUR NEW HORSE MANURE APPLICA-TIONS. Then: "Just Holes" stores.

Such is Mr. Lauren's power of suggestion. Once Ralph Lauren was a boy from the Bronx — a boy named Ralph Lifschitz, until his family changed the name when he was sixteen years old — and then he was a tie designer, and now, of course, Ralph Lauren is a way of life.

As Mr. Lauren strolled through Sotheby's auction house on a recent day, looking for appointments for his new Ralph Lauren department store, he was spotted by a young man wearing not one but two Polo shirts — the knit shirt beneath the pink button-down — as well as Polo horn-rimmed eyeglass frames and what one must assume were Polo trousers, Polo socks and Polo loafers.

The young man stood transfixed at the sight of Mr. Lauren, looking as if he had glimpsed his Creator.

Hundreds of stores and boutiques throughout the world sell Ralph Lauren shirts, ties, suits, wallets, skin lotions, address books, wool undershirts, tuxedos, suitcases, duffel bags, pillowcases, towels, napkins, shower curtains, dinner plates, flatware and you name it. Has he thought about Ralph Lauren food served in a Ralph Lauren restaurant? "Absolutely!" he said. To his credit, he did turn down a proposal for Ralph Lauren coffins.

The world's first Polo/Ralph Lauren department store at Madison Avenue and 72nd Street will soon be followed by more new stores in Italy, Switzerland, Spain, Austria, Greece, Canada and Mexico, among others – global Laurenism.

Critics accuse him of not designing at all, but sewing his name and logo on preppie styles. When Mr. Lauren was once asked what made his sheets different, he answered, "The difference is, you will want to buy them." His customers seem to be buying a measure of confidence and security, with the little polo pony symbol or the Lauren label being their assurance of at least an image of quality. They are also buying what Mr. Lauren has described as an "old-money look."

On the visit to Sotheby's he asked a representative of the auction house why the paintings of horses, hounds and hunters in red coats and high hats were so popular. "Because of the interest in a return to tradition," the representative explained, "and an interest in the aristocratic look." Mr. Lauren replied in his soft voice, "I can appreciate that."

He describes his styles as "antifashion," from the western wear to his traditional lines. He is described as the "most American" of designers, and he seems to understand better than many that, although American men may want a touch of style, they fear looking like dandies and, indeed, tend to regard fashion as just another horse manure application.

"American men," he said, "want a bit more style than just the office uniform, but they don't want distracting clothes that indicate they are too much into themselves.

"I am not complimented," he added, "when someone says, 'I like your shoes' or 'I like your tie.'"

His advertisements look for all the world like propaganda posters for the nuclear family and the American Way of Life. They often depict rugged individualists – handsome, WASPy and aristocratic – standing ready in their simple $260 sweaters to defend home, family and country club.

When Mr. Lauren discusses his clothing, he speaks of "honesty," "integrity" and "realness," and he says things like "My ties represent all that I stand for." He talks of "standing by" his ties when Bloomingdale's said they were just too wide. He stuck by his instincts until Bloomingdale's and the rest of the world came around.

The forty-five-year-old Mr. Lauren, who has been married for twenty years and has three children, not only espouses Laurenism but lives it. One of his "life-style groupings" of products for the home is called Jamaica, and he has a house there. His Montauk house is said to sport much of his New England and Mariner collections, and the Thoroughbred grouping should do nicely when he builds on his Pound Ridge estate.

Another grouping is titled Log Cabin, of which he has several in a compound on his ten-thousand-acre RRL Ranch in Colorado. Mr. Lauren also has sixteen hundred beef cattle out there, with hides bearing the RRL Ranch brand. Soon, all cattle will want them.

EUGENE LANG'S "I HAVE A DREAM" PROGRAM

S ITTING ON THE dais, Eugene Lang, a multimillionaire industrialist, suddenly realized the commencement address he was about to deliver was complete balderdash, to put it nicely.

He was about to tell sixty-one sixth graders in a warm Harlem auditorium that he had also attended P.S. 121, a half century ago, that he had worked hard and made a lot of money and that – quick, the No-Doz! – if they worked hard maybe they could be successful, too.

Instead, Mr. Lang, a magnate with a no-nonsense style, stepped to the podium and told the graduates that if they stayed in school, he would pay the college tuitions for each and every one of them: college educations on the house!

There was stunned silence, peppered with a few audible gasps. Then students, parents and teachers cheered and mobbed him. "I have never kissed so many strangers," Mr. Lang recalled. He told them that he was thereby earmarking $2,000 for each of them toward college tuitions, that he would add more money each year that they stayed in school and that their college tuitions were assured.

The speech was five years ago. There has been no publicity of any kind about this at Mr. Lang's behest.

The students are now all in the eleventh grade, and they are stopping by Mr. Lang's office these days to tell him of their preparations for college aptitude tests and to discuss colleges they might want to attend.

All fifty-two of the students still living in the New York area have stayed in school and are doing well enough to qualify for college. This is considered remarkable, given the high dropout rates for students such as those in this group, who are black or Hispanic and predominantly poor.

Mr. Lang said that the nine other students moved away but that two were keeping in touch with him and said they planned to take advantage of his offer.

"Dropping out is what's normal," said Darryl Gallishaw at a gathering of several of the students recently at the Youth Action Program center in East Harlem, where they were being told about free preparation for the Scholastic Aptitude Test and free tutoring for their classes.

"Around here, you are big and important if you drop out," said Aristedes Alvarado, another of the students.

Several students said they thought Mr. Lang's concept had worked, because many children in the neighborhood put ideas of college out of their minds at an early age, thinking it a luxury beyond the reach of their parents.

There are tuition-free colleges, of course, but the students said many in the group had not thought of attending college at all until Mr. Lang's inspiration – and several said they might well have dropped out of high school by now.

Also helpful, they said, was the constant attention paid them by Mr. Lang and by Johnny Rivera, twenty-three years old, who works at the center. Mr. Lang pays Mr. Rivera to watch over the program on a day-to-day basis, with Mr. Rivera asking the students how things are going in school and occasionally visiting their homes to talk with their parents.

"Naked money can have an arrogance," said Mr. Lang, who has remained in close touch with the students since his speech. They visit him from time to time in his office at the headquarters of his company, Refac Technology Development Corporation, in the Chanin Building, at 42nd Street and Lexington Avenue. They talk to him about everything from math problems to problems with parents and friends.

Mr. Lang's promise has taken on a name: the "I Have a Dream" Program, with annual reunions, meetings, a newsletter and, most recently, a camping trip.

Students in the program are viewed a little differently. "Other kids envy us and tease us sometimes," said Mr. Gallishaw. "Like saying: 'You got an old man miser looking after you.'

"My junior-high-school teachers were always after me to keep my grades up," he continued, meaning the teachers did not want him to spoil his chance. "I keep quiet about being in the program now."

Some of the students said their parents' interest in their schoolwork had been greatly heightened. "My mother is after me all the time about homework," said Leonard Quinones. "She said if I blow this opportunity, she'll kill me."

"My parents are dropouts," said David Nieves. "They want me to go all the way now."

"You can't get into drugs and sex and stuff and do this, too," said Mr. Gallishaw. "My friends started doing drugs, so I switched to this group of friends," he said, looking around at the other students in the program.

"Sometimes you see that happening to your friends," said Mr. Alvarado, "and you wish other classes and other kids had what we have."

Telesforo Rivera is the one student who is considering not going to college. He may join the Army instead. The others tease him about it, but gently. Mr. Lang has told them it is their choice.

An irony is that Mr. Lang now expects many of these students will qualify for scholarships. "Hell, a lot of them will get full scholarships," he said. "Colleges fight over good minority students."

He happens to know. He is chairman of the board of managers of Swarthmore College, a trustee of the New School for Social Research, a member of the Advisory Board of Columbia University's Graduate School of Business and chairman of the Conference of Board Chairmen of small, independent liberal-arts colleges.

He believes the concept has now shown itself to be successful and wouldn't mind seeing some other wealthy people adopt classes of their own.

"The great thing about this," said Mr. Lang, a bit of a penny-pincher who flies coach class and eschews limousines for subways and buses, "is that nothing is leeched off for fund-raising expenses or anything else. You write a tuition check to a school."

Mr. Lang, sixty-six, lives in New York City and has three children and four grandchildren. Lately, this president and chairman of the board has been sitting in his office in an old Art Deco skyscraper, thinking that there is more to life than just making money: "I asked myself: 'Am I to just sit here and keep proving to myself what I already know? That I can take money and make more money with it?'"

Philanthropic work, he said, now occupies "more of my time than my stockholders would like.

"I don't like to see a bridle put on the human spirit," said the self-made millionaire, "in business or school. A view that one can't afford college so why try is a bridle."

The students recalled that they were falling asleep during the sixth-grade graduation and that they were thinking, "Oh, no, more balderdash," to put it nicely, when Mr. Lang stepped to the podium. And he almost gave it to them, but instead they heard what one of the students called "maybe the greatest speech ever made."

None could recall the next speaker on the program.

Postscript: This article brought widespread publicity to Mr. Lang's program, prompting the U.S. secretary of education to fly in to see it for himself, and more than a hundred others to sponsor classes nationwide. In June 1987, twenty-seven of the fifty-one students still living in New York graduated from high school, with twenty-one more expected to graduate by December 1987, and twenty-five of the twenty-seven June graduates had been accepted by colleges as diverse as Barnard and La Guardia Community College.

DAVID SCHARF,
COMMANDANT
OF CATERERS

He DOESN'T KNOW who catered the D-Day invasion, but David Scharf figures this has to be about the closest thing to it.

The Allied forces weren't dining on his chicken liver pâté or his kosher moo goo gai pan either. They ate C rations and liked it.

Mr. Scharf is catering a Hasidic wedding this Sunday with twenty thousand guests expected. If you aren't invited, you should realistically consider yourself not all that close to the family. The affair is at the Jacob K. Javits Convention Center and is the center's first wedding.

This being the height of the wedding season, Mr. Scharf is catering other soirées that same day, including a somewhat smaller one in which twenty-nine Russian immigrant couples are being married simultaneously at a hotel in Teaneck, and other affairs on Long Island.

Mr. Scharf will be airborne on Sunday, hopping by helicopter from one wedding reception to another and commanding by radio-telephone his armies of workers, his convoys of potato salad.

Tractor-trailers will move out with about four tons of food from the Bensonhurst commissary of David Scharf Caterers Inc. at 2200 hours (10:00 P.M.) Saturday, bound for the Javits Center, where a crash effort is under way to make the kitchen kosher. A team of twelve rabbis is supervising the scouring of the kitchen, to include the cleaning of the twenty-six huge ovens with blow-torches to remove any non-kosher residues.

Most guests will arrive at the affair via thirty hired shuttle buses from the Borough Park and Williamsburg neighborhoods of Brooklyn, although some guests have already begun to arrive from several foreign countries for this wedding of the only daughter of the Grand Rabbi of the Hasidic Munkaczer dynasty, Moshe L. Rabinovich.

The Grand Rabbi's son, Chaim, was married in 1984 at the New York Coliseum to a woman whose cousin had been married earlier that same week at the Nassau Coliseum. Leaders of these ultraconservative, fundamentalist groups explain that the weddings are of such monumental proportions because followers see them as tantamount to royal weddings.

The 1984 Nassau Coliseum wedding of the Satmar sect was attended by about twenty thousand people and probably holds the modern-day wedding reception record for sandwiches: eight thousand.

Mr. Scharf's pre-ceremony smorgasbord and post-ceremony sit-down dinner will include 200 pounds of Waldorf salad, 1,000 stuffed peppers, 540 pounds of moo goo gai pan and mountains of cantaloupe supremes, relish boats and sautéed peapods in mock butter sauce, to be served by 240 waiters. He scoffs at the sandwich record, noting that his affair will feature gourmet dishes served on china, not sandwiches on paper plates.

Because the dishwashing machines at the center are not kosher, he will truck an estimated 35,000 dirty dishes back to Brooklyn to be washed.

Borough Park, where the group's synagogue and schools are, is all abuzz this week with talk of the wedding. Women are baking for a week of receptions to follow the wedding, out-of-town guests are sleeping on couches and rented roll-away beds, and bleachers are being built inside the synagogue.

Printed posters on lampposts tell of the wedding and of the availability of a cassette tape "at your local cassette shop" of the music that is to be played at the wedding.

"Everyone in school is very excited," said Moshe Deutsch, eleven years old, especially about the reception that is to last until about 4:00 A.M. Monday. "We have practiced songs and have made signs to take to the wedding. A boy from Australia who came for the wedding is in my class this week."

There is plenty for them to be excited about. "The dancing gets absolutely wild," said Yussie Ostreicher, a friend of the family. "Men balance chairs, ladders, candles and bottles on their heads while they dance. I've seen them light their hats on fire and wear them burning while they dance."

The bride, Frima Rabinovich, nineteen, and the groom, Rabbi Yosef Horowitz, twenty, are fourth cousins. Their marriage was arranged, and they have met only twice, once when they were introduced in the company of their families, and once more at their engagement party in the company of a thousand people.

They will be married outdoors in the middle of 11th Avenue (which will be closed to traffic) on a stage made of truck trailers. Men and women will be separated by police barricades, just as they will celebrate in separate halls during the reception and dinner at the Javits Center, and just as they are separated in the synagogue, which they enter by separate doors – in keeping with Orthodox tradition.

"If most of the gifts aren't monetary," said Mr. Ostreicher, a friend of the family, "the bride and groom may have to go into the appliance business."

And what if more than twenty thousand people show up and threaten to overrun the smorgasbord? "I'm finished!" Mr. Scharf said. Don't believe it. This veteran of thousands of wedding reception battles is ready for the tactical deployment of hundreds of pounds of Hawaiian chicken should the situation on the ground become desperate.

THE HANGER KING

So, TELL US, Mr. Hanger —

"Please," Bernie Spitz interrupts, "call me Bernie."

People are always making that mistake. Mr. Spitz, a.k.a. "The Hanger King," owns The Henry Hanger Company, and people logically assume when they meet him that he must be Henry — last name, Hanger.

"You wanna talk about hangers today?" Mr. Spitz says eagerly, standing in his dazzling hanger showroom in the Garment District.

A large sign reading WELCOME TO THE HANGER WORLD OF HENRY HANGER really understates the case. This is a hanger *cosmos* with more than eight hundred styles on display. And you thought they were just wood or wire.

In this big city of small worlds — with its own flower district, diamond district, fur district, kitchenware district, used musical instrument district, songwriting district and so on — Bernie Spitz is a legend in the hanger district, located around 34th Street and Seventh Avenue, where he has his showroom.

The man claims to have *introduced* the plastic hanger to America. He *pioneered* the slacks rack. He has a home in Beverly Hills, if he does say so himself.

At sixty-eight years old, with more than fifty years in the business, Mr. Spitz sparkles, and doesn't have a wrinkle on him; not on his face and certainly — certainly! — not on his clothing, which he keeps neat on the most fantastic hangers imaginable, while the rest of us are tossing our clothes on doorknobs and piling them high on unused exercise machines. Like no one else, he wears a two-inch, diamond-studded hanger on his lapel.

He admits to one big mistake, hanger-wise. In 1954, while at the Peninsula Hotel in Hong Kong, Mr. Spitz discovered a strange sort of hanger in his closet, one that had a small knob on the top, rather than a hook, and was useless when stolen. He brought one back and, like some dreaded Asian virus, the "ball and hook" idea escaped, spreading throughout the hotel-motel industry, ruining his replacement-hanger business and, of course, making it virtually impossible for guests to hang their pants on a hanger on the shower rod to steam out the wrinkles.

Bernie has tortoiseshell hangers, key-lock coat hangers, thin hangers for small New York apartments, ultraheavy Italian wood hangers, satin-padded hangers, full-bodice hangers with hips and breasts, and – don't get him started.

"But my claim to fame is the unbreakable hanger!" he proclaimed, dropping to his knees in his office and pounding the floor with a Henry hanger.

There are hangers in the showroom bearing such names as Esprit, Swatch, Calvin Klein and Liz Claiborne. "A garment well displayed is a sale half made," Mr. Spitz said of these and other companies that order custom hangers for their clothing.

He said that he does not – would not – sell those cheap wire dry-cleaner hangers that people use to break into cars. He has hangers that sell for $1,800 per dozen – solid brass – and he has customers who buy them, two dozen at a time. One customer, Marvin Davis, the millionaire businessman, has three or four thousand Henry hangers.

"You gonna hang a $5,000 dress or a $3,000 suit on a wire dry-cleaning hanger?" Mr. Spitz asks. Not us.

"I could never work for another hanger company," said Norma Shinsky, executive liaison of the firm. "Not now. This is where the excitement and the glamour are in the hanger business. Famous people and the finest hotels use our hangers. If you need a thousand custom hangers tomorrow, you got 'em."

Perhaps because there is just nowhere else left to spend the stuff, Bernie Spitz says people are "putting a lot of money in their closets."

"There are people who call themselves closet decorators who come in here now," he said. "They want beautiful hangers, hundreds of them all the same, covered in fabric to match bedspreads and curtains.

"Hangers have become status symbols," Mr. Spitz said, just like the designer furs and clothing that hang upon them – status symbols upon status symbols.

When he was sixteen years old, his business cards read, "Call me Bernie, the youngest hanger salesman in America." His father (yes, Henry) had started the small business during the Depression, and when Mr. Spitz was eighteen his father sent him and his brother Herbert, sixteen, on the road to drum up some business.

They ventured where no hanger salesmen had gone before, tens of thousands of miles, meandering and cold canvassing through upstate New York, out across the Midwest, trading in the old car for a flashy Packard convertible in Oklahoma City, then wheeling week after week throughout Texas, before heading on out to California.

"It's been a wonderful life," said the tanned, gold-bangled Bernie Spitz. "There's never a dull moment in the hanger business, as you can imagine!"

NELSON DOUBLEDAY'S NEWFOUND FRIENDS AND RELATIVES

His FRIENDS ALWAYS said they were busy washing the dog, rotating the tires or sharpening the scissors when Nelson Doubleday, Jr., owner of the Mets, used to call.

"It was like the commissioner of sanitation calling to offer you a free ride on a garbage scow," one acquaintance recalled.

They knew what Mr. Doubleday wanted when he called in the early 1980s, back when the Mets had a firm hold on last place. He wanted to invite them to a Mets game, to build attendance and give him someone to sit with.

"It was lonely at Shea," Mr. Doubleday said yesterday. "People snubbed me. I often sat alone."

Today, Nelson Doubleday stands as perhaps the most popular man in New York. Yesterday, on the eve of the opening game of the World Series at Shea Stadium, the telephone in his Park Avenue office rang incessantly, and amazingly enough, each of the callers – hundreds of them – claimed to be a close friend, an old friend or, if that didn't seem to be working, a blood relative of Mr. Doubleday's.

They were anxious to see him again, very soon, and wondered what he was doing Saturday night, when the Series began, or perhaps Sunday evening, when Dwight Gooden was expected to be on the mound.

He took a call from a "distant cousin," then a "close friend"

of his from a store where he bought some candy in Massachusetts, followed by a former St. John's basketball player, who argued that he had probably given Mr. Doubleday great pleasure in
watching him play and that maybe Mr. Doubleday should repay
him with complimentary World Series tickets.

And there was the young man who had promised his grandmother on her deathbed that he would get her tickets to the Series. She didn't sound like she'd be much fun at the game.

Friends say that no one has more fun at a ball game than
Nelson Doubleday.

"Nelson! Nelsuuuuuun!" Three Mets fans wearing T-shirts
and holding cups of beer leaned over a railing at Shea Stadium
during a recent game and yelled down at Mr. Doubleday, who was
scampering up the aisle from his seat in the stands to buy a hot
dog.

He stopped, craned his neck upward, answered their questions about why he didn't move so-and-so up to third in the batting order and why he thinks Astroturf stinks. He argued a few
points with them, but not vehemently. "It isn't smart," he said, "to
argue too much with three guys standing over you with cups of
beer."

He excused himself, saying that he had to have a hot dog
and that the line wasn't getting any shorter between innings.

Mr. Doubleday, who has been called, "the most powerful
sports investor in New York" because of his large personal invest-
ment in the Islanders and controlling interest in the Mets, sits in
the stands and waits in line for hot dogs and beer.

"That's Doubleday?" a fan asked incredulously, looking at
this preppie, patrician man — Princeton by way of Deerfield Academy — whose shirttail had come untucked from all the bounding
around, as he waited in line.

The fan remarked that most baseball owners — the owner of
another New York baseball team, for example — "wouldn't dare
leave his bulletproof glass luxury box. I think he has sandbags and
a machine gun up there," the fan said, referring, of course, to
Yankees owner George Steinbrenner. To be sure, Mr. Doubleday
has a luxury box with two color TVs, comfortable chairs, a bartender and a buffet table of imported wines and delicacies, but he

said that he still prefers to spend as much time as possible out in the open air.

Mr. Doubleday said he sits in his seat in the front row at the edge of the Mets' dugout "so I can get a feel for the game." He does not speak to the players, except for maybe an occasional hello before a game. He does not call the dugout during games as some owners do and does not visit the locker room after the game. "That's not my ball game," he said.

Said Raymond Davidson, an artist with Doubleday publishing company, who attends many games with him, "I think he realizes that there is something spiritual that goes on with a team that no one should disturb."

An usher, Jimmy Sansaverino, noted that the fifty-two-year-old Mr. Doubleday has always sat in the stands, taking the bad comments with the good. "He has always been the same," said Mr. Sansaverino. "He has calmly said that it would take four or five years to build a winner, and now he has."

Mr. Doubleday, whose ancestor Abner Doubleday is the legendary, if not the actual, inventor of baseball, said he doesn't mind when a fan criticizes the team. "They bought a seat," he said. "It's their prerogative to tell the owner what they think."

Balancing a cardboard tray of beer cups, he was stopped by fans offering congratulations. Small children in blue Mets caps asked for his autograph. "Dear Billy," he wrote, "nice to see you at Shea – Nelson Doubleday."

Fans recommend their nephews as bat boys, and they recommend players the team should acquire. "The day I make a trade for the Mets, we're all in trouble," Mr. Doubleday said.

He said he learns things from talking with fans such as problems with ticket scalping and traffic congestion, and he even receives ideas worth thinking about on how to improve the team. But talking to the public can backfire, he added, recalling the fabulous young ballplayer in California who, after a search of several weeks by team scouts, was found in a league for seven-year-olds.

He took another call in his office yesterday and told the caller: "Tell him the commissioner took all the tickets. Tell him anything. I've never heard of this guy."

He shook his head and said he had seen every conceivable ploy to get through to him to ask for tickets, including the one where someone comes in under the pretense of writing a piece about him.

Pity.

IN BROWNSVILLE, CHRIS ARMSTRONG MAKES IT MORE THAN JUST A GAME

JUGHEAD STEVENS THREATENS the very future of the softball game, as he wallops one pitch after another downrange in suborbital flight, the balls still rising as they clear the tall chain-link fence around the playground, then crashing down on the cars, buildings and residents of Amboy Street in Brownsville.

Little kids try to retrieve the balls quickly so the game can keep going, but as Jughead rockets them onto rooftops and into an adjacent backyard occupied by two vicious guard dogs, there are breaks in the action.

Perhaps thousands of other schoolyard softball games are in progress on this summer evening in New York. "But this is a little more than just a game," explained Chris Armstrong, as he watched sixteen-year-old Jughead and the rest of the Brownsville Invaders practice.

This is Mr. Armstrong's team. He organized it eight years ago, when he was just fifteen years old. He and the ballplayers point out that there is nothing else for youths to do in the poor Brooklyn neighborhood: no Boy Scouts, no movie theaters, no YMCA, no park activities, no shopping district.

"I was fed up with being bored," said Mr. Armstrong, a heavyset man whose shirttail is out after a day of work in an office. "Everybody was bored and getting into trouble. The crime rate here is sky-high. The police statistics show the crimes are committed by young men — boys, really."

At the age of seventeen Mr. Armstrong decided he wanted a lasting program and, after long hours of studying how in the library, he drew up papers, without the help of a lawyer, to form the Brownsville Youth Organization as a nonprofit corporation.

The group fixed up the playground behind Public School 183, but it is still a field of broken concrete and sinkholes, one of them six feet in diameter and filled with water, right next to second base. Smack dab in left-center field stands an old handball wall.

A recent game was interrupted by two men running onto the playing field brandishing handguns. "It's like the OK Corral around here," Mr. Armstrong said.

After forming the group, Mr. Armstrong and Linda Fuller, who is now his fiancée, set about seeking contributions of money and material from local businesses. The softball team became a league and then two leagues, and Mr. Armstrong also began a football program. The organization now receives contributions from two hundred businesses, from Chase Manhattan Bank to Rudy's Coffee Shop-to-a-Meal.

Mr. Armstrong has developed a public-relations group made up of several of his ballplayers. They attend dinners and ceremonies at which they accept donations and give thank-you speeches.

"You meet a lot of important people," said Kemah Jones, a fifteen-year-old player. "The food is great, too. But you have to play it off a little, you know, and not pig out."

Mr. Armstrong has also assembled a board of directors that includes officers of large corporations, including banks and utilities.

Three hundred youths from nine to nineteen years old are playing in the softball leagues this summer, and the organization says it has two thousand participants in all its programs. Mr. Armstrong lets the youths do everything – coaching, umpiring and acting as league commissioners – "to give them a dose of real life." He has the players do league work on his home computer to get them interested in computers.

Kemah does the play-by-play for the softball games. He is part of a video and sound crew that Mr. Armstrong has assembled to produce and direct the videotaping of the games, do pregame and postgame shows, play-by-play and commentary.

Kemah also coaches a team of younger players and is involved in a new youth theater group that Mr. Armstrong is setting up. Kemah said he might also get on the staff of the organization's newsletter.

Mr. Armstrong, who accepts no money for his work, has written to several large Long Island aerospace companies, requesting their cooperation in an aerospace-careers program he is trying to develop.

He has also secured space in two basements across the street from the schoolyard and is furnishing them so that the organization can start a school-tutoring program this fall. He makes regular checks of the report cards of those in his programs.

Next, Mr. Armstrong wants to purchase a sixteen-unit apartment building a block from the schoolyard that the city is going to auction. The price of real estate in Brownsville is going down, he said, and he believes the organization can buy it for about $7,000. He said he would refurbish the apartments and rent them to poor people for about $150 a month.

Mr. Armstrong has become something of a father figure for many of the local youths. Many have no fathers at home and turn to him with their problems at all hours of the day. He walks the streets, and when he sees members of his organization out late, he tells them to go on home.

Neighbors say the softball games have become quite the neighborhood events, with the annual all-star game a regular street festival. Mr. Armstrong has worked out a deal with the New York Mets to let the most valuable player of the all-star game sit in the Mets dugout during a game at Shea Stadium.

After years of work Mr. Armstrong has convinced the city to resurface the field behind the school and tear down the old handball wall. "It will be a symbol that someone cares about Brownsville," he said.

After practice the Invaders stood around in the glow of sodium-vapor lights, leaning on bats and talking baseball. An adult from the neighborhood stopped by and said: "I thank God for this. It gives the kids something to do and keeps them from getting into trouble and getting hurt. These boys didn't ask to be born here."

MUGGERS, MURDERERS AND THE DOUBLE-PARKED

MAFIA RUBOUT
SPARKS INTEREST

"Is THIS THE spot?" Janet D'Amico asked as she joined the crowd.

"This is *the* spot," Akeem Reynolds, who seemed to be there for the day, said emphatically, "from now on."

There was no formal ceremony, but a patch of pavement in front of Sparks Steak House, on East 46th Street near Third Avenue, took its place in the annals of New York Mafia folklore yesterday as the place where Paul Castellano was murdered.

Or in the vernacular, this would be The Spot outside the posh East Side eatery where "Big Paul" Castellano — reputed Mafia chieftain, kingpin, czar, *capo di tutti capi* and graduate of the infamous 1957 Apalachin, New York, crime caucus — was rubbed out in a hail of bullets as he stepped from a chrome-plated black limousine in his $200 loafers, elegant dark-blue mohair suit and fat gold pinky ring.

"A classic!" proclaimed a man in the crowd, an aficionado of mob rubouts.

"Oh, let's eat here!" squealed Donna Stern, a visitor from Chicago, when she learned that she had happened by The Spot that she'd heard so much about on television.

There were cries of anguish from regular patrons who believed that all the publicity over the killing of Big Paul and his chauffeur would make the restaurant so popular that they'd never get a table again. "This is a terrible, terrible thing," said one of them, Bill Kirchner, an advertising account executive, as flashes from cameras in the crowd flared outside.

A man who described himself as the owner of a restaurant in the neighborhood remarked that he "would have dragged the bodies around the corner to my place" if he had realized the gangland killing would bring so much publicity. He looked upon the throngs and the television crews gathered to look at The Spot and said tour buses were sure to follow.

A crowd gathered there all day yesterday, pointing to possible bloodstains (some of which were apparently antifreeze and oil drippings), discussing every detail of the slayings and saying "only in New York."

Only in New York, they said, do these gangland-style slayings still occur with any regularity. Only in New York does everything seem to revolve around eating and restaurants. Only in New York do people step over bodies slumped in the street for two hours to get into a popular restaurant.

"I'll bet when he arrived and was gunned down, someone rushed in to get his table," said Rick Nelms, another onlooker.

Mike Cetta, who owns Sparks with his brother, Pat, and who spent much of the day being interviewed in front of the restaurant, said he was thankful the shooting took place outside, rather than inside. "We do not want to capitalize on this tragedy in any way," he said and paused. "Any way you could put down that we were recently named the best steak house in the city?"

"Are you network or local?" he asked a crew from a local television station. "Oh well, I'll give you an interview. I gave one to CNN."

Regular patrons of the restaurant dined on scampi, beef scaloppine and cabernet sauvignon, while bemoaning the wave of popularity they were certain would wash over the place.

"Look at Umberto's in Little Italy," said one, referring to a restaurant singled out in guidebooks as the place where Joey (Crazy Joe) Gallo was gunned down in 1972.

Other diners recalled the murder of Carmine Galante in Joe and Mary's restaurant in Brooklyn in 1979 and Giuseppe (Joe the Boss) Masseria at the Nuovo Villa Tammaro restaurant in Coney Island.

A police raid at La Stella in Forest Hills in 1966 resulted in thirteen arrests and a visit by the *New York Times* food critic, Craig Claiborne, who gave the restaurant a two-star rating.

Mr. Nelms suggested that New York restaurant guidebooks include a new category – for those where Mafia hits take place. Said Ralph Cappo: "I always eat at these places. Would Mafia dons eat at crummy Italian restaurants?"

Traffic stood still on East 46th Street and horns blared as gaping motorists and pedestrians blocked traffic. Officer Al Rapisardi of the 17th Precinct arrived by scooter and worried that Sparks – "like a Radio City or a theater district" – might now require extra attention.

A man in the crowd complained to him that the blood had been washed away from the scene of the crime, and Rozanne Albergo asked the officer how it was that hit men could make a quick getaway during rush hour in midtown while no one else could.

Television crews from around the world elbowed each other out of the way for a shot of something red on the curb. "They did a beautiful job," a member of the crowd commented to Anthony Mason, a television reporter for Channel 2, referring to the killers. "Very professional."

"This is a big story in Japan," said Shoji Hiroyuki, a sound man with the Nippon Television Network. "We have our own Mafia in Japan now, you know. Japan is becoming very Americanized."

"They love it in Brazil, love it!" said Paulo Arujo, a television reporter for the Globo Television Network of Brazil, who stooped down and talked into his microphone while pointing to the red stuff on the curb.

People arrived from throughout the city and the suburbs to view The Spot. Some professed to have inside information on the slaying. Others professed not to know their own names, explaining that it might not be healthy for them to talk to reporters about the mob.

People couldn't seem to bring themselves to be in a somber mood. "We came to see the blood, face it," said Michael Brooks. But others said they were there to see the television news celebrities. And still others asked if there would be a new Monday-night special on the menu, or if the restaurant would be offering a new Rubout Cocktail, with six shots in it. One customer checked his coat at the restaurant and asked if he could get a flak jacket in return. "Ha, ha," said the unsmiling coat check attendant.

"This is history," said Tulsi Das. "Years from now I can tell my grandchildren, 'I was there.'"

John Quinn smiled, nodded his head and said, "And they say the Mafia doesn't exist anymore."

Akeem Reynolds was giving tours of The Spot, pointing out Big Paul's blood, even making a distinction between that blood and the chauffeur's blood.

Street vendors had noticed the increased traffic along 46th Street, and one of them, Emilio, was selling wool scarfs to passersby. A tourist asked with a smile if the scarfs were official souvenirs of the occasion.

Emilio seemed annoyed at that comment, but when a tourist arrived with a camera and was upset that the bodies and the blood were gone, Emilio offered with a smile to lie down in the street for $5.

SENSATIONAL CRIME SELLS SENSATIONALLY

Oh, TO BE young, attractive and under arrest in New York.

The calls are pouring in now to Jack Litman, the attorney for Robert E. Chambers, Jr., the man charged with the torrentially publicized murder of Jennifer Dawn Levin. "This is great," the callers are saying, "just great."

"'This one has everything,'" Mr. Litman recalled them saying. "'Everyone is excited about it. People are talking about it on the Coast, in Chicago, Texas, everywhere. It's great.'"

The calls began coming in just hours after Ms. Levin was killed in Central Park, and they are still coming in more than three weeks later. They are coming from all manner of film makers, TV docu-drama producers, book publishers, book packagers, authors, screenwriters, literary agents, playwrights and a variety of go-betweens.

Rumors in the entertainment industry are that more than one hundred film and TV-film offers have been made, although Mr. Litman set the number at "about a dozen" of what he considers "real offers."

The callers are telling Mr. Litman, who won't let them talk to Mr. Chambers, that they want to tell this story "with sensitivity" and "in the best of taste." Some are telling Mr. Litman that if he signs with them, he can play himself on the screen. "There is no accounting for bad taste," said Esther Newberg, a literary agent who has not entered the fray.

Mr. Litman said that he will not discuss the deals with them until after the trial is over, but those in the entertainment business said such a project might bring hundreds of thousands of dollars from book and film contracts. He acknowledged that if Mr. Chambers is found guilty, New York State law would prohibit his client from profiting from any of this.

When human tragedy occurs in New York – a city that is the center of the publishing world, one of two coastal centers of the film and television industries and a city where most waitresses seem to have agents – the scramble for rights, options and exclusive interviews often begins. "It's like personal-injury lawyers flocking to a car accident," said one agent, "but more ghoulish."

The murder of Jennifer Dawn Levin, it seems, is about to take its place among dozens of other New York area crimes in recent years that have been turned into entertainment.

"If the Chambers–Levin case occurred in Iowa or someplace like that," said an independent film producer, "this deluge would not have happened." He might have added the Bronx. Four people were murdered in the Bronx on the same day as Ms. Levin but received little attention from the news media.

"This case has all the elements," said Connie Clausen, a literary agent, one of those who is "very excited" about "The Preppie Murder," as she calls it. Not a bad working title, she thinks. About the case, she said, "It has money, sex, a defendant who is movie-star handsome, a lovely girl and kids who seemingly had everything." She admitted there might be a problem of having no hero for the story, one of the concerns that has kept some agents and producers away. "But," Ms. Clausen said, "you can always make the lawyer the hero in a pinch."

Lisa Wager, an associate editor at Dolphin Books, said that she finds herself asking, "Is there a book in this?" not only when she reads newspaper articles and listens to news on the radio but even when a friend is talking to her about something. "We like to think," she added, "that we are part of a sophisticated literary world and not in the business of processing dirt. But dirt sells."

"It all begins with the sensational newspaper accounts," said Mr. Litman, who said that on many days he has received fifty telephone calls from reporters, along with the calls from tipsters, threateners and tarot-card readers. Writers have interviewed him for pieces they said would appear in *New York* magazine, *Mademoiselle* and *Vanity Fair*. "This is upscale crime," one agent explained.

A television station, WNYW, has run two segments concerning the murder of Ms. Levin on what it refers to as an "entertainment-news" program called *A Current Affair*. A spokesperson, Isabel Fernandez, said the show is "part entertainment, part news" and has run pieces on Joey Heatherton, fashions, Miss America, AIDS and Henny Youngman.

"The people calling me about rights and options," said Mr. Litman, "seem to view this as having to do with a morality malaise in the latter twentieth century. They view it as being about people who are too affluent with no solid family structure, kids set to sea too early with inevitable results.

"Tragedy, according to classical definition, is grandiosity flawed," Mr. Litman said. "That this happened on the Upper East Side behind the Metropolitan Museum between two people who went to prep schools has a lot to do, of course, with the publicity."

"The reaction must have something to do with the popularity of *Dynasty*," said one film producer, who said he had overheard a spirited discussion in the Russian Tea Room of the adaptability of this crime to television. "The popularity of *Dynasty* and Polo shirts," he added.

"To be completely venal about it," said an agent who represents a newspaper reporter who had been contacted about rights to his stories for TV films, "the people involved in this crime fit the demographics that TV is shooting for."

The agent noted that the newly released book written by Sydney Biddle Barrows, popularly known as the Mayflower Madam, hit the best-seller list immediately upon publication. Ms. Barrows, who was prominently displayed in a New York newspaper this week, demonstrating her workout regimen and sharing her health secrets, said on a network television program yesterday morning that the day she was arrested for running a call-girl ring was the best day of her life.

HANGING ON
BERNHARD GOETZ'S
EVERY BITE

"ENOUGH ALREADY!" snapped a middle-aged man, waving off a reporter and striding into his apartment building.

The man lives at 55 West 14th Street, in the same building as Bernhard Goetz, who three weeks ago was just Bernie, a mild-mannered, bespectacled neighbor in the electronics field but who is now Bernhard Hugo Goetz, the "Death Wish Vigilante," who shot four black teenagers on the subway, folk hero of millions, and for the moment, perhaps, the most talked-about man in the country.

"Enough already" seemed to sum up the feelings of the reporters who have been staking out the apartment building since Mr. Goetz surrendered, as well as those of the building's tenants and employees whom the reporters have been badgering for even the most minute morsels of information.

The middle-aged man who yelled that had made the mistake of saying he had witnessed Mr. Goetz eating a meal in the New Courtney Restaurant next door. The reporters pressed for details. What had Mr. Goetz ordered?

"It was a sandwich," the man answered. "Turkey, I think."

A follow-up question, concerning the presence of lettuce, tomato and mayonnaise on said sandwich, set the man to yelling and running into the apartment building. And so it remains an open question whether the sandwich was the number 1 Triple-Decker Sliced Turkey with Bacon, Lettuce, Tomato and Mayonnaise or the Monte Cristo Turkey Sandwich on French Toast. It could even have been the Open-Faced Hot Sliced Turkey with Gravy and Cranberry Sauce, for all the press knows.

At least readers knew exactly what Mr. Goetz had eaten for lunch the day before. A newspaper and a television station had acted on a tip that Mr. Goetz had made an excursion to New Jersey, and each sent news teams to retrace his steps. *The New York Post* published a photograph of "the type of toy fire engine Bernhard Goetz purchased" at a Toys 'R' Us store in Union, New Jersey. (Mr. Goetz said he had promised it as a gift for a child.)

The newspaper also published a photograph of Irene Wienckoski, a waitress at the nearby Mark Twain Diner, who had served him lunch: "turkey sandwich on whole wheat and a glass of orange juice."

A pattern of turkey sandwiches was beginning to take shape in the Goetz case.

One television viewer, however, insisted that Channel 4 reported the turkey was on rye — not whole wheat. In *The Post* Ms. Wienckoski said: "He left me a three-dollar tip on an eleven dollar bill. I was impressed, because he was so generous."

"There is nothing left to report," said one of the reporters staking out Mr. Goetz's apartment building. The reporters said they were left with the likes of reporting on turkey sandwiches because Mr. Goetz was not granting interviews.

The Post did corner Mr. Goetz in the New Courtney coffee shop and managed to obtain a few mumblings from him that were artfully written up as an interview and offered under the front-page headline: EXCLUSIVE INTERVIEW: "DEATH WISH" VIGILANTE TALKS.

The story began:

"Bernhard Goetz gave a firm handshake.

"He was told the subways will never be the same.

"'I hope not,' he said and returned to his toasted sandwich and cold slaw."

That was all he said. The paper is to be congratulated on its scoop — yet certainly readers are entitled to know what kind of toasted sandwich? And what is this "cold slaw"?

The legions of reporters were finally told to leave the apartment lobby this week. "I mean," said a woman who lives in the building, "there is really nothing more to say. I told one of them I had seen Bernie leaving the building this week, and the reporter asked, 'Did you happen to catch his shoes?'

"Some of the people in this building," she said, "have become absolute hams and spout off to the TV cameras on things they know nothing about."

José Barquet, a porter at the apartment house, said some tenants and employees had been offered money for anecdotes. Mr. Barquet said he had been offered $500 by newspapers to obtain a photograph from Mr. Goetz's apartment and $1,000 to let them into the apartment. Several building employees said a newspaper had illegally broken into the apartment.

Mr. Barquet said a representative of *The National Enquirer* had offered to pay him a lot of money to tell about Bernhard Goetz's personal life — "more than thirty thousand dollars, if the story is good enough," he said.

"This is a very competitive newspaper war," said Michael Shain, a *Post* reporter who had been on a stakeout of the rear entrance of the apartment building for twelve hours on a recent day. "There is a lot of loose money floating around on this story, money for access, money for information from cabdrivers, that kind of thing."

The building superintendent, Agustin Barquet, said he was happy that only a few reporters were now covering the building.

"There were armies of them," he said. "We had to call the police to keep from being overrun. They would have taken over the building and beaten down Mr. Goetz's door.

"Now there is not much more for them to learn, and they ask about who Mr. Goetz voted for, whether he has taken a shower or what kind of shoes he is wearing. The judge and jury aren't going to care about that."

He told the reporters he had visited Mr. Goetz, who had been eating a sandwich. "What kind of sandwich?" a reporter in the group shouted. "I didn't try it," was Mr. Barquet's reply. "They have had their stories," he said, "and now it is time for them to be quiet. There is a lot of baloney now," he said, hastening to add, "Not the sandwich, the questions."

Four carloads of reporters and photographers remain, focusing on the front and back doors and the exit from the parking garage. "We are all sick of it by now," said one photographer. The reporters agreed they were still there because the reporters from other papers were still there.

John Randazzo of *The Daily News* had been staking out the back door of the building for nine hours one day, to no avail. "I've picked up absolutely nothing today," he said. "I went to the restaurant, because he reportedly ate a sandwich there. I couldn't find out if it was a ham or a cheese; that's the kind of day it's been."

JURY DUTY AND
THE CREATIVE EXCUSE

IT'S NOT JUST the heavy crime
that bothers New Yorkers; it's the perpetually nagging jury duty
that goes along with it.

Residents of Manhattan serve on jury duty far more often
than most other Americans, local court officials say, because
Manhattan's residential population is but a fraction of the swollen
population during the day, when crime also swells.

About sixty-four hundred people are summoned each week
by the county clerk's office, and this being New York, a lot of
them are not about to take this obligation of citizenship lying
down.

Hundreds pour into the clerk's office at 60 Centre Street on
Mondays and Thursdays, complaining that they are too busy or
just too darned important to serve or that their biorhythms are
too far out of sync at the moment to possibly judge another human being or that their dog is ill — quite possibly terminally ill.

One man wore a BERNHARD GOETZ FAN CLUB T-shirt recently in hopes of being deemed too opinionated to serve. Several each week lean over the counter at the clerk's office and say,
confidentially, that they are insane.

Some seem to feel better if they throw things, and Jack
O'Neill, senior court officer, sits at the door of Room 139, pistol
on his hip, to make certain things do not get too far out of hand.
"I can sense someone is really getting angry," he said, "when they
tear off the doors to the office and start throwing them at us."

The hard-core cases wind up in the office of the Clerk of the County of New York himself, Norman Goodman. The clerk since 1969, Mr. Goodman has heard it all. And he has given his gentle, firm lecture on citizenship to presidents of the largest multinational corporations, famous fashion designers and stars of stage, screen and television – not to mention a recent visit by a member of the heavy-metal group Twisted Sister, who finally served graciously.

Mr. Goodman is adamantine in his insistence that all who are called must serve – eventually. He allows three six-month deferrals with no questions asked. He has been known to offer people shortened stints on jury duty and routinely allows aspiring actors and actresses to go to auditions if they are waiting in the jury pool to be selected for a trial. He allows those summoned to pick a date sometime in the next six months when they can serve, and he has them come in then.

"You have to be flexible," he said. "This is a city of entrepreneurs, of models and actresses and free-lance musicians with crazy schedules."

But when a choreographer pleaded in his office this week that she needed yet a seventh six-month deferment because she is working on a show that is about to open on Broadway, Mr. Goodman gave her the civics lecture and told her to report for jury duty next week.

A man with fifteen deferments said he manages a $1.5 billion investment fund and would be happy to serve as early as 1988. Mr. Goodman told him to report next week, too. He promised to sue Mr. Goodman.

A young man told Mr. Goodman he was a member of a religious sect that will not allow him to sit in judgment of another man. "Jesus said, 'Judge not, lest you be judged,'" said the young man. Mr. Goodman responded: "Jesus also said, 'Render unto Caesar what is Caesar's.' I'm Caesar."

Another man came in with a psychiatric report saying he could not make decisions and should be dismissed from jury duty. When he told Mr. Goodman that his occupation is floor manager of a large brokerage house, Mr. Goodman shouted: "C'mon! You make hundreds of decisions every day." The man will serve.

"Chuck Scarborough [a local TV newscaster] served a few days ago, and John Chancellor and Ralph Lauren and Jackie Onassis and Robin Byrd of Channel J [who dances around in a scanty outfit several evenings a week on cable television], so why not these other people," he said.

Of the two thousand people in the jury pool at any given time, about fifteen hundred come in with medical excuses and about fifteen are bona fide, Mr. Goodman said.

On his desk he has a medical dictionary, in which he often can't seem to find the ailments prospective jurors complain about. He also has a medical directory listing doctors and their specialties. "I don't like a note from a urologist telling me he is treating a man for a severe heart condition," Mr. Goodman said.

Some who come to the office have legitimate medical reasons for dismissal, and others try to get out of jury duty because their employers will not pay their salaries while they serve. The county pays jurors $14 per day for serving, and Mr. Goodman said their average length of service is five and a half days.

A lot of the complainants coming into Room 139 are upset that some people are exempt from jury duty and they are not. Full-time members of the clergy, practicing lawyers, dentists, psychologists, elected public officials, the insane, the governor's secretary, police officers, nurses, people over the age of seventy, felons and licensed embalmers are among those exempted, along with full-time mothers – not mothers who work outside the home.

Timothy P. Sullivan, deputy county clerk, said he thinks the problem of citizens trying to get out of jury duty is worse now than he can ever recall.

"New York is becoming a town of younger professionals," said Mr. Sullivan. "It is a stereotype that these people are self-involved and not civic or community minded, but we find this to be absolutely true. They can't serve on jury duty because they will lose a step in the race at the office." Sometimes they cry about it, he said, and when he tells them they can't have their way, "they scream and yell and throw coffee.

"Sometimes people ask about alternative service," said Mr. Sullivan, "and I suggest maybe we could set something up –

burying the dead for two weeks at Potter's Field or emptying bedpans at Bellevue. They take the jury duty."

Mr. Goodman said his faith is reaffirmed every day in the jury system. "People become extremely recalcitrant," he said. "But they often apologize for giving us a hard time and say the experience was rewarding. It helps if they have a juicy trial to tell their friends about."

SIDEWALKERS

SIDEWALK CAFÉS AMID HONKS AND FUMES

THIS WAS NOT Christine Jerard's idea of a good time. "I'm so hot," she whined, perspiring in an outdoor café yesterday as the temperature rose into the nineties. "Let's go inside where it's air-conditioned."

Her companion, John Melsner, did not speak but fixed her with a terrible glare that seemed to say she was probably just perspiring to prove her point.

Mr. Melsner was feeling cool, and in more ways than one. Outdoor cafés can do that to a person. He was sipping frothy green drinks and settling comfortably into café society at the Café de la Paix on Central Park South. The waitresses said Mr. Melsner's condition exemplified "the sophistication factor" in the sidewalk-café business, noting that he seemed to be smoking each cigarette in an ever-more-continental fashion.

Although looking snappy in their black bow ties, the young waitresses were wilting a bit in the steamy heat and grumbling about the hot spell that is driving away business and gratuities as surely as did the two preceding months of rain. "New York weather is awful, isn't it?" said Julie Ross, a waitress who moved here from San Antonio four months ago.

Such are the vagaries of New York café society. "It's always something," said another waitress, Bennett Brady. "Even when it stopped raining, that big pothole was still filled with water, and cabs hit it and showered our customers – usually the ones in white dresses."

One must be hearty, these waitresses maintained, to be a member of café society in New York. Boulevardiers must not only brave inclement weather and pothole showers but must suffer unaccomplished street musicians, the attendant fragrance of horse-drawn cabs, kids with big blaring radios, lost dogs, beggars, purveyors of stolen wrench sets, honking horns, bus fumes and — last week — a little window-washing fluid that rained down upon the turkey-on-croissants. "You have to take orders between honks," Ms. Ross said.

Tara Feehan, another of the waitresses, says that sometimes, when she is serving a sandwich with potato chips, a gust of wind comes up and the chips sail away. Napkins take frequent flight. Other sidewalk cafés report regular takeoffs of their colorful umbrellas. Passersby in need of home furnishings sometimes carry off tables and chairs.

For all of this, many New Yorkers believe that sidewalk cafés, which increase in number every year, are one of the nicest things about the city.

"They are civilizing," said Joseph DiCarlo, owner of the Sarducci Restaurant at Seventh Avenue and 16th Street, which has a popular sidewalk café. "People love to watch the street life. We've had people walk by here naked. I have to remind customers to go back to work."

"I love the cafés," said Sheila Yudin, sitting in a sidewalk café on Mulberry Street. As she spoke, a large automobile, built before emission controls, spent a great deal of time going forward and back trying to fit into a tight parking space not four feet from where she sat. "Hemingway in Paris," she had to admit, "it is not."

Joe Pozzuli, of Joe's Pizza on Bleecker Street, explained that his two small outdoor tables were always "jumping outside and inside," depending on the presence of city inspectors. He said it was too expensive and time-consuming to obtain a city outdoor café license.

Only 171 of the sidewalk cafés in New York are licensed (the most ever), according to city officials, who noted that six city agencies are involved in a licensing process that can take from four months to a year if neighbors object. Increasingly, they do object, concerned that there will be no room left on sidewalks for pedestrians. City officials said that even a place the size of Joe's Pizza, with three tables inside and two outside, would pay about $1,100 for a license.

New York's sidewalk cafés range from those set behind fences and shrubbery, such as the Café du Parc across from the Metropolitan Museum of Art, down — no offense — to the dinette set outside Casa di Pizza on Mulberry Street placed there by Luigi Silvestri, the congenial host, manager, amateur opera singer and cook.

Uninvited and unshirted, Mr. Silvestri joins his guests at the table to get away from the hot pizza oven and yells *"Heyyyyyy-yyyyyy! Babeeeeeeee!"* at women passing by who somehow are able to resist his charms. One of his outdoor customers leaned the back of his chair against an old green Chevrolet Impala station wagon parked in the street.

Pat DiCori, at the sidewalk café of Bruno's bakery on La Guardia Place, said sidewalk cafés were the only places one can enjoy a drink with a dog. She was having cappuccino with Plaza Poo, her dog. "I wish outdoor cafés were open all year round," she said. "You could wear your coat."

Marlene Resto, a waitress at the bakery, noted that the outdoor café was anathema to the restaurant rule of rapid turnover, and she talked of café queens and kings, Nancy and Harvey to name two, who can dawdle over a cup of coffee for hours. "Also," she said, "bums pick up your tips."

"People think they're very European," she said, "sitting out here drinking cappuccino. But when the garbage truck pulls up, it kind of takes away from the atmosphere."

Daren Snell, sitting in the Café de la Paix sidewalk café, said that she was enjoying the sidewalk show, having spotted fur coats the likes of which she'd never seen, as well as Cindy Garvey, Bernadette Peters, Tiny Tim and countless men stopping to dig through a nearby trash receptacle.

Michelle Mellinger was having a cool drink at Caffè-Primavera, at Mulberry and Spring streets, which uses a popular formation of two rows of tables on a narrow sidewalk, with a slit of daylight down the middle for pedestrians.

Ms. Mellinger recalled dining at a place with the same setup on Columbus Avenue when a passerby, "a wise guy," strolled past and snatched the broccoli from her plate. She hates broccoli and did not press charges.

TOFUTTI, AND
OTHER SIDEWALK FARE

NIGHT AFTER MIDDLE of the night, his wife would tell him to give it up, David, and come to bed. But David Mintz of Brooklyn would not come to bed. The world was out there waiting, he said, just waiting for a soybean-curd-based frozen dessert. He could not, would not, rest until Tofutti was invented.

It was not easy for the fifty-three-year-old Brooklyn restaurateur. Experts told him that the nondairy dessert was an impossibility. Neighbors had called him "the mad scientist," and some of them meant it. He had to repeatedly let out his belt during years of testing and tasting.

Along the way, Mr. Mintz invented kosher beef stroganoff — kosher beef stroganoff! — which was like defying gravity. The mixing of beef and sour cream in the same dish is a most flagrant violation of kosher dietary law, so Mr. Mintz substituted blended tofu for sour cream, with almost no change in the taste of the stroganoff, or so he claims.

"Have you lost your religion?" customers yelled at him in his kosher restaurant. When he introduced tofu cheesecake, a few customers swore it was the real thing, swore it violated kosher laws, threw down their napkins and walked out.

Others called him a fool, and he began tacking up informational posters headlined: WHAT IS TOFU?

Yesterday, Mr. Mintz was tasting vindication and cappuccino Tofutti as he watched fifty young men and women in a training session in midtown preparing to take to the streets of Manhattan today with their Tofutti carts. "We are making history today," said Mr. Mintz, obviously moved. Even as he spoke, Tofutti was making an appearance in Paris at the Salon International d'Alimentation, a food show.

If you were to develop a taste for, say, a dried pear while walking down the street in New York, you could buy one from a street vendor. Or maybe you'd like some pistachio nuts, or an Italian sausage, pizza, bagels, cookies, knishes, an egg cream, an Italian ice, a complete picnic lunch, tacos, Brie, hot potato salad, bean-sprout vinaigrette salad, crêpes with blueberries, skewered cantaloupe, tempura, Yum Yum hot dogs, hot chestnuts, falafel, chow mein, souvlaki, shish kebab, spinach-and-ham quiche, pâté de campagne with cornichons, or blue cotton candy.

Street vendors have been spotted selling all of that and more. Carts down on Wall Street were selling "Bird Burgers" (ground-turkey burgers) — albeit not very many and for not very long. The Tofutti umbrellas are blossoming at the height of the New York street-food season.

"Beat 'em!" David Braff, food service consultant and trainer of street vendors, yelled to the eager young charges in their spanking new white Tofutti uniforms yesterday as Mr. Mintz looked on. "Beat 'em with a smile. Beat 'em with courtesy. Beat 'em with fewer calories per serving if you have to, but beat 'em!"

Go head-to-head on the same corner with Italian-ice vendors, he told them. Don't knuckle under to a Chipwich.

Mr. Braff urged them to smile and wash their hands and polish their carts, while warning them of occupational hazards such as quick-change artists and altered currency, as well as armed robbers and jealous vendors of lesser products.

Mr. Braff also talked about "mental obstacles" that must be overcome on the part of salespeople and customers. Many trainees said the greatest obstacle this product would have to overcome was anti-tofu sentiment. "I hate tofu," admitted a Tofutti trainee, Diana Mayo, twenty-one years old. "I worked at a health-food store and it made me ill just to look at it. Luckily Tofutti isn't like tofu at all."

"Tofu is scary," said Jennifer Downey, eighteen, another

trainee. "It is weird and foreign and it sort of floats." She agreed that Tofutti is different.

Mr. Mintz, who grew up in the Williamsburg section of Brooklyn and now lives in Sheepshead Bay, developed tofu recipes during the late 1970s for his restaurant, which he sold after forming Tofu Time, Inc., two and a half years ago. Local residents recall lines outside his kosher restaurant on Church Avenue in Brooklyn, which was famous for employing actual Jewish grandmothers in the kitchen. His classified advertisements read: GRANDMOTHERS WANTED.

He had not thought of marketing Tofutti as a "no cholesterol" or "no lactose" food — slogans now emblazoned on the side of the carts. He had never heard of lactose intolerance then, but now states confidently that forty million Americans suffer from it. "They should not suffer," he said. "They should eat Tofutti."

Soft, frozen Tofutti, which tastes rather like ice cream, has been available for some time in stores. The street-vendors' variety will sell for $1.25 for five ounces and will be available in five flavors. The company, which went public in December, began in one room, with a phone that, optimistically, had call-waiting. "I would get a call for five gallons," he said, "and deliver it in my car."

He has something of a lab at his office in Bensonhurst, with little brown bottles of papaya extracts and raisin-juice powders and larger containers labeled Frodex 10, Lodex 5 and Centpro 70. He enjoys going down there and stirring up all sorts of fanciful concoctions.

"I like a pineapple–sweet potato Tofutti," he said, "but the public may not be ready. I like the idea of mango, and I love hazelnuts, and watermelon is one of my favorites. I absolutely love garlic, but I don't suppose . . ."

He is working on a "revolutionary" Tofutti shake. Ovens are being brought in so that he can perfect a meatless hamburger that tastes like the real thing. This tofu visionary foresees a time when tofuburger franchises replace McDonald's and Burger King, a time of tofu TV dinners and, possibly, of tofu cigarettes. His lights burn late into the night.

CITIZEN PRUNER CORPS
TAKES TO THE STREETS

MARIANNE HOLDEN COULD not
restrain herself any longer. She whipped out her trusty twelve-
inch folding saw and attacked the Japanese pagoda tree.

"It feels sooo good," she said, standing on her tiptoes and
spitting sawdust as she removed an extraneous limb, good to be
out of the office in her flannel shirt and hiking boots doing some
serious forestry.

A wise guy walking by yelled "Timberrr!" when the little
branch dropped to Fifth Avenue.

New York's Citizen Pruner Corps — more than a thousand
pruners strong — is on the march again, armed with shears, saws
and certificates authorizing them to prune with impunity.

"This is our favorite time of year," said Diane Nisita, a member of the corps, who prunes away on West 82nd Street, "warm
enough to get out and prune, but before the sap runs."

Ms. Holden is the commandant, if you will, of the corps.
Her title is actually executive director of the New York City
Street Tree Consortium, which gives the course that leads to the
pruning certificate, issued by the Parks and Recreation
Department.

Their lot is not just to prune street trees, however, but to
cultivate the soil around them, to water and feed them and to
serve as their guardians against the likes of vandals and dog walkers, as well as those who would chain their bikes to the trees or
nail messages on them.

Ms. Holden said that some of the trees are too attractive and invite trouble, much like people who wear gold chains on the subway. The Kwanzan cherry, for example, is so beautiful when it flowers that people strip off the branches.

In Papua New Guinea, trees are the leading cause of injury to people: people falling from trees, trees falling on people and of course the coconut-related injuries. But in New York, it is quite the opposite, as the city's approximately 600,000 street trees — trees planted along the sidewalks — come under constant assault by the motoring public, pedestrians and pets.

Not to mention the "god-awful growing conditions," in the words of one arboriculturist, which include carbon monoxide fumes, lack of water, and soil that is not really soil at all but some hypercompacted concoction of cement dust, salt, broken concrete, smashed glass, dog excrement, "McD.L.T." cartons and other rubble.

Ms. Holden said examination of street trees shows the growing roots reaching out of the burlapped planting soil, meeting the rubble and turning back into the burlap.

And there is precious little even of this nonsoil, which quickly gives way beneath the sidewalk to sewers, drains, the IRT and BMT, telephone cables, gas pipes and vaults.

"Because of the dogs," Ms. Nisita said, "it is not quite so exhilarating to run one's hands through the spring soil." Corps members said one of their tasks was to inform dog owners that pet waste is not good fertilizer.

Construction projects kill the trees en masse in New York. Sodium-vapor lights keep them up all night. "It's quite amazing they live at all," said Ellen Levine, a corps member on West 101st Street.

They do not live long. About thirteen thousand street trees die each year, and this is the first year in some time that a significant number will be replaced. Their lives are only about seven years on the average, according to one study, rather than the half century or more they might live in the country.

Some New Yorkers think that is where trees belong, outside the city. Although corps members spread the word about the benefits of trees (producing oxygen, filtering the air, reducing noise and — finally, something New Yorkers can appreciate — improving property values), some New Yorkers still do not want trees and they go so far as to cut them down.

A passerby watching Ms. Holden prune said he saw no real reason to have trees around that do not have "bananas or something" on them.

There is evidence to suggest that trees under attack — by insects, for example — emit airborne chemical warnings to fellow trees, which make defensive chemical changes. But this does not help much when an Econoline van drives down the sidewalk.

Not to add to citizens' worries, but this city suffers an ever-widening "Prune Gap," which the Pruner Corps is attacking. Although the Parks Department is pruning a lot more trees now than it once did — about 40,000 trees last year — the department reports that 100,000 a year need pruning.

Pruning, not unlike going out for a quart of milk, can be adventuresome and sometimes dangerous in New York. "People yell at you," Ms. Nisita said. "They are accustomed to being suspicious."

And pruning, not unlike saying "Nice day" in public, is also controversial and can draw a crowd of argumentative people debating which limb should be lopped.

"The neighbors are fascinated when they realize I'm not doing anything harmful," Ms. Levine said.

Ms. Holden is now registering people for the next pruner certification course to begin this month. "Be an artist, not an executioner" is one principle the course teaches.

"People who like to prune do get carried away," said Justine Fevola, a horticulturist who has taught the course. One man, who is not a course graduate, has been spotted in Brooklyn trimming little street trees with a chain saw.

Robert Meneke asked about the course but decided not to get involved in pruning.

It seems a man he knew took it upon himself to clip a dead limb from a tree in front of his apartment building, cut his hand, fell out of the tree and landed on a passerby, who thought he was being attacked. The passerby slugged the pruner, who staggered back into the street and was almost hit by a taxi before he fled, only to be brought down by a neighborhood dog that bit him and tore his pants. Mr. Meneke concluded that pruning was just "too dangerous."

STREET PERFORMERS

MICHELLE AND DENISE SILBER open tonight on Broadway. The twenty-one-year-old twins, who sing and strum guitars, will play the Astor, adjacent to Shubert Alley at Broadway and 44th Street: the Astor Parking Garage.

They have been booked to play for patrons of the arts who wait in long lines for their cars after the theaters let out. They played the garage for a few weeks last summer, and as a startled tourist remarked to them while taking their photograph, "This would not happen in Baltimore."

In New York, street musicians and other performers seem to be everywhere at this time of year. Most New Yorkers apparently think that these buskers lend a festive air to the city, although there are those who believe, as does Hilton Coughlin, who was walking past a street band, that "street musicians stink." Asked to amplify, he said, "They disturb the peace and block the sidewalks."

Break-dancers perform for tourists entering the Empire State Building. A cellist plays on subway platforms. Trumpeters, flutists and a violinist are currently playing on subway trains. Some are startlingly fine; one saxophonist is so bad he solicits loose change to stop playing. It is a small price to pay.

People eat fire on the sidewalks of New York. "You have to," explained William Shaw, who thought he could come to New York and make money by juggling on the Avenue of the Americas, but people just walked right past him. He started juggling fire, and more people paid attention but not enough. He finally had to start eating the stuff.

The voice of a talented lyric tenor echoes down the block in Little Italy. Mimes perform for those waiting in line at movie theaters, And a violinist serenades those coming outside to smoke during Broadway intermissions. Another violinist was playing Vivaldi in a Times Square subway station recently, heard a train coming, announced that he would "try to finish it for you," flew through the remainder of the piece and received an ovation from riders boarding the train.

Ronald Grunwald, a visitor from Philadelphia, observed a nine-piece band setting up recently on a Times Square sidewalk. "Whole orchestras! Amazing," he said.

Some musicians and other performers come to New York from throughout the world to play New York's streetcorners as if they were famous nightclubs and music halls: Columbus and 72nd, 59th and Fifth; Broadway and Liberty — wherever there are crowds and wherever the cop on the beat allows.

A passerby dropped fifty cents into Ray Peters's saxophone case on the sidewalk at 59th Street and Fifth Avenue and said: "You're exceptionally good, young man. You'll make the big time some day." "Madam," Mr. Peters called after her, "this *is* the big time." Mr. Peters came from England to play the sidewalks of New York, working his way up from the lesser byways to this, the Carnegie Hall of streetcorners.

"In other cities street musicians are regarded as panhandlers," said Desmond Valentine, a jazz saxophonist who plays the Wall Street area during noon hour. "But here, you can make more money on the street than you can in clubs. Musicians are discovered on these sidewalks. Thousands of people go by."

Go they do, thousands an hour in many spots, creating a mass market for opera singers, comedians and steel drummers; vendors of hot dogs, Chipwiches and falafel; hawkers of Leatherine handbags, Senegalese umbrellas and battery-operated plastic roses that light up (a significant improvement on nature); proselytizers for various religions; pickpockets, three-card-monte players and big-league beggars — one of whom holds a sign reading MY ANALYST SAYS I MUST GO TO JAMAICA.

"In New York, you can be discovered anywhere," said Michelle Silber, even in a parking garage. She said that they received numerous offers to play in restaurants and at private parties, and that an agent had them make a demonstration tape of three songs.

A flutist on Fifth Avenue finished playing and announced the streetcorners where he will next be appearing. A street group known as The Uncommon Jazz Ensemble puts out a newsletter for its fans. The group's leader, sixty-one-year-old Hassan Hakim, said he played the Savoy, Birdland and the rest of the best clubs with Louis Armstrong, Count Basie, Miles Davis and Dizzy Gillespie, to name a few, and said he prefers the street. "There is no hassle from club owners," he said, "and frankly, we can make just as much money out here."

Technically, the street performers can be run in for blocking sidewalks, soliciting money or making too much noise. There is still the lone sidewalk minstrel, but now there is also the rock-and-roll group that booms top-forty music powered by Honda eight-hundred-watt portable generators.

Police Officer Kiane Wittine said that on a nice summer evening the 20th Precinct, which covers the Upper West Side from 59th Street to 86th, receives about fifty complaints concerning street musicians and other sidewalk obstacles. "For many of the area's residents," she explained, "it's no longer interesting to see and hear the same street entertainers every night."

Sam ("Play It Again Sam") Brown has been playing his tenor sax on the streets for more than twenty years. He brings smiles to hundreds of faces, but very few drop a coin into his open, battered instrument case.

"I play only love songs," Mr. Brown said, "because — you wouldn't believe this — everyone in New York is a romantic. Why do you think we are allowed to play? New York is a city of romance."

By contrast, Davo Bryant, a twenty-one-year-old jazz drummer, arrived seven days ago from Albuquerque, New Mexico, having left home to play on the streets of New York. He played for the first time Sunday with a group of five regular street musicians at the corner of 59th Street and Fifth Avenue — an auspicious beginning. The saxophone player, Chris Zimmer, had come from Frankfurt to play street jazz. Monky Kobayashi, the drummer for a band playing across the street, came from Tokyo.

"New York is a city of opportunity," Mr. Bryant said. He sees crowds everywhere he looks, and they all seem to him as though they are waiting to hear someone play.

The group finished playing, emptied the instrument case and began stacking quarters, dimes, nickels, pennies and subway tokens — about $40 each. There were notes in the case from people who wanted them to play private parties. The lead guitarist, Mark Lampariello, had two notes from admiring women.

As Mr. Bryant packed up his drums, Brian Miller, bass guitarist and the leader of the group, said to him, "Be at Liberty Park on Wall Street tomorrow morning at ten-thirty."

Liberty Park, as the plaza at Broadway and Liberty Street is known, is a showplace for bands, comedians, mimes, escape artists and you-name-it who cater to Wall Street workers on their lunch hours.

That day, about one hundred people in dark suits ate hot dogs and Chipwiches and tapped their feet as they watched Davo Bryant, Brian Miller and the rest of the group perform.

Gil Callan, who works at Dean Witter, said he and many of the others in the briefcase brigades daydream a bit about being as free as the street performers seem to be.

Mr. Shaw, the fire-eating juggler who joined the outdoor circus that is New York, said it is nice to set your own hours and to work outdoors. But there are problems: rainy weather and occasional burns. He'd like to get into computer programming.

TRENDOIDS:
THE CHIC
AND THE DEAD

GETTING IN

"To NOT GET IN," Laura Barclay explained simply, "is to die."

Ms. Barclay lives, thanks to her ostrich-feathered turban. The doorman at the Area dance club spotted her topfeathers in the roiling sea of human desperation outside the club one night this week and commanded one of his lieutenants to pull her through the pressing crowd, up the steps from social oblivion and into the fashionable club.

"Oh, thank you, thank you, thank you," Ms. Barclay said, as if Joe Brese were the doorman on the last helicopter out of Da Nang. Mr. Brese has the power to save social lives. With a point of his finger and a word to a security man, he determines who shall pass into this rock club, now enjoying the fleeting status of New York's hottest.

The Chosen thank him, kiss him, hug him and push gratuities into his hand. After a year at the door, his status in Manhattan's downtown hemisphere is such that he can no longer pay for meals in restaurants or for clothing at boutiques, so eager are those in the know to ingratiate themselves.

Those he has not selected have pulled guns on him nine times, knives six times and a baseball bat once. A few days ago, a full bottle of wine was hurled at him, crashing against a wall eight inches from his head. He stays a safe distance from the crowd to avoid kicks and jabs. It really is that important to them.

"This could only happen in New York," said the mild-mannered Mr. Brese, thirty-two years old, who has worked throughout the country and was lured here by the club's owners from his home in San Francisco. "New York is a city of money, power and big egos that bruise easily."

At an hour when most of New York was going to bed – the club does not even open its doors until 11:00 P.M. – the fashionably late crowd outside Area swelled to several hundred, spilling out onto Hudson Street near the Holland Tunnel and mingling with squadrons of arriving taxis and limousines.

Mr. Brese stood at the top of the stairs, wearing a black beret and a long black coat that lent him a vaguely monklike air. As if mounting the steps to a temple, a burly security man slowly walked to him and said quietly: "E. Randolph. Says he's on the list." That would be The List – a computer printout made anew each day, containing the names of those who shall positively be allowed in.

Mr. Brese looked down at the list on his clipboard. Finding no Randolph, he shook his head and said, "Not here," just as he had shaken his head when a man claimed to be "Mick Jagger's son," Jade, who happens to be a girl. Someone in the crowd jumped up and down yelling, "Joe, Joe, it's me!" And with that, those who had not a clue as to his name began yelling to get his attention: "Joe! Joe! Joe!"

Mr. Brese pointed to a woman and commanded one of the security people standing in the small, cordoned area at the bottom of the steps: "Dmitri! The woman in the red hat." As she squeezed toward the front accompanied by three friends, Dmitri grabbed her hand and opened the velvet ropes for her and her three friends – while simultaneously holding off a dozen others who said they were with her but were not.

It is not so unusual for single men, who have more difficulty getting in because of their great numbers, to pay a fee to such a woman to say they are with her.

Mr. Brese selected people quickly, as if assembling a bouquet. Of course, the two women wearing clear plastic dresses and white tape over their breasts were selected, as were those with big, fluorescent, feathered earrings that looked to be deep-sea fishing lures. But also, he chose a few well-manicured Wall Street

types in pin-striped suits. Celebrities, regular customers and Mr.
Brese's friends certainly had an edge, as did the distractingly attractive, the obviously rich and anyone arriving in a stretch limo.

He turned down dowdy women who looked like they were
out hunting up a draft beer and young men in T-shirts and jeans
who looked as if they had come over to mow the lawn. Rowdy
men rarely make it in, even though that has meant excluding
offspring of the rich and famous who try to have Mr. Brese fired
the next day. He said he prefers people who show a little imagina-
tion in their dress — the man in a fake-fur tuxedo being an
example.

"It's hard to describe," Mr. Brese said. "Sometimes it comes
down to the way a person walks or the looks on their faces."

Loved ones must sometimes be left behind. "My husband is
right back there!" screamed a woman being ushered in. "He has
all my money. I won't be able to buy a drink." The security people
told her to move along, and an hour later, she was still tugging on
Mr. Brese's sleeve, asking, "Any hope for my husband? Any hope
at all?"

At a quarter past midnight, twelve hundred people were
packed in, and Mr. Brese had cut the intake to a trickle. Outside,
the size of the mob mounted, undulating and pushing, with those
in the front row barely able to stand.

"More rope!" shouted one of the security people, who
wanted to widen the cordoned area around the door.

"More stanchions!" shouted another, sounding like a deck-
hand on a ship in a stormy sea.

The crowd kept pressing in until the security people stood
back to back, pressing back against the crowd.

"Not one more, Michael!" Mr. Brese yelled to the assistant
doorman, Michael Clancy. "No one gets in until you move back!"
Mr. Brese yelled at the crowd.

Finally, however, it appeared to Mr. Brese as if they might
overrun his position, and he pulled down the heavy rolling steel
door to this converted warehouse with a crash.

Standing inside, catching his breath, one club employee
asked: "What do they want? It's as if we were giving something
away."

Clearly, they were, something intangible. When some semblance of order was restored, Mr. Brese reopened.

At 2:00 A.M. a man who had been standing out there for an hour shouted that his civil rights were being violated, and as he walked away, he said he would see the doorman in court.

At 3:00 A.M. one of the few remaining rejects yelled obscenities at Mr. Brese.

At 4:00 A.M. two men from London, who said they had been in the country just two hours, pulled up in a taxicab and asked, "Is this the place?"

Several hundred people still dancing at 5:00 A.M. on a weeknight were sure that it was.

HAIR

"WHADDYAWANNADO, LISA?"
Cheryl Mintz asked Lisa Lester, hanging out at the apartment, both as bored as they could be.

After a long silence it came to Ms. Lester like a bolt from the blue: "Let's get haircuts!"

They were out the door in nanoseconds to the Astor Place Barbershop, for an exciting and potentially perilous adventure in hairstyling.

A Frozade lemonade cart with a big umbrella sat outside the shop at 2 Astor Place, just off Broadway, serving the throngs who await their turns in the shop. Cheryl and Lisa, both twenty-five years old, submitted their names to Joe Gallo, Jr., who is the doorman — that's right — at the barbershop. If he loses his job, he's dead. He's the only one in the business.

Customers bribe him to try to get in sooner. The two young women did not seem to mind waiting. They peered inside, along with everyone else, watching haircuts — an activity said to be popular in small towns but certainly new to Manhattan.

But what haircuts! The Guido, Detroit, Punk, Mohawk, James Dean, Fort Dix, Sparkle Cut, What-the-Hell, Spike and Spina di Pesce (Spine of the Fish) — most of them created right here, in this barbershop in the East Village, a neighborhood that some residents contend is the spawning ground for everything new: art, music, haircuts — all that is important.

"Hair," stated Marjori Boyman, a student from the Fashion

Institute of Technology who was awaiting a cut, "is the most important thing." Period.

Cheryl and Lisa were a little nervous. "Girls come in here literally shaking," said Enrico Vezza, who owns the shop with his brother, Frank. Their father opened the old-fashioned barbershop with its twirling barber pole in 1940, and the two sons have worked there for more than thirty years.

The shop was losing money and about to go out of business two years ago. "The neighborhood was run-down," Enrico explained, "not to mention that no one was getting haircuts. *Cops* were not getting haircuts."

But one momentous day Mr. Vezza began noticing more young people in the neighborhood, young people with short hair – beautiful, closely cropped hair that required regular professional attention. He hung out a sign that read ASTOR PLACE BARBER STYLIST, instead of "shop," kept prices cheap – $6 to $8 for men and $8 to $10 for women – and now stands clear of the front door for fear of being knocked down by the stampede.

He just keeps cramming more and more barbers into the little shop. Recently, they took out the coffeepot to make room for another barber, and now there are twenty who cut twelve hours a day, seven days a week. They have plans to build a loft for ten more chairs. The garbageman asks for more money for picking up the hair outside the back door, four times a week.

Paul, Enrico's son, sits on a ladder just inside the front door. When he spots a barber chair opening up in this assembly line of distinctive haircuts, he picks up a hand microphone attached to a speaker on the sidewalk and – above the din of buzzing electric shears, the clip-clip-clipping and the blaring rock music – calls the next customer: "Carole."

"Oh, God!" said Dr. Carole Burns, a bit weak-kneed, "I hope they'll at least listen to me." Dr. Burns moved to New York a few days ago from Columbus, Ohio, and is feeling a bit dowdy. Franco, her stylist, is a recent immigrant who has honestly never heard of Ohio. That does not help. She does not want anything radical, she told him, just something a bit more fashionable. "I want to experience New York," she said, "and this place is part of it."

The truth is, there were people reading *The Wall Street Journal* in the shop, two conservatively dressed stockbrokers receiving good old everyday haircuts with just a hint of style. But one peacock-blue spiked hairdo with shaved white sidewalls can erode all confidence.

"I don't want to look like that!" said Josephine Pierangelino, gazing about the room. "And, God, please, not like that, that, that or that!" Like a ride on a roller coaster, it had seemed like a great idea to the sixty-year-old woman before she sat down. Her daughter, Gail, with a modified Guido – short sides, slanted Valentino sideburns and wet curls dangling on her forehead — had talked her into it.

"It is not like a doctor," her barber, Joseph, said calmly. "If *he* makes a mistake, you die." Mrs. Pierangelino informed Joseph that if he gave her a punk haircut, he would be the one to suffer from injuries incurred on his flight through the front window. She liked the haircut, and they both lived.

"Easy, easy," Joel Smolinsky said to his barber, Mario Macchiarulo. "I have to look for a job." He left with a haircut suitably short, he said, not for job interviews but for basic training.

Asked what people back home would think of her slicked-back, short-sided cut with two razor-line V's cut into the nape of the neck, Naomi Palmer, a visitor from Saratoga Springs, New York, said, "They will think that I have been to New York, that's what." Her barber, Nick Scalici, said some of the older barbers had experienced some difficulty adjusting to customers' requests for Lightning Bolts and other designs carved into their hair. He smeared a big green glob of styling gel on Ms. Palmer's head and sent her back to Saratoga Springs, smiling.

Marie-Dominique Bucher, visiting from Paris, snapped a photograph of her mother, Genevieve Lassus, having her hair cut, and said: "This is a crazy place. New York is a crazy place. We wanted a souvenir of New York to take home."

Cheryl Mintz and Lisa Lester bounced out of the shop laughing and sporting new short haircuts that are fashionable but will still allow them to keep their jobs. "A haircut can change your life," said Ms. Mintz.

Two suburban women entering the shop expressed both fear and hope over that proposition.

WALKING
UNDERPANTS

"**S**o," ONE CUSTOMER lacing up a pair of Cushionaire-soled Step-Flex shoes said to another, "how long have you been walking?" And the second one replied, "Oh, about a month."

This was not a couple of toddlers shooting the breeze at a day-care center, but rather two middle-aged men in business suits trying on expensive walking shoes (or "walking systems," as some are called) this week at the Urban Hiker, a new store billing itself as "America's First Walking Store."

Jogging is said to be out. Too hard. You could get hurt. Walking is said to be in.

The Urban Hiker, on Amsterdam Avenue at 85th Street, is a store for what the owners call "serious walkers." It carries dozens of styles of walking shoes ($45-$135), complete walking outfits ($60-$165) and walking accessories (such as imported, high-tech walking poles made of ultralight steel that telescope down into your briefcase).

A customer, Marshall Lieber, dropped in to ask if the store carried "walking underpants." It does. Mr. Lieber already has Pro-Walker walking shoes, a walking shirt, walking shorts, a walking sweat suit and walking socks. (Sure: the Rockport Walking Sock, $7.50.) Raymond Rosario, the store's manager, can talk for a long time about walking socks: "Notice the bulbous toe," he said, then pointed out the padded heel, the arch support and so on. There are walking hats, too, and walking gloves.

And how does all of this walking-wear differ from, say, jogging outfits? "In subtle ways," George Pakradoonian, Jr., the store's owner, said with a smile. "Walking suits have maybe a little more style to them, perhaps, because, like, you might want to go in some place."

"Stores," interjected a customer, who said she felt much better now about shopping, telling herself she was actually "health-walking."

"You could stop for lunch on a walk," Mr. Pakradoonian said, suggesting a new facet of exercise regimens.

"Yeah," another customer said. "Would you have a walking shoe I could wear from the couch to the refrigerator during commercials?"

"Walking is not difficult," Mr. Pakradoonian asserted. Take his word for it. "People have been walking for centuries," he said. "People can talk while they walk."

"Also, you could walk the dog," another customer said helpfully.

"Walking relieves stress and burns calories," Mr Pakradoonian said. And there are those who believe it can do a lot more than that. One of the store's customers is David Balboa, whose business card reads THE WALKING PSYCHOTHERAPIST, M. S. W., C. S. W., M. B. A. He has developed psychotherapeutic walking that combines race walking with the Brazilian samba.

In the store is a book titled *The Walking Book* with such chapter titles as "Meet Your Feet" and instructions in how to walk: "Step 2: Defying gravity, we lean forward to overcome inertia." Mr. Rosario also gives instructions in the store on how to walk.

There is a copy of a slick new magazine called *Walking*, which carries articles on how and where to walk and what to wear. There are ads in the magazine for a "walking video" and a book titled *Walk, Don't Die*, which "shows you how jogging kills, calisthenics cripple, diets debilitate and aerobics disable."

Mr. Pakradoonian, who is twenty-seven years old, was working at his father's shoe store, George Boys, on West 116th Street, when he came up with the idea for a walking store. "My father thought I was absolutely nuts," he said.

He recalls his father, George Sr., saying: "Everybody walks!

Why do you need a store to take a walk?" Mr. Pakradoonian explained that his father was very old-fashioned but conceded, "When I first saw that *Walking* magazine, even I thought, 'Enough already!'"

"People say to me, 'Why can't I put on a pair of cutoff jeans and go for a walk?' I say, 'Go ahead.' OK, we're in the fashion business. How many people that you see in Adidas jogging suits are jogging?"

By the way, he was asked, isn't the term "walking shoe" redundant? "Not in the least," he replied.

Despite the new store, the advent of walking publications and the recent formation of dozens of walking clubs in the city, many New Yorkers continue to walk (to the bus, to the store, etc.) without a prescribed walking regimen and without true walking outfits.

Herb Vincent, who passed by the store, would not dignify the question of how long he had been walking with an answer. He did say, however, that he does not feel the need for a $165 Gore-Tex walking outfit and $100 Vibram-soled shoes "to take a &*%?X) walk."

The customer who wanted shoes for trips from couch to refrigerator agreed but said he liked the overall "no sweat" direction that fitness seems to be taking in this country and that he looks forward to perhaps one day reading a magazine called *Standing* and to shopping at a store called the Urban Napper.

THE RETRO RESIDENT
OF THE
BOUTIQUE HOTEL

Bianca, Brooke, Bjorn and Beulah slept here, at Morgans, a new hotel on Madison Avenue just opened by Steve Rubell, of Studio 54 fame, as host to the hip.

So, who the heck is Beulah? Beulah Baer: a sprightly ninety-six-year-old who would not leave when her old building was converted to this "boutique hotel."

She has a *People* magazine she has been reading to help her figure out just who in the heck all these people in the halls and on the elevators are anyway: Halston, Calvin Klein, Diane Von Furstenberg. She thinks she recognized "that British fella," that rock-and-roll singer. Mick Jagger? "That's the one," she says with a smile.

Beulah says everything but her is up-to-date – up to the nanosecond – at Morgans. The men who open the door for her and the desk clerks who take her messages are fresh faced and tucked into uniforms by Georgio and Calvin. Mr. Rubell sends them for haircuts to the Astor Place Barbershop, the East Village shop specializing in all that is important today, hairwise.

Fashion models are being photographed up in the bathrooms, which are designed by André Putman, described by *Vanity Fair* as today's "most exciting interior designer." The bathrooms have stainless-steel sinks – from airplanes. The rooms are equipped with lots of electronic equipment. Zolatone, known as "Monet in a can," is on the walls – not some old wallpaper. There are no

229

spreads on the beds; bedspreads are not happening. Avant-garde Mapplethorpe photographs are happening, and his signed works are on the walls of every room. Calvin's jumpsuits are on the housekeepers. Bianca Jagger is in the elevator. There she goes now.

Beulah Baer is up in Room 407. She has been there for fifty-eight years, the first one to move into the new building, between 37th and 38th streets, in 1927. Miss Baer — "Never married, too busy" — stepped into the elevator one day this week, unfazed by a man with a spike haircut. "Good morning," she said cheerily. Heading out the door, she said to the doormen: "See you later, boys, I hope" — a reference to the vagaries of life at ninety-six.

"The staff is all so friendly," she says. Mr. Rubell says he hires them that way, explaining: "None are from New York."

"There used to be so many trees in the neighborhood," Miss Baer says, walking along Madison Avenue using her cane, "and Steve Rubell is planting trees in front. He is such a nice young man.

"It's a late-night crowd at the hotel," she says, over split-pea soup at a restaurant around the corner. "I guess they act kind of silly sometimes, but so did I. I loved the nightlife. I can sleep as late as they do."

Later, she told Mr. Rubell: "Now you tell me if I cause too much trouble. I can be kind of bad sometimes. Really. I have friends in, and sometimes they stay late. We do a little drinking."

"Beulah is a good biblical name," says Miss Baer, who was raised a Southern Baptist. "I should be a better person, but you kind of go with the crowd.

"I like my cocktails," she explains. "Gin. We used to stir it up in the bathtub during Prohibition. I was seeing a handsome captain from Governors Island then. Handsome. I always liked older men. They seemed to have more sense and more money.

"I had a lot of beautiful relationships," she says with a wink.

"I don't throw my bottles in the trash," she says. "I wrap them in brown paper and sneak them out to a public receptacle. I don't want to get Mr. Rubell in trouble. He doesn't have a liquor license.

"But I look for the good in everybody," she says. "When you

say nasty things about people, you're saying something nasty about yourself. Remember that.

"I went to Studio 54 once," she says. "I didn't see Steve. I just wanted to check it out." Ah, but she was younger then, she notes — about ninety.

"I read about that birthday party the Jaggers had here for their daughter," she says, "but I didn't go. I don't feel like getting dressed up, and you don't get excited about celebrities when you've been in New York as long as I have.

"I used to be somebody, too, you know," she says. She came to New York in 1919 to open the city's first passport office. "Wealthy and famous people were the only ones who traveled abroad," she recalls, "and I met them all."

She has books autographed by Edith Wharton and, in her scrapbook, autographs and notes from the likes of Lillian Gish, Douglas Fairbanks, Mary Pickford, Lionel Barrymore, Sophie Tucker and Hedda Hopper. She has saved several newspaper articles written about her, in which she is nicknamed "The Passport Lady." Will Rogers wrote about her for *The Saturday Evening Post*, and she wound up in *Who's Who of American Women*.

She lives on her government pension in a room that has not been redecorated. Mr. Rubell says he cannot afford to put a lot of money into a rent-controlled apartment for which Miss Baer pays him $78 a month. Says Miss Baer: "It's fine with me, and nobody ever suggested I leave.

"But," she says, turning to Mr. Rubell, who has dropped by, "you'd better fix the bathroom the workers messed up and paint the closet. Those guys took my little footstool, and I can't reach the Ritz crackers!" Mr. Rubell says that he will, right away, and Miss Baer smiles and says, "Isn't he nice?"

She does enjoy the same housekeeping services as the other guests. "I like the fancy little soaps and the luxurious towels," she says and notes that she could order up a steak from the twenty-four-hour kitchen at 5:00 A.M. if she wanted one, just like Rod Stewart does.

By all accounts, the hotel had become rather seedy, with half-day rates and a lot of prostitutes, before Mr. Rubell and his partners purchased it.

"That stuff didn't bother me either," Miss Baer says, "except for the night one of the ladies pushed a man out the window and he landed on the roof outside my window. They took one of my lovely monogrammed sheets and wrapped him up. I never got it back."

She says she is looking forward to the opening of the stylish restaurant at the hotel.

"They might be surprised to see me at the bar once in a while," she says, riding up on the high-tech elevator, "but I'll be there."

"Hey," says a young man in sunglasses and a red leather outfit on the elevator, "Go for it."

Postscript: *Miss Baer died in 1986, but she thoroughly enjoyed her celebrity after this article appeared, including an appearance on* Late Night with David Letterman.

THE PUPPY PLAY GROUP
FOR THE
SOCIAL ANIMAL

MINNIE JUST SEEMS so much better . . . adjusted . . . since she joined the puppy play group.

Everyone says so. The women who own the dogs in the Upper East Side group were all talking about it in the gray dawn this week as they led their dogs to a regular morning session along the East River.

"Yes, Minnie is really coming out of her shell," said Christine Apuzzo, Minnie's owner.

"Minnie is just like all other dogs," remarked Sari Mason, whose dog Moira is also in the group. "I may be anthropomorphizing here, but dogs need dog involvement."

"They're social animals," added Lillian Kraemer, whose little dog Alexander was padding along the sidewalk at 6:20 A.M. "People are fine, but this group lets the dogs have social contact with their own species."

Minnie, a small white dog in a long-legged sweater, lived in the suburbs for many years, it seems, and has had some difficulty adjusting to city life. "Minnie was my father's dog," Ms. Apuzzo said. "He died. It was a traumatic experience for the dog."

The group walked down some steps, crossed a bridge over the Franklin D. Roosevelt Drive and occupied a strip of cement with some broken park benches at the riverside just north of 51st Street. The owners are all working women — three single, two married, no children — and they talked about their dogs' being unhappy that they aren't home all day.

Minnie often starts barking when Ms. Apuzzo goes to work and doesn't stop all day. The problem has been alleviated somewhat since she joined the group. Also, Ms. Apuzzo bought Minnie a brand-new dog collar that administers an electroshock every time the dog barks.

"I hired animal counselors," Ms. Apuzzo said as the women distributed coffee purchased at a nearby deli. "One told me Minnie had to be desensitized to doors and had me spending hours walking around opening and closing doors in my apartment. I felt crazy.

"Another one told me to tape inflated balloons to the door to stop her scratching. And he told me to have a party for the dog and sit on the floor with her. I said: 'But the dog sits on the furniture.' Another counselor told me I had to train my voice to sound like a low growl when I reprimanded her. I did that."

The women said they met while walking their dogs last spring and formed the group, which now meets seven days a week, "to foster happy, well-socialized dogs who can relate well to other dogs," according to Ms. Kraemer.

"'Xander is a very small dog," Ms. Kraemer said of Alexander, "but he has been in group since puppyhood and is quite un-neurotic.

"There is a social aspect to the group for us, too," she said. "I think we've worked through the dogs in our relationships. We see each other for parties and dinners now."

On Sundays, Domosan, Sofia Goldin's Akita, goes to the country, but two other dogs, Radar and Mo, join the group for expeditions to Central Park for group sessions, which normally constitute running around, some scolding and some positive reinforcement. Six dogs and six owners cram themselves into a Honda for the trip. The dogs sometimes visit each other at home for play dates.

Over the noise of traffic whizzing by ten feet away, the women chatted in dawn's first light this week about dental benefits, a lynch mob of tenants after a superintendent, dogs preferring cat food to dog food and the real gold medallion that Alexander wears. Domosan stalked a pigeon. Toby, Ellen Politas's dog, chased Moira, said to be his girlfriend.

"The dogs really look forward to seeing each other," Ms. Mason said, "although I could be anthropomorphizing."

Ms. Kraemer took out some photographs of Alexander's birthday party in which the dog was wearing a party hat and Ms. Kraemer was carving a birthday steak for the dog and his dog guests.

"I didn't have a birthday party for Moira this year," Ms. Mason said. "I feel like a terrible mother."

"It's difficult for a single working woman to raise a dog in the city," remarked Ms. Kraemer, a lawyer, who is single. "There are a lot of pressures on a dog in the city. Yes, sometimes I wish I lived in the suburbs for the dog's sake. Everything normal in New York, like these dogs playing, must be organized." Someone mentioned schools for dogs in the city, but none of the owners said their dogs were gifted.

"I have to have two sets of dog walkers – at noon and four – and they're not easy to keep," Ms. Kraemer said. "One of them just went back to Yugoslavia."

The women walked back across the bridge, up the steps and across 51st Street, meeting and greeting other dog walkers they see almost every day, and stopping to talk dogs.

"Oh, Minnie always goes to group," Ms. Apuzzo said. "Group has made a new dog out of her."

THE 50,000 HOMELESS; THE 7 MILLION MERELY CRAMPED

CENTRAL PARK TREE: 5RMS, NO FEE, GREAT BREEZE

"**T**HIS IS NEW YORK," Frank Serpe, a city official, says with a shrug. "People live in trees" — something those in other parts of the country have long suspected.

And why shouldn't they? New Yorkers live just about everywhere else: on sidewalk gratings; in million-dollar apartments the size of walk-in closets; under expressway ramps; in permanently berthed boats; wherever they can.

Life is good in the trees, Bob Redman reports. He lived in a spacious, five-room split-level house in the top of a towering beech tree with spectacular views of the city skyline and all of Central Park — in fact it was *in* Central Park. Imagine what the rent would be.

Alas, Mr. Redman awoke one morning to the sound of Mr. Serpe, director of horticulture for Central Park, yelling: "Come down! The party's over!" Mr. Serpe had about ten Parks Enforcement Patrol officers with him. "There are a lot of lunatics," he explains. Mr. Redman came down from the tree house, and the officials huddled to decide what to do next with their captive.

"The department had been looking for this guy for eight years," Mr. Serpe says of Mr. Redman, twenty-two years old, who began building tree houses in Central Park eight years ago while a teenager living with his mother on West 82nd Street.

Over the years, city workers found his latest tree houses and tore them down, often while Mr. Redman secretly watched from a distance and laid plans for his next structure. In all, he built thirteen tree houses, all of them in Central Park between the latitudes of 79th and 86th streets, each more lavish than the last.

The final one included ladders and rope bridges – one leading to an adjacent tree – as well as benches and tables he had made.

Mr. Serpe ordered the tree houses torn down under a policy banning such structures as potentially harmful to trees. "But we marveled at the spectacular workmanship," he says. "The last one had floors strong enough to hold a truck, and with not one nail driven into the tree."

Mr. Redman says he has always loved trees, which some would say is a curse for a boy growing up in Manhattan. "I like to be in trees," explains Mr. Redman, who recalls going to Central Park to climb them when he was eight years old. "I like to be up, away from everything. I like the solitude" – something he says is difficult to find elsewhere in the city.

"I loved most to go up in the tree houses and look at the stars," says Mr. Redman, who named all of his tree houses after his favorite stars and called the last one Epsilon Eridani. "The view at night, of the city lights and the stars, is beyond description."

Friends heard about his fantastic tree houses and asked if they could visit. He let them come, as many as twelve at a time, but he asked that they try to arrive unnoticed and that they not make much noise. They brought sandwiches and radios and books and flashlights.

He posted rules, prohibiting branch breaking, fires, litter and loud noise, among other things. "Failure to comply with the above rules," the notice read, "will be considered a threat to the existence of the Spacecraft Epsilon Eridani."

He didn't want his tree houses spotted by authorities, because construction was difficult. He scrounged scrap lumber — one thousand pounds of it went into the last tree house — and carried it, little by little, into the park, where he hoisted it into the trees. Entry to the various houses was often forty feet above ground, with several levels above that. Mr. Redman shinnied up the trees and dropped ropes for visitors to climb. He is lean and lithe, with powerful arms and legs, and can scale tall, branchless tree trunks with remarkable speed.

Mr. Redman selected trees off the beaten paths. He built the houses high up and camouflaged them with green paint and branches. The last house was in a tree just across 79th Street from a Parks Department office and equipment yard, yet it went unnoticed for four months. Others lasted as long as a year.

Something of a legend grew among denizens of the park — urban folklore, about sightings of a young, handsome man who dwelled in the trees, according to Dick Drost, a man who says he lives a good deal of the time in the park. Like other park dwellers, however, Mr. Drost stays on the ground, which Mr. Redman doesn't understand, given the dirt, the rats and the crime.

Although Mr. Redman sometimes spent weeks at a time in the tree houses, he dwelt some of the time in his mother's apartment on West 82nd Street, but that is not the stuff of which legendary tales are made and will not be dwelt on here. He said that his mother, Mary, feared for his safety in the park after dark. Eventually, she also became concerned that he was not preparing himself for a career.

His brother, Bill, sometimes brought his set of conga drums to the tree houses and played them very late at night. This is the stuff of which legends are made. "It freaked people out," says Mr. Redman. Mr. Drost recalls rumors that there might be whole tribes of drum-beating tree dwellers in Central Park.

Mr. Redman recalls hearing the screeching and screaming of animals and human beings late at night in the 840-acre wilderness and feeling quite safe high in the trees. "During storms," he adds, "the tree house swayed and creaked, and it seemed like a ship at sea."

On the day of Mr. Redman's recent capture, as park officials and enforcement personnel huddled to decide his fate, Mr. Redman offered to help the workers dismantle the tree house.

"I told him I supposed that was all right," says Greg Owens, the tree-care coordinator for Central Park. "Well, he walked right up the tree. It was amazing."

"Wow! This guy has potential!" Mr. Serpe says to himself, concluding that rather than locking Mr. Redman up, maybe they should offer him a job.

And they did. He promised not to build more tree houses in the park – he lives with his mother now – and recently Mr. Redman became a professional tree climber and pruner for the Central Park Conservancy.

He often amazes his colleagues by racing up tree trunks and walking in the trees.

Climbing and trimming in Central Park this week, Mr. Redman says that he cannot believe a job so perfect for him could possibly exist and that his mother has certainly been pleasantly surprised. It is beyond the wildest dreams he ever had, sitting up in the treetops, swaying in gentle breezes and watching the stars.

APARTMENT ANGST

For nine months Gail Pollock has been looking for an apartment in Manhattan. She has been scouring neighborhoods, canvassing door-to-door, begging, checking the obituaries and making offers of cash, cases of Scotch and blackberry pies – to no avail.

She has sought professional help, but when she tells rental agents that she is looking for – Get this one, Harry! – an afford-able apartment in Manhattan, they nearly spit out their coffee and fall off their chairs.

If she were looking for, say, a nice, exorbitantly priced, claustrophobia-inducing apartment in a bloodcurdling neigh-borhood, they would certainly be happy to help.

A Buddhist chants and a Bible group prays for divine inter-vention in Ms. Pollock's quest. The agents say she'll need it. The woman is looking for a $500-a-month studio.

She met the Buddhist, the Bible-group members, lots of nice men who said she could live with them, and little old ladies who invited her in for tea as she trod the streets of New York looking for what she acknowledges is "a needle in a haystack."

The twenty-nine-year-old film editor moved here from Seat-tle – not from outer space, as one agent suggested – to pursue her dream of a career in the film industry. Part of that dream is to live in Manhattan in a small studio apartment.

On a recent and typical day in her relentless campaign, Ms. Pollock, who now shares an apartment with three roommates, rose at 5:30 A.M. to buy the morning newspapers for the latest apartment listings. She used to begin at 4:30 A.M. but found that her telephone calls at this hour irritated tenants, who had often received ten calls already.

For a time she combed the obituaries and called the bereaved. But she learned that if the doctor who had signed the death certificate didn't get the apartment, there always seemed to be a neighbor down the hall who immediately called a friend in need of an apartment to say, "The old geezer finally died."

After looking for ads in the papers, Ms. Pollock stopped next this day at a copying shop, where she now receives a warm welcome and a volume discount, having ordered in recent months about six thousand fliers offering a $700 reward for a lease on a rent-stabilized apartment.

When someone answers this appeal, posted on poles and stuffed into mailboxes throughout Manhattan, she jumps on her bicycle and races to the apartment. She bought a bicycle for this purpose, and after it was stolen while she was apartment hunting, she acquired a second.

She has temporarily stopped working so that she can answer the calls instantaneously and so that she can spend more time looking. She was able to spend only three to five hours after work canvassing the neighborhoods, often continuing the search until midnight. And when she is out searching, she frequently calls the answering service she hired so that she wouldn't miss any responses to her fliers.

Even so, she often arrives at the apartments to find several dozen other hopefuls there bidding up the price, as well as tenants asking $2,000, $5,000 or $15,000 under the table — cash, right now — to give up the place.

She knows that reasonably priced apartments are out there. There are an estimated 1,150,000 rent-controlled or rent-stabilized apartments in the city, but getting one seems to require the luck and the up-front cash of a lottery jackpot winner.

In her price range she has seen some real doozies. She had an inside tip on a $470-a-month apartment in a beautiful building on lower Fifth Avenue, but it turned out to be a dark, ten-foot-by-ten-foot tomb, with one closet converted to a bathroom and another closet with a hot plate described as a kitchen.

Often the apartments are in what a realty agent might call a "changing neighborhood." One was a wreck of an apartment with "potential" near the Williamsburg Bridge. Ms. Pollock asked the superintendent last summer, "How many times have you been mugged?"

"This year?" he replied. "Four times."

With the year only half over, and factoring in a few more muggings because she is a woman and because she frequently arrives home late from work, Ms. Pollock decided four was probably too many.

She has become a familiar sight in many neighborhoods, and as she went about posting her fliers this week, several people called out to wish her luck. She was "papering" the Chelsea neighborhood, stopping along the way to call on building superintendents. She has paid several of them $25 or $50 to notify her if an apartment becomes available, but others have apparently paid more. She contacts some of those on her roster several times a month. One of them, Rafael Rodriguez, said that he has come to admire Ms. Pollock's perseverance and would call her first.

Some of Ms. Pollock's friends have suggested that she go on a television talk show to appeal for an apartment or that she rent a large billboard or establish a relationship with a man with a nice apartment and move in with him.

One of her friends has given up on the film business to sell computers, in large part to pay for a nicer apartment. Others have given up on New York altogether and moved back whence they came, where life is easier. They suggest she do likewise and offer to pick her up at the airport.

"I'm staying," she said resolutely, taping up a flier that was flapping in a chill October wind. "When you get knocked down, you just have to get back out there and hustle. It gets insane, but this is New York, and this is what you have to do."

HOMELESS
HAROLD

A VEXING NATIONAL problem
has come to roost on West 11th Street, and it is Harold.

Harold might be more easily described as "homeless" if he
were not so insistent about having one. "My home is New York
City," said the unkempt man with long, scraggly black hair, who
appears to be about twenty-five years old. "I live here like everybody else."

Not quite. He lives on a nicer street than most, a pictur-
esque block lined with trees, heavy ornamental iron fences and
million-dollar brownstones and town houses – albeit on the sidewalk, rather than in the elegant homes.

He is wintering on a choice sidewalk location, a grating with
an updraft of balmy, tropical exhaust. "Feels like it's from the
laundry room," he said, the laundry room of St. Vincent's Hospital and Medical Center. Harold often leaves shoes and other be-
longings there to hold his claim on the spot, and he tries to return
in early evening, "before someone else takes it."

What is almost too good to be true is that there is a house on
his little patch of property, a big metal box, about four feet square
and five feet tall, designed by a neighbor across the street to
cover the grate and keep people like Harold from sleeping there.

It is in the shape of an old cash register, with a curved front
that makes for terribly uncomfortable lounging. But Harold
found a way to sleep on the top part of the box and, later, a way
to get inside.

The presence of Harold and others like him on the block has prompted some spirited discussions among block residents, some of whom find their concern for the homeless heightened and others who now think "the homeless should be locked up," in the words of one.

"It's different," said one passerby, who stopped yesterday morning in front of Harold's box, "when they live in front of your house than when you see them on the TV news." A woman companion asked, "Why doesn't he get out of here and go to a shelter?"

Others on the block, such as Steven Gaines, can be sharply critical of neighbors who react this way, but Mr. Gaines said it was also a mistake to romanticize the homeless. He said the issue of the homeless living on the block was far from cosmetic. "They foul the streets in every conceivable manner," he said.

There is, for instance, the matter of the absolute wild man who lived on the sidewalk for about two years who had the habit of waking the neighborhood nearly every night, yelling loud, graphic obscenities. "The man's voice was unbelievably deep and strong," said Harriet Heyman, another resident. "It was like Walter Cronkite gone berserk."

Many neighbors railed against hospital officials to do something about the screaming man on their property, but no matter how many times the man was chased away or escorted to shelters and emergency rooms by the police, he always returned. Mr. Gaines and others asked the hospital to put some barbed wire on the grate, which months later the hospital did.

"Then," said Dan Sorrenti, a spokesman for the hospital, "we received calls from neighbors saying how inhumane it was to put up the barbed wire. It's a real catch-22 situation."

Not to mention that men still put pieces of cardboard over the barbed wire and sleep there. Police Officer Gerard Barry, who answers many of the neighbors' calls, said it is difficult for the police to do much if the homeless men refuse to be taken to a shelter.

"It's a terribly uncomfortable position to be in," said Carl Stein, who owns a town house across from Harold's box, "to be sitting in your living room warm and comfortable and know a man is on your doorstep freezing."

Mr. Stein said his seven-year-old daughter frequently had nightmares about the screamer. "For my wife and I," he said, "it's a real dilemma. If having the homeless on the sidewalks is simply unsightly and an inconvenience, that's one thing. But when does an inconvenience become so great that it interferes with the way we live?"

Mr. Stein is an architect, and part of his work is redesigning living spaces as shelters for the homeless. "I have learned a lot," he said, "mainly that the homeless are not all deinstitutionalized mental patients by any means. A lot of them are people who can't afford housing, who cannot find a job."

"It becomes the law of survival," Mr. Gaines said. "When I can't sleep or work, it becomes me or them. The problems of living in New York mount up. I start to think about leaving. I love this city. I want to stay here."

"Part of you aches for the people on the sidewalks," said Cynthia Story, another neighbor. She said she had offered some of the men on the street clothing but that they had refused the offers. "People in New York are hardening to seeing the homeless out there. They are so common that we stop looking at them. That's what is frightening."

"I'm happy the screamer is gone," Ms. Heyman said, "but it concerns me that no one can do anything for him. It seems we just don't care enough. That's the bottom line."

"It is," Mr. Gaines said, "the character and nature of people in this city not to care, to walk on by and not look, to not start up with somebody.

"The terrible thing is that after we asked for the barbed wire and got it and the screamer left, I felt sorry for him. I felt like we had evicted him from his home. I wonder where he is and if he is all right."

Out on the sidewalk yesterday morning, Harold was rising on a sunny, almost springlike day. The sidewalk next to his box was littered with cigar butts. Harold apologized, saying that he had entertained some guests the previous evening and had not had a chance to clean up.

OF MURPHY BEDS,
CASTRO CONVERTIBLES
AND CRITICAL CLOSETS

RICHARD GLAVIN HAS a terribly tiny foot-by-three-foot kitchen. If he lived somewhere else, his friends would pity him, but in New York they are jealous of his having a separate kitchen space.

Mr. Glavin explains that he is going a little crazy. Like so many other New Yorkers, he tells of once living in a nice, normal apartment designed for human habitation before moving to Manhattan and a typical apartment with the bedroom, home office, dining room and living room all squished into one.

A cat's scratching post might seem a small thing in another city, but here it takes precious space where Mr. Glavin could put a little chair and maybe have somebody over to talk to. The scratching post must go, and Jasper, the orange cat, must be declawed.

"That's the kind of price we all pay," says Mr. Glavin, speaking to Jasper, "for living in New York." If he lived in any other city, he says, he would have a dog.

Getting rid of the scratching post was the idea of Meg Forman, an apartment space consultant who advertises: "Expand Your Apartment. I'll redo your apartment to create the visual illusion and physical experience of much more space." Ms. Forman is an industrial designer who says her experience in the area of microengineering prepared her well for working with Manhattan apartments.

Her new career is blossoming, she says, as only it could in

New York — a city where a reasonable amount of living space is an unaffordable luxury and where people at the next restaurant table check your watch. It's a city of Pullman kitchens, Murphy beds and Castro Convertibles and a city of answering machines — because who wants to stay at home in an apartment the size of a NASA nose cone, living like an astronaut?

Ms. Forman sits on Mr. Glavin's bed and talks about how she takes things off walls, throws out heavy drapes, rearranges traffic patterns, stacks things and does a lot with mirrors. She charges $125 for what is normally a one-day job.

"I didn't always live like this," says Mr. Glavin, sinking into reverie about his abode in Washington, D.C., which had high ceilings and a sun porch. Now he talks of having perpetually bruised hips from banging into corners of furniture. He has a long cord on his phone and takes it up the fire escape to the roof — his recreation room.

"You start thinking thoughts," he says, "like, 'I could put three albums on one tape and save room.' But you can only be so ingenious. Eventually you have to throw things out."

"There is no room for sentimentality," says Kelly Reid, another of Ms. Forman's clients. "I have a few postcards from friends that I have to get rid of because they clutter up the place."

Ms. Forman suggests that Ms. Reid might want to paint palm trees on the brick wall across the three-foot air shaft from the two windows in her studio apartment. "That might make me more angry about not having a real view at these prices," says Ms. Reid.

They decide to try putting rice-paper shades over the windows with little lights behind them to simulate sunlight, and perhaps with paper leaves back there that might cast shadows on the translucent paper. Ms. Forman also wants to put a rice-paper shade with a bulb behind it next to Ms. Reid's loft bed to simulate a window.

Ms. Reid balks at a suggestion that she put the television set out of the way under the desk and watch its reflected image in a mirror on the wall. "Wouldn't that be a little weird?" she asks. Ms. Forman also suggests placing Ms. Reid's dresser on rollers so the room can be changed for varying occasions.

"Closets become critical," Agostino Rocchi proclaims solemnly, speaking of apartment space problems. He would. He is co-owner of Creative Closets, on Broadway near 88th Street, a closet boutique that sells and installs closet organization systems for ever greater volumes of storage. He has a client with 120 pairs of shoes. He has clients with special storage needs, like for harpsichord covers. He says business is booming.

Daniel Farina, a customer in the store, marvels at the scented coat hangers and comments that his bedroom is actually not as large as a display closet in the store. Mr. Farina contends that he once heard of a hypnotist in New York who worked with clients who felt claustrophobic in their apartments.

Mr. Rocchi says he has learned to approach closets cautiously in this town, much in the manner of the bomb squad. He opens closet doors slowly and carefully. When possible he has the owner open the closet and take the brunt of any avalanche. "The New York apartment," he says, "has to serve as attic, garage, basement, extra room and place for dressers there is no room for."

He and his partner, Curt Bohlen, have "before" and "after" display closets in the store, at least in part so they have a place to put the clothes they can't fit into their closets at home.

One customer, Jean Hart, called the store, desperate, with no place to put anything in her new apartment. After living in Los Angeles and Chicago, she says, she felt as if she were moving into a glove compartment. Mr. Rocchi made an emergency call to her apartment, and Mr. Bohlen installed the closet organization systems yesterday.

"I feel as if I am in a Japanese culture here," she says. "If you move you step on somebody's toes. There is nowhere to put anything. I have a car that I'm having to leave outside the city. I guess I'd better just kiss that good-bye."

WELL-TO-DO'S
AND DON'TS

CAN AND
BOTTLE PICKERS

IN SOME FARAWAY place, the mother and child might have been out for a stroll picking wildflowers. "There's a red one!" five-year-old Mark Williams shrieked. He skipped to the curb, picked the red beer can from the gutter and handed it to his mother.

The child regarded it as a game. His thirty-year-old mother, Yvonne, looked weary. She had risen early again this day to collect empty bottles and cans on the streets of the East New York section of Brooklyn.

Collecting the five-cent deposits has become a major source of income for many of the city's poor in the fifteen months since the state's bottle and can deposit law – supported by conservationists to clean up streets, highways, parks and streams – went into effect.

"It doesn't mean as much here," said one collector, David Malone, as he surveyed the impoverished block. "That ain't no picture postcard." Nevertheless, the streets of the neighborhood are cleaner, residents say.

The collectors begin lining up outside Aces Beer and Soda Distributors, set among the abandoned buildings and rubbish-strewn lots of East New York, about 7:00 each morning. The doors open at 9:30. The collectors turn on a fire hydrant around the corner to wash the bottles and cans so that they will be accepted.

They bring their take in bags and boxes and shopping carts.

A man nicknamed Caravan Charlie has tied three shopping carts together and pulls them like a mule. Others have fashioned elaborate carts from wood, roller-skate wheels and milk trays for this line of work.

About a dozen people stood in line yesterday morning. In warm weather, when collecting is not such an arduous task and when people consume more beer and soda, lines of fifty to seventy-five people stretch around the corner at Atlantic Avenue and Eastern Parkway. Fights sometimes erupt over who is ahead of whom.

On days like today, they place their carts and boxes in a line and take refuge from the cold in the Wash and Dry Laundromat. They keep a close eye through the window on their hard-earned collections because there are those who would steal them. They each have their reasons for being here. Mrs. Williams said she needs the money for food and is trying to save for her son's Christmas present.

Gilbert Gonzales needs a bottle of wine. "I'm an alcoholic," he explained, shivering in the December wind on the shady side of the street. "I'm going into a detox program. Not today."

"We need some soap powder," said Annie Mae Keyes, who had brought ninety cans and bottles. If all are brands sold by the distributor and if they are clean and in good condition, she will take home $4.50.

Irving Goldsmith needs his dignity. "You've got to keep trying," said the forty-three-year-old man as he and his wife placed their bottles and cans in small boxes, as required by the redeemer. They come nearly every day and were there the day before in a chill rain. "You develop a keen eye for the can and the bottle," said Mr. Goldsmith, who said he always hopes for a mother lode in a trash can.

"I don't want welfare," said another man in line. He said that a cup of coffee and a grilled cheese sandwich cost him $2.20 across the street at the Jumbo Donut Shop — a small price to pay each day for his pride.

Although the law states that each shop selling beer and soda must redeem the deposits for the brands they sell, many merchants in the neighborhood send the collectors to Aces. "They don't want us around," said one of the men in line, referring to the other stores. Indeed, they do not.

Osvaldo Duran, who owns a bodega around the corner, accepts empties but is not happy about it. "These people come in when I'm trying to make sandwiches for people," he said, "and they are no good for business." He said that containers take up space that should be used for merchandise and that they draw cockroaches and rats.

The owners of Aces make the same complaints. "They have taken the garbage off the streets and put it in our stores," said Sal Rossi, one partner in the business. "We're in the garbage business."

"So are we," said one of the collectors. "The government decided to give us the garbage. There are folks who can afford to throw the cans away, and there are folks who can't afford not to pick it up. I guess it's a blessing."

Aces accepted only half of Mr. Goldsmith's cans and bottles, so he made just $2.75 after lugging the containers to the store from his apartment about two miles away. He and his wife walked away dejectedly, with the wind whipping empty cans and plastic bottles around their feet. They were on their way to the food store, where they said they would shop for something for dinner for themselves and their three children.

Yvonne Williams and Mark walked away after collecting a few dollars. "He wants a tricycle for Christmas," she said, turning her back on the boy so that he could not hear. "I'm saving as fast as I can."

Suddenly she screamed angrily at the boy: "Get out of there!" He looked up from a garbage can that he was looking into for bottles and cans.

She swatted him and snapped, "We're not going into the trash!" Then she hugged him and for a moment looked as if she might cry.

RESTAURANT ROW SOUP KITCHEN: A TALE OF TWO CITIES

HE FOUND THE cheesecake rich and creamy, the ambience pleasantly informal and the service most accommodating, yet Ernie said he could not help but be a bit disappointed that the luxurious chocolate-mousse cake with shaved walnuts was not on the menu yesterday at the St Luke's Lutheran Church soup kitchen.

"After all," Ernie said, "this is Restaurant Row." He was among the customers at a soup kitchen amid the cavalcade of chic restaurants (twenty-one of them) lining West 46th Street between Eighth and Ninth avenues.

Joe Allen, a restaurant one door down, often sends over pumpkin pies and chocolate-mousse cakes. Orso, another trendy restaurant adjacent to the soup kitchen, donates pasta primavera. Crepe Suzette donates some of its finest French breads from time to time, and Carolina sends smoked ribs and breasts of chicken that are prepared on a mesquite-fired, open-hearth grill.

Le Périgord, a few blocks away, catered Thanksgiving dinner at the soup kitchen: cornish hens, pumpkin tarts, the works. Barbetta, Café de France and Crepe Suzette have sponsored benefits for the soup kitchen.

"We have a prix-fixe menu," said the Reverend Dale Hansen, pastor of the church, "fifty cents." The chocolate-mousse cake alone is $3.95 at Joe Allen. The fifty-cent price is for the luncheon for the elderly. The late-afternoon meals are free.

With prices like that, it is no wonder to Pastor Hansen that his restaurant is probably the most popular on the block, serving about 67,000 meals a year, including those delivered to the homebound.

Usually, the soup kitchen serves soup. But the cook, Mel Marrant, feels an obligation to serve fresh, homemade soup, not the canned stuff. "This is Restaurant Row in New York," he explained, above the piano that accompanied the diners.

"When they serve something really special," said Nettie, a customer, "the place is packed for days afterward. The word travels through the streets like wildfire. This soup kitchen carries the finest reputation in the city."

But it would. This is Restaurant Row. In a city that is often said to have been split in two – half rich, half poor – the sidewalk outside the soup kitchen provides as good a juxtaposition as can be found.

This week a man in a tuxedo and a woman in a fur coat, on their way to Barbetta, stepped over a man in tattered clothing who was lying on the sidewalk, waiting for the soup kitchen to open.

"Soup smells good, doesn't it," Pastor Hansen said to the man, when he came in from the wet snowfall. The shivering man responded, "You have no idea."

Pastor Hansen tells his patrons they can have all the refills they want, to save them the trouble of sneaking them, and he gives containers of soup to go to those who want them.

Many of the restaurants along Restaurant Row are frequented by an interesting clientele. Some are known for attracting famous actors, others for attracting writers, arbitragers and even Mafia chieftains. The soup kitchen has its own cachet. At one table this week, a group of older women, all of whom said they had once been Broadway starlets, Ziegfeld girls and the like, tried to one-up each other with talk of their glorious pasts. "They fight for the microphone when we have a sing-along," Pastor Hansen said.

Another table drew older connoisseurs of the grape, and yet another was occupied by a group of what Pastor Hansen called "the young alcoholics, under thirty years old." Drug users and pushers also frequent the establishment, although Pastor Hansen throws out anyone caught practicing their bad habits on the premises.

A young, blond woman in black leather pants, a tight red sweater and a red beret, accompanied by two black men, was identified by a worker in the soup kitchen as one of the prostitutes from the corner, Eighth Avenue and 46th Street.

The restaurant owners on the block do not complain about the soup kitchen's clientele. Pastor Hansen said this was because these people were already here and because the restaurant owners knew that Pastor Hansen spent much time running off undesirables, such as the prostitutes who do business — complete transactions — on the front steps of the church.

"It's a long way from Wausau," said Pastor Hansen, referring to the Wisconsin town where he had his previous ministry.

The church is also affected by its proximity to the theater district. The soup kitchen has its own theater-ticket desk, where customers can buy tickets for whatever they can afford.

"We don't get a lot of tickets to *Cats*," Pastor Hansen said. "Most are to off Broadway or off-off Broadway or off-off-off."

Using volunteers and modest contributions, the church keeps a dizzying variety of programs going to serve the polyglot neighborhood. They include providing clothes for those who need them, counseling for battered women and children, English lessons for Hispanic people and an alcoholism program.

"We had to open the church up to the community," said Pastor Hansen, who arrived here twelve years ago to find the church chained shut like a fortress.

Pastor Hansen has been stabbed twice, once by a man who knocked on the door, asked for food and demanded money after Pastor Hansen fed him.

But he keeps opening the door.

TANNED
AND TITLED

"**W**HERE ARE THE princesses?" yelled a frantic Bruce Lynn.

Mr. Lynn, a publicity man, had maintained his cool all evening but was suddenly seized by the awful fear that there could be a serious case of Titled-Nobility Shortfall (TNS) at this gala tenth anniversary celebration of a tanning salon.

But of course, that didn't happen. "Ah, Prince Roffredo Gaetani Lovatelli!" shrieked Vittorio Assaf, an owner of the tanning salon, gleefully sighting royalty.

TNS is just a temporary social condition (albeit an aggravating one) in New York City these days. There are just too many titled people running around for a few not to wander into a good party, especially one held, as this one was, at the Tunnel, a dance club enjoying the always-fleeting status of one of New York's hottest.

"Is this the Sigourney Weaver affair?" someone asked, and was told, no, that the Sigourney Weaver affair was at the other end of the club. And no, it was not the birthday party for Dustin Hoffman's daughter Karina, either. That was in the basement, where the party with David Byrne, of Talking Heads, had been the night before. And so on.

Isabella Rossellini was scheduled, or so Mr. Lynn said, to make an appearance at this party Thursday for the Portofino Sun Centers in Manhattan, but she did not. Someone said it was just as well, since Ms. Rossellini is not tan anyway. (Remember?) And this group was looking and talking tan.

Prince Lovatelli remarked, through an interpreter, that it is important to have a tan, even if you are a prince. "Perhaps even more so," said the interpreter, adding a personal note.

Concurring with the prince were Marquis Fabio Della Gherardesca and Count Davide Silvello von Moser. The nobility was starting to roll in now — along with fifteen hundred untitled guests — to the great relief of Mr. Lynn and Mr. Assaf. Mr. Assaf said he was moved that so many important people had come to pay homage to his tanning salons and to "tan-ness," generally. Cissy Houston, Whitney's mother, performed at the party, and she was far from the most tan person at the party.

"Having a title and a tan seems to be the thing in New York," remarked Harrison Gladstone, a party guest. "Everyone with a foreign accent is claiming to be a count or an archduchess from Italy or Austria or someplace. And they all say they've just returned from St. Maarten, even though it may have been a trip to the tanning parlor."

Said Mr. Assaf: "Even if you do go to St. Maarten, you should come in for a pretan. The worst thing that can happen to a person is to get sunburned on vacation."

Probably the most tan person at the party was Don Richman. "People ask me all the time where I've been vacationing," said Mr. Richman, "and I tell them 'Portofino.' They ask, 'But isn't it rather cool at this time of year?' thinking I mean Portofino, Italy, and I say, 'No, not really.'"

Many of those at the party stood in line for treatments on two of Mr. Assaf's tanning machines that had been brought in. The guests were dropping bons mots that sounded vaguely familiar, like "You're never fully dressed without a tan" and "You can never be too rich or too tan."

"I would never go out in natural sunlight," remarked a tan guest, Leonard Benjamin. "Too many UVB and UVC rays."

"I understand there can be certain health hazards to tanning," said another guest. "But if you look bad and hate yourself, why would you want to live?" Mr. Assaf asserts that his tanning machines are completely safe.

Kersti Bowser, an Elite model, said she takes the rays at Portofino, too. She said that she is half Swedish and half black and has to keep the Swedish half in check.

"You must have a tan to be successful" explained Arthur Appleman, a lawyer who visits the salon three times a week. He said he used to take just facial treatments, "but my hands looked funny, so I now do full body.

"When you are tan, you look rich," Mr. Appleman said. "When you look like you have money, people in New York want to give you more money. And women like you better, a lot better. You look rich to them, too."

"It would be impossible to overestimate the value of my tan," offered another regular customer, although his wife estimated that her tan cost about $3,000. She has been on a Regular Tan Maintenance (RTM) program at the salon for eighteen months.

Mr. Assaf was upset. He said he had been so busy planning the party that he had not had time for a touch-up tanning treatment. Someone said he'd better get his priorities straight, and he readily agreed.

A woman told Prince Vittaliano Borromeo how honored she was to meet him. "His family owns Milan," someone whispered to her.

The woman turned to a man standing next to the prince and asked, "And are you anybody?"

"No, I am not," the man answered.

But Mr. Assaf said the man possessed something as important as a castle in Europe or some old crown jewels in a drawer: When all around him in New York City look pale and sick at this time of year, he has a tan.

THE MILLIONAIRE'S CLUB OF EAST HARLEM

ON A DREARY, drizzling October night in Spanish Harlem, raucous laughter wafted out of a little makeshift shack on a rubbish-strewn lot.

Rafael Quinones, standing on the corner nearby, broke into a smile at the sound of the laughter and said: "Sounds good. Nice to know somebody's having some fun around here."

They were having fun at the Millionaire's Club, one of the city's newest nightclubs. It is on New York's Upper East Side, but too far up, up where the Tofutti bars and designer-fur salons give way to bodegas and housing projects.

"Just trying to get something started," said Angel Gonzalez, a member of the new club, slapping down a domino — whack! — in a spirited game. "Things were getting bad around here."

Mr. Gonzalez and a few other men in the neighborhood cleared debris from the vacant lot at 102nd Street and Second Avenue, then constructed a clubhouse from scraps of lumber, tin, paneling, linoleum carpeting and anything else they could get their hands on that resembled a building material.

One side of the clubhouse flips open to the sidewalk, and the men sat out of the rain slapping down dominoes, throwing back cans of beer and tumblers of Cuba libres, listening to hot salsa music on the radio and watching the world go by.

As darkness fell, activity on the sidewalk picked up, with kids from the nearby housing projects coming to hang out at the small Ponderosa grocery store or outside of Garcia's Barbershop. Young men strutted by in clouds of after-shave lotion, looking to buy or sell illegal substances. Young women doused in makeup strutted by, looking to make some sales of their own.

An elderly woman, a Mrs. Stewart, walked past wailing loudly. Her granddaughter had been murdered – her throat slashed, people said – the night before. Those on the sidewalk said they had heard about it. Some of them answered her anguish with blank stares, while others turned their backs.

"This is a rough neighborhood," said Celestino Concepción of the seeming indifference. "We can't mourn them all."

Neighborhood residents said that the simple little shack had somehow managed to lift the spirits not only of the fifteen club members but of the entire neighborhood. The club has become something of a community center, performing all sorts of functions, from the organizing of neighborhood softball games to taking up collections for medical bills and funerals.

The shack is apparently sacrosanct, having been granted immunity from vandalism and theft. The members are viewed as the elders of the neighborhood. Most of them were pioneers of Spanish Harlem, immigrating from Puerto Rico in the late 1940s and early 1950s, when the neighborhood was predominantly Italian. Most are raising families here. People in the neighborhood call this the Millionaire's Club, the members said, because the neighborhood residents are so poor that they view these men, who are lucky enough to have jobs and are able to chip in a few dollars a week for beer and a weekend cookout, as rich.

Some people in the neighborhood are envious of the men who gather in the shack – in the grand tradition of suburban-country-club envy. "It's all relative," said Benny Roldan, a club member.

Victor Fallas, owner of the Ponderosa grocery store a few doors down, and Juan Garcia, owner of the barbershop, both said they liked having the clubhouse there because the neighborhood is now a lot safer at night.

Electricity has revolutionized the club. Since Mr. Concepción agreed to run an extension cord out the window of his building next door, the club not only has electric lights but has acquired a television. Dominoes stopped at 8:30 P.M. this week for the World Series.

Another major change has been the installation by one of the club members, Perfecto Matos, of a bathroom connected by a pipe to the sewer in Mr. Concepción's building. "This changed everything," said Mr. Roldan, "because we drink beer here and now the members can stay longer at the club."

No women are allowed. "Our wives let us spend a lot of time here," said José Maldanado, the chef at the cookouts, "because they know where we are and not out carousing." One of the wives has promised, however, that the first time she spots a woman on the premises she will come in and tear the clubhouse down.

The club started out as just a couple of boards leaned together. Then someone brought over a hammer and nails, and a room ten-feet square was built. The club's popularity demanded the addition of a small front porch and the acquisition of more portable coolers for beer. Recently, another addition was made, doubling the size of the club.

For many members, the club recalls clubhouses they had when they were children in Puerto Rico. For others, it recalls the fraternal spirit they remember from street gangs they belonged to when they moved here: the Sea Hawks, the Viceroys, Dragons and others.

The program of activities offered by the club has expanded to include excursions to Yankees and Mets games for members and for neighborhood children, as well as fishing trips to Brooklyn, weekend softball games and neighborhood cookouts on the lot.

There is a new owner of the lot, who has let them know he would like them off the premises. But they are going ahead with plans to winterize the club, converting a fifty-five-gallon drum to a stove.

"Who knows what could happen," said Mr. Concepción, who said there is interest in holding fund-raising events for a neighborhood excursion to Puerto Rico and having a neighborhood Christmas party at the club. One child said he was collecting books and would ask the men if they would start a neighborhood library.

The members don't know about that. They want to make sure the original purpose of the club is not perverted: to drink beer, play dominoes and laugh a lot.

Anything beyond that, they say, is asking a lot from a pile of boards.

YOU AND
YOUR FUR

"THE NEW YORK woman," said Beverly Stein, tossing off a raccoon coat and slipping into a silver fox in the showroom, "is the queen of the fur-bearing kingdom."

And when the weather turns cold, there is no ensuing dormancy in the species, no thought of retiring to a cave or of burying oneself in a muddy pond bottom for the winter. Cold air and thoughts of the new social season instead send thousands of women scurrying to the Fur District to take their coats out of cold storage or to buy new ones. With all of the fur-bearing women scampering about, the neighborhood takes on the look of the prairie-dog village at the Bronx Zoo.

When the flocks return to the Fur District, winter is nigh in New York, explained Leon Kassman, co-owner of Davellin-Balencia, where two thousand furs are for sale on the showroom floor and twenty-nine hundred are in cold storage. "This is a rite of autumn," said Mr. Kassman, who adds extra help for the rush at the 29th Street store, which he has to keep open seven days a week at this time of year.

"A bunch of us," said Mrs. Stein, "have lunch every year and then come and get our furs." Mrs. Stein's companion, a woman named Deanie, said: "You panic. It's warm and then — bingo! — it's cold, and you've got to have your fur. Otherwise people take pity on you for not having one."

Mrs. Stein often trades in her fur coats for new ones, and her used coats go to fur thrift stores, which she thinks is "just grand because then everyone can afford a fur."

"A fur is an incredibly high-priority item in New York," said Mr. Kassman. "Secretaries and nurses have to have them. Some customers are buying more than one."

Delores Reichman said that in her hometown in Pennsylvania, a fur might be considered ostentatious for someone in her position, a schoolteacher, "but not here. I wouldn't even know how to go about being ostentatious in New York."

"I consider finding a good furrier as important as finding a good doctor," said Adrienne Malis, who was slipping into a silver fox. Her husband looked on as she tried on furs, and he said repeatedly – loud enough for all to hear – that money was no object.

"If your wife doesn't have a fur," he said, "it does not look good for you as a man."

David Leinoff, co-owner of the store, said that despite husbands' grousing about their wives and girlfriends – mistresses are still a sizable market segment, he said – buying fur coats is "all an act. Most sales are made to women to fulfill a man's ego, to show that he has made it."

Mr. Leinoff said that this should be the greatest year ever for fur sales, noting that luxury is in vogue and "the ecological issue" – people making ethical objections to the wearing of animal skins – has all but disappeared. "The people who were out on the picket lines are now in the showrooms," he said.

"People still hassle you occasionally," said a customer in a fur coat, "but I tell them that as long as they're still eating hamburgers – hamburgers are cows, you know – maybe they should just shut up about it."

"I object to the wearing of animal skins on economic grounds," said another customer. "I can't afford them."

"Excuse me," a clerk said to a customer trying on her fur coat after taking it out of storage, "I didn't want to say anything, but what I'm seeing here is not 'now.' The fur is, and pardon me please, somewhat dated." The customer in the crowded showroom greeted the appraisal with enthusiasm and began trying on new fur coats.

Some customers had to make agonizing decisions. Pity poor Deanie, for example, torn between two furs with money as no object. She left without a fur coat, but luckily she has two at home.

And then there was Mrs. Malis, who was replacing her raccoon coat because "raccoon weighs very heavily on you, you know?"

Mrs. Malis's husband said he buys his wife fur coats "because she is more attractive, feels more attractive, is happier and I therefore have a happier home life."

"I have furs, of course," said Mrs. Malis. "This is just something to knock around in," she said, referring to the $5,000 silver-blue Norway fox coat she was holding. She was buying it, she said, largely "because I already tried everything in the brown family."

Jeanne Hoeflich's problem was that she had reached the conclusion that "mink is just too common, no longer a status fur." Another woman chimed in, "Yeah, my cleaning lady has one." Phil Verner, a salesman, added, "We call the dark brown and black minks 'The Uniform,' because everyone in New York has one."

Pat Fulmer tried on a natural mahogany Danish mink and said, "My husband owes me this for making me come with him from Atlanta to New Jersey on business for a year."

She said she did not wish to be a snob, but, "I want female pelts. Male pelts are wider and less expensive, and I would not want to find myself in a group of people who knew that my pelts were male."

Some of the customers talked of the relative status of furs, particularly someone else's. One talked of another woman's fur as "looking like something she hit on the highway," and another said that a mutual friend "waddles around in that big beaver coat until you think she's going to build a dam in the living room."

Billi Sloan, another customer, had her own problem: lynx lust. She was trying on a $4,500 short-waisted jacket of American lynx mix, Finnish raccoon and white Norwegian fox. "This is just something to throw in the closet," she said, pointing to what she really wants, a $40,000 Russian lynx coat.

Her companion, Hope Siegel, noted that life is not completely fair. "I cannot wear cats," she said, because of an allergy.

She bought a Finnish raccoon coat instead — "just something to wear with jeans."

One of the many women buying themselves fur coats said, "I got tired of waiting for some man to come along to buy me one." She is thinking of sending it to herself with a card reading, "From Sugardaddy to my Baby."

A friend chided her about buying a fur coat, recalling that ten years ago that same woman had criticized people "for such unconscionable extravagance."

"That was then," the woman responded, "and this is now."

THE GIFT
OF GLOVES

On a crisp, sunny morning this week a jaunty little man with a canvas bag slung over his shoulder walked briskly through the Bowery handing out pairs of gloves. In his wake the sidewalk was dotted with men who had stopped to slip on the gloves and take a moment to admire them.

"Who was that guy?" asked a man on crutches, rubbing his gloved hands together.

"Gloves," answered another. "That was Gloves."

Gloves Greenberg. For twenty-one years Michael Greenberg has performed a simple act of charity, walking through the Bowery between Thanksgiving and Christmas, giving gloves to those who don't have them.

"How much do they cost?" asked the next man.

"A handshake," replied Mr. Greenberg.

"Say what?" said the man. "You don't want us to join a church or anything?" Mr. Greenberg smiled, handed the man a pair of red wool gloves and shook his hand.

"Say," said the man, sheepishly, "you wouldn't happen to have something in dark brown, would you?" Mr. Greenberg exchanged the gloves and was on his way.

Every payday throughout the year, Mr. Greenberg buys three pairs of gloves to give away during the holiday season. In recent years word of his charity has spread, and people have been mailing him gloves. Girl Scout Troop 1646 of Floral Park, for example, held a glove drive and sent him twenty-one pairs and sixteen unmatched gloves.

But mostly he receives envelopes in the mail containing one glove, the mate to which has been lost. Most of these are righties, he noted, saying that for some reason he can't quite figure out, people lose left gloves four to five times as often as right gloves.

He has a mountain of sixteen hundred gloves in his small Greenwich Village apartment, which a friend refers to as Greenberg's Glove Compartment. He matches them all. Some wait years for their matches to come in, but he refuses to give away unmatched gloves.

"Oh, look!" he said, leaping from his chair in the apartment and grabbing two red mittens. "A match!"

So exhausting is this task that this year he held a Fourth of July glove-matching party. "The more we drank," he explained, "the easier it was to find what we thought were matches."

The multicolored mound contains ski gloves and work gloves and gardening gloves and gloves intended for the driving of expensive sports cars and gloves to be worn with ball gowns and little red mittens and rabbit-lined chamois gloves. There are gloves bearing tags from five-and-ten-cent stores, as well as those with labels from Fifth Avenue designer shops.

The fact is, he doesn't want any more gloves, and he has been returning money from benefactors. "I would," said Mr. Greenberg, who distributes the gloves as a memorial to his father, "just like to see others doing the same sort of thing, something other than just writing a check for a tax-deductible contribution."

Mr. Greenberg, who works for Grey Advertising on the Revlon account, always carries a few pairs of gloves in his briefcase in the event he sees someone who needs them.

He hopes to give away as many as three hundred pairs on trips to the Bowery between now and Christmas. He could give them all away in a couple of hours if he went only to missions, but he prefers to seek out those who withdraw and would not otherwise have gloves.

They sometimes recoil when he approaches. It sometimes

takes him fifteen minutes to persuade some of them to accept the gloves. "These are not my gloves," said a tottering old man. "I cannot take them. No one has ever given me anything. What do you want from me?" Finally, the man accepted them.

"Happy Thanksgiving," Mr. Greenberg said, greeting a bare-handed man. "It's cold. You need some gloves. They're yours." Some snatch the gloves quickly. Others are more cautious. But all of them this day took the gloves and immediately put them on.

"This is strange," said Bob Bose, a recipient who stood shivering on East Third Street. "People don't give something for nothing in this town. But this man, he didn't ask me questions or hold them out and tell me I had to do something to get them. My hands were cold. Now they're not, and bless him."

Some of the men were clear-eyed and well groomed; others were dirty, disheveled and staggering. Mr. Greenberg stooped to place a pair of gloves next to a man who slept on the sidewalk at the corner of Houston Street and the Bowery.

The fifty-six-year-old Mr. Greenberg recalled being raised during the Depression — without gloves — in Williamsburg, just across the bridge from the Bowery. He said his father had taught him, "Don't deprive yourself of the joy of giving."

Occasionally, Mr. Greenberg has seen someone on the Bowery he recognizes. "It brings tears to your eyes," he said. "You are reminded that these are human beings whose lives have turned."

He has given gloves there to a man who had been one of his teachers at Brooklyn College — an economics teacher.

"I was handing out gloves," Mr. Greenberg recalled, "and I saw a man who had been a leading baritone at the Met when I was an extra, a spear carrier. He didn't recognize me, of course. The lead singers at the Met would never have associated with the likes of us.

"I wanted to say, 'You were so wonderful!'" But Mr. Greenberg feared he would embarrass the man, who silently took the gloves and walked away.

"I've seen them wiping windshields with the gloves," said Mr. Greenberg, "and selling them for whisky money. That is not my concern. When you give a gift, you let it go."

THE OUTDOOR
TYPE

"**S**WEETHEART," SAID JOYCE
Grant, who looked out from behind ultradark, wraparound sunglasses as she spoke to the clerk in the camp store through a cloud of her cigarette smoke, "you don't have to tell *me* about summer camp. I was Camper of the Year."

Summer camp season has arrived in Manhattan, an unlikely place for it to turn up, and many urbane New Yorkers are making annual visits to the Camp Shop, an exclusive outfitter on East 54th Street. Some admit to not knowing a canteen from a mess kit, and others believe that – denied a minimum daily requirement of Bloomingdale's and exposed to fresh air – they would never last in the countryside. Carbon monoxide supplements might help.

But they come to the store to outfit their children and pack them off to summer camp. "We are, of course, always anxious for the children to return from camp," explained Sandy Pessin, a parent from East 75th Street, "but we have a wonderful, wonderful time when they are gone. My friend Sheila held a 'Thank God They're Gone' party last summer."

The store carries equipment with the logos of 265 camps and will pack a trunk right down to the bar of Fels Naphtha soap – "everything but the kid," said Harvey Kamer, the proprietor – and ship it to any one of the Winnebagos, Waganakis, Mah-Kee-Nacs or Wi-Co Su-Tas. Moreover, the shop sews York Boil-Proof Name Tapes into every sweater and shirt, every pair of underwear and pajamas, and every measly little sock, as required by diabolical camp regulations. "We hate to sew name tags!" Mrs. Pessin said. "That's why we're here."

The deadline nears for shipping the trunks, and it is nearer still for orders that include the name-tag service. The Camp Shop is jammed. On a recent day, parents were double-parked outside the elegant little limestone building with a tasteful little brass sign reading THE CAMP SHOP INC.

An occasional limousine deposited a camper at the door. Some were accompanied by nannies. A few parents arrived with the measurements of children who are away at boarding schools and not even stopping off at home before going to camp for the summer.

The waiting room was filling up. Mr. Kamer was giving directions to someone on the telephone: turn right on Fifth Avenue at Gucci, past Glaser Furs, past the Margot Gallery.

Five machines are sewing in name tags all day, every day now. One of those sewing was once heard to mutter, "Shouldn't their mothers be doing this?"

Ms. Grant, the Camper of the Year, who now resides on East 57th Street and in North Miami, Florida, was there with her husband, Joey Martino, and her stepdaughter, Danielle Martino, who had to be outfitted for eight weeks at Camp Robindel in New Hampshire.

Ms. Grant removed her pink leather jacket, revealing a pink, tie-dyed rhinestone and metal-studded sweatshirt, and got down to business. "How many T-shirts are the other kids getting?" Ms. Grant asked Mr. Kamer.

"Twelve," he answered.

"We'll take fourteen," she said.

Ms. Grant, who did not remove her sunglasses indoors, denied her Camper of the Year honors were from Camp Bloomingdale's or Camp Fiorucci. It was "a real camp": Camp Pakatakan, as she recalls — give or take an aka.

Joey Martino recalled attending a free Police Athletic League camp out in the semi-wilds of northern New Jersey when he was growing up.

"This will be five thousand dollars before it's over," he said, "what with the flight and the hotels for visitation."

"Joyce and I are going to camp, too," said Mr. Martino, slapping his stomach. "Camp La Costa," he said, referring to the luxurious southern California spa.

As Danielle, eleven years old, self-consciously modeled shorts and T-shirts and endured the measuring and weighing process, she did not say a word.

Asked about camp, she said she might be lonesome, not knowing anybody. "You'll know somebody," Ms. Grant said. "Your camp is next to the one my friend's son goes to."

At one of the other two tables in the small salon, there was concern about divorced parents and visiting day. Mr. Kamer said that because of the problem, some camps no longer have visiting days and that others have separate days for mothers and fathers.

At the third table there was talk of "the best" camps and "the right" camps. Eric and Judy Mower, who live at 63rd Street and Park Avenue, said they had reacted against "all this silliness about the social cachet of a camp."

They are sending their ten-year-old daughter to a camp that Mr. Mower described as "a real camp, not a resort, not a fashion show." Mrs. Mower said she was going to pack her daughter's trunk and even sew in the name tapes.

"I have some tapes left over," she explained, to which Mr. Mower responded, "You know that's not the reason." They smiled at each other.

Mr. Kamer breezed in with the bill for Danielle Martino: $935.55. "You're not funny, Harvey," said Ms. Grant, pulling a wad of $100 bills from her purse and throwing them on the table.

Mr. Martino turned to Danielle and said: "I don't know if we can afford to come up and visit you. I could send you a videotape of me. Seriously."

"If you do that," Danielle said, "I won't write to you, ever."

LOOKERS

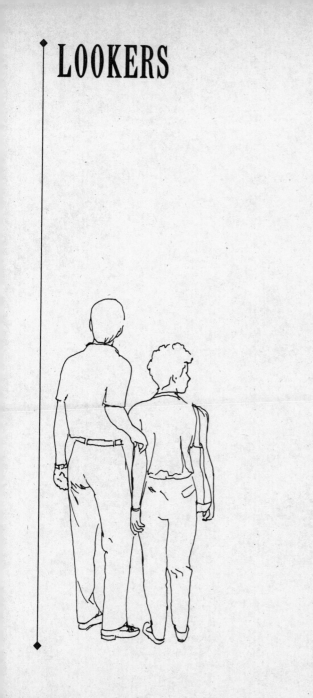

DECALS –
GIVING POVERTY
A PRETTY FACE

S ARAH TORRES SAYS they're "an outrage"; Allie Regner thinks they're "kind of fun"; Steve Saltiel calls them "really stupid"; Wilmer Cintron thinks them merely "dumb."

Believe it or not, the city is placing large vinyl decals depicting shutters, potted plants, venetian blinds and window shades over the yawning, broken-out windows of abandoned city-owned buildings that face the Cross Bronx Expressway. The decals are the talk of the neighborhood.

Residents of the Crotona Park neighborhood agreed that while the city was at it, why not expand the program to provide designer-clothing decals to place over the tattered apparel of impoverished residents, large Mercedes-Benz decals to strap to their sides and New York strip-sirloin decals for them to eat.

"They should fix up the buildings," said Mr. Cintron, "and have people living here, not decals."

Decals are all the city can afford, said city officials, who explained that federal "deep-funding" programs for housing have been shut off and that there is no money for rehabilitation, not even enough to demolish the buildings.

"In one sense, yes, this is a terrible thing," said Robert Jacobson, director of the Bronx office of the City Planning Commission. "Decals aren't going to solve people's problems, aren't going to give them jobs."

But in a roundabout way, many officials believe, the decals

might help do just that. They are trying to improve the image of the Bronx in the hope of attracting business to new industrial parks in the borough, to provide jobs for local residents. The decal plan is part of a $300,000 federal grant to help the city improve the images of run-down neighborhoods.

Mayor Ed Koch, asked for comment on the decal program, said yesterday that he had suggested it four years ago as a way of putting abandoned properties "in cold storage" and making neighborhoods more livable until money for restoration becomes available, which might take years.

"I recognize that it will take hundreds of millions of dollars to restore all of the abandoned buildings in the city of New York," the mayor said. "In a neighborhood, as in life, a clean bandage is much, much better than a raw or festering wound."

The landscape along the expressway, a cavalcade of urban blight, is thought by many city officials to be an embarrassment to New York and to the Bronx in particular. Mr. Jacobson said many people know the Bronx only by what they see from the expressway — driving through from New Jersey to Long Island, or from the Middle West to New England, praying that their fuel supplies and tires hold.

He said he read an article by one such person recently, who wrote of the South Bronx, "You could drop a bomb here and no one would notice."

If the decals, to be placed along the expressway between the Harlem River and the Bronx River Parkway, give people a false impression, Mr. Jacobson said, so do the abandoned buildings. "Behind those buildings," he said, "are 600,000 residents of the South Bronx. There are 100,000 to 150,000 jobs here."

He said that abandoned buildings also give the impression that the government doesn't care. "We do care," he said. "Hundreds of millions of government dollars have been spent on housing in the South Bronx."

Still, it all seems pretty peculiar to neighborhood residents. "Somebody doesn't care," said James Trebillcock, a resident of the area, "or they'd be making homes for people rather than making missiles and giving us decals."

Here, in the poorest congressional district in the country,

residents said life is improving. Most point first to the partially built Bathgate Industrial Park, which they say is successfully attracting businesses — "with financial incentives," said Xavier Rodriguez, chairman of the local community board, "not decals."

Mr. Rodriguez is unconvinced that decals will help attract businesses. Moreover, he is worried that the decals will make the buildings look just presentable enough so that their rehabilitation will be delayed.

Residents and the few remaining shopkeepers along Claremont Avenue in the neighborhood recite a litany of other improvements that have been made, including the refurbishment and scheduled reopening of the swimming pool and tennis courts in Crotona Park as well as the cleanup of the park's pond, which has been stocked with trout. Trout fishing in the Bronx — Mr. Jacobson said he liked the sound of that.

Residents talk of the repainting of a building overlooking Charlotte Street — a street that has been a national symbol of urban decay. The building used to be called "The Last Hope Apartment Building" and is now "The New Hope Apartment Building."

It is across the street from the bizarre sight of two suburban-ranch-style homes, the first of about ninety scheduled to be constructed.

They talk also of rubble-strewn lots that the city has planted in grass and wildflowers and of the Don Quixote apartment building, thriving in a sea of abandoned buildings.

The police said crime in the area is decreasing. "Sure it is," said Mr. Saltiel, owner of the I & H Meat Market, "if only because there aren't any people left. For entertainment we watch that building over there burn. It has burned four times in the last two months. Every time a building burns, I lose six or seven customers."

He, too, believes the neighborhood is improving, but largely, he said, "because it couldn't get any worse. The only answer is to tear everything down, and that's what they're doing to make way for the industrial park," he said. He holds some faint hope that someday a row of houses on Fulton Avenue, which are scheduled to receive decals, will be rehabilitated and have "real life," rather than the "semblance of life" that one city official promises the decals will provide.

He envisions workers at the industrial park raising families in these buildings facing Crotona Park.

A few people, such as José Ceballos, who works at the meat market, favor the decals. "I grew up here and saw it go down," he said. "Now we're moving up. Anything to make us look better, I appreciate. I think it lets people know the city at least hasn't forgotten us."

On the other hand, there are those such as George Palermo, who said, "The decals just show the Bronx is not a priority."

Sarah Torres, vice-president of a tenants' group at the large Claremont Village public-housing project nearby, called the decal program "a shameful cover-up of the housing shortage."

At a window for illegal betting in a candy store on Claremont Avenue, a woman said she didn't like the decals. "This ain't Disneyland," she explained.

Diana Simmons stood examining a six-story red-brick apartment building on the Grand Concourse to which the city has already affixed decals. She said she liked them, because "the building looks nicer, and with it sealed up, guys can't rape girls and do drugs in there like they used to."

Mae Cooper was also examining the trompe l'oeil windows. "I went by in a car," she said, "and the building looked so good I came over from my place on Jesup Place to see if I could rent an apartment."

Told that city officials said the decals in this neighborhood away from the expressway were designed to lift the morale of residents and show them the city cares, Mrs. Cooper replied, "That may work, for a little while."

She looked at the windows again. Some showed colorful pots of plants on the sills, some had shutters half open, some had the shades half drawn. "Nobody's home," she said, and walked away shaking her head.

MODELS

WITH THE EXCEPTION of Grandma Braden, who said the girl could use a little meat on her bones, everyone always said that Maggie Braden, cheerleader and beauty queen, was the prettiest girl in town.

Yesterday, for the first time in her life, waiting for an elevator up to the Wilhelmina modeling agency, the nineteen-year-old from Ohio began to wonder if she was pretty enough.

"You come to New York," said the blue-eyed blond, eyeing the competition, "and you start thinking what it was like for those girls back home who were never asked to dance."

Yesterday was an open call at the agency for aspiring models, many of them probably the fairest that their own hometowns had to offer. The singular beauties had come from throughout the country to New York, the world's modeling capital, and were herding aboard an elevator at 9 East 37th Street that carried one comely cargo after another to a twelfth-floor reception area.

Some of the aspirants held romantic notions of a glamorous industry they have seen depicted on television, of being on the next plane to Milan or Paris and of becoming millionaires overnight. It happens.

Most held a more realistic view, however, including Julie Anne Warner, who said that modeling may sound glamorous to the folks back in her hometown of Rockville, Maryland, but that "once you're in New York, it's all business. There are hundreds of beautiful girls around. I walk 150 blocks a day in a sweatshirt and sneakers, stopping six, eight or ten times to try and get work."

They could hear a cacophony of telephones from the frenetic booking rooms – which had the air of telephone rooms in brokerage houses or bookie joints – whence the agency's two hundred or so models were being dispatched. Twenty booking agents answered calls for a certain model or a certain model type – bookings that ranged from catalog jobs to lucrative cosmetics advertising, paying from $150 an hour to $3,500 a day.

Sherry Carter, twenty-one, of Cleveland Heights, Ohio, looked around the room and had the unnerving feeling she had waited too long. Indeed, she was told in her interview that she looked too old and sophisticated in photographs.

Ginny Samardge, who conducted the interview, explained: "Sophisticated is not selling in New York. The look is young, clean and fresh."

"I've had good success in Cleveland," said Ms. Carter, her hands shaking slightly, "and got up my nerve to try and crack the Big Apple. You can get away with being not quite tall enough or slightly too old in other cities, but in New York you have to be absolutely perfect – five feet eight inches to five feet ten inches tall and fifteen to twenty years old."

Courtney Rainey, a fresh-faced seventeen-year-old model recently signed by the agency, breezed through.

"Oh, God," one of those in the reception area sighed, admiring the young model and comparing herself unfavorably to her. But even Ms. Rainey said she still had plenty of reason to be nervous, moving from Miami to compete with an estimated fifteen hundred other models in New York.

Karen Hilton, director of the agency's women's division, said that she was a former social worker and that an important part of her job is to counsel and even be a surrogate parent for young models, some of whom are younger than Ms. Rainey.

"They are all accustomed to having everyone drooling all over them," she said, "and when they are rejected for jobs in New York – and they all are – withdrawal sets in fast."

The staff must also counsel some of those who come for the open calls and break down when they are turned away, however tactfully. Of the thousands of candidates who show up each year at the open calls, held three times a week, the agency signs only about twenty, and many of them wash out quickly. Many are determined to make it, and some of those rejected have returned under new names with dyed hair or sculpted noses.

Dan Deely, director of the men's division, recalled a variety of tactics employed by the aspirants to stand out in the crowd, including one man who arrived in a housedress.

Bill Weinberg, president of Wilhelmina, said one woman signed with the agency and had a successful career in television before it was discovered that she had for years been disguising her lack of height at the agency by wearing bell-bottom pants that concealed seven-inch heels.

The crowds of aspiring models vanished in a matter of minutes. Dan Dillon stayed longer than most. People in Temple, Texas, told Mr. Dillon that he was just too darned handsome to be working at a local savings and loan association, and he began a modeling career in Dallas before arriving in New York last week, trying to hit it big.

Tall, dark and dimpled, his only conceivable flaw is that he looks too much like Tom Selleck – something that women in the office contended was impossible. They were happy that he was invited back for a follow-up interview. Others were rejected as being slightly too short of neck, waist, calf – or just too short altogether – as too narrow of lip, too thin of hair or having eyes set slightly too far apart. But Julie Anne Warner was just right.

Ms. Warner, who was Miss Washington, D.C., in the 1983 Miss U.S.A. contest and has done modeling for hair products and swimsuits, was signed by the agency and fairly drifted out the door on air.

"She is all-American," said Ms. Hilton, "perfect for selling American products on television. She is going to make a lot of money in New York."

Maggie Braden arrived late and was told that the open call was over. As she waited on the twelfth floor for the elevator back down, she said that the sight of so many gorgeous women had completely shattered her confidence. She just hoped that she would have the courage to come back and try again.

Standing alone, away from the group, waiting for the elevator, Maggie Braden looked like the prettiest girl in town.

THE SECRET
OF THE
BEST-DRESSED LIST

"YEAH," SAID Charles Richman,
picking up the phone at the Fashion Foundation of America.
"This is Fashion. Whaddyawant?"

This is a busy time at the foundation, which has just announced its forty-fourth annual list of the world's best-dressed men, featuring President Reagan, Prince Charles and, inexplicably, the mayor of Jersey City, who indicated that this is the kind of honor that can ruin a man in his community.

Calls were coming in from reporters throughout the metropolitan area and beyond, with only Mr. Richman there to field them. "I am the foundation for the most part," he explained to a visitor, digging through stacks of cascading papers to find the ringing phone.

The foundation is in a small, altogether unfashionable office at 44 Court Street in downtown Brooklyn, manned by Mr. Richman. He describes himself as an "old public-relations warhorse" and claims to have invented best-dressed lists back in the 1930s, coming out with the foundation's first in 1941. Today there are many best-dressed lists, but his still attracts worldwide attention.

Mr. Richman said press agents, politicians and tailors for the stars clamor to have their clients placed on the list. Sometimes they offer him money, which he says he refuses.

Those named to the list have often used the honor to further their careers, going on to do commercial endorsements and even to start their own lines of clothes, he said.

Anthony R. Cucci, mayor of Jersey City, was wearing flexible-waist, polyester-blend slacks when he learned of his selection. He said he was stunned and perplexed and had no plans for a collection of Cucci wear, although the name does have a ring to it.

His selection left those in New York's fashion industry scratching their heads yesterday. "Talk about a dark horse," said a spokesman for Bill Blass. "What is his look?"

The door of the foundation's office reads BROOKLYN RECORD, with "Fashion Foundation of America" in smaller letters below. The *Brooklyn Record* is a small weekly newspaper published by Mr. Richman. Inside, telephone numbers are written on the walls and the paint is peeling.

Rooting through the piles of paper, Mr. Richman produces thank-you letters from past winners and wives, including those from several first ladies: Jacqueline Kennedy, Mamie Eisenhower and Pat Nixon. There are lots of buried photographs of people receiving foundation certificates: Bob Hope, Cesar Romero, Jack Benny and Jimmy Stewart.

Mr. Richman is guarded in answering questions about how he compiles the list. "I see photographs in the papers," he said. "I talk to tailors on the phone, or sometimes we have a few drinks and kick the names around."

He scouts the finalists to make sure they are somewhat dapper, and then "I make my recommendations to the committee," although, he admitted, there is no committee per se.

"It's an informal-type thing," he explained, one in which he plays "a primary role." He said that another man, John Tudor, "is a key figure" in compiling the list.

He said the list has become a hobby. "There's no money in it," he said. "I have no ax to grind. We put the owner of Luchow's on once, and he invited me to lunch. That was nice. I get to meet famous people — Elizabeth Taylor, Rosalind Russell, people like that."

Told that Mr. Cucci was perplexed by his selection, Mr.

Richman said, "He had been recommended and observed" and was placed on the list "as a nice-looking man who is interested in making neckties with an imprint of Jersey City and the Statue of Liberty."

Admittedly, he said, Mr. Cucci "was not like Prince Charles, an open-and-shut case," or Ronald Reagan, named to the list for the third time, "because his clothes fit just as well this year when he came out of the hospital as when he went in – incredible!"

Fit is most important to Mr. Richman, who said the foundation placed Pope John Paul II on the list a couple of years ago. "He just wears religious garb, of course," he said, "but he looks marvelous in it, doesn't he?"

Also included on the list this year are the commissioner of baseball Peter Ueberroth, the actor Jason Robards, the pianist Bobby Short and the singer Boy George. Mr. Richman said that they would all probably receive their honorary foundation medals by mail, "although we will hold luncheons if they pay for them."

Mr. Cucci said he learned that he was on the list while in Atlantic City, on New Jersey's gold lamé coast, at a meeting of the New Jersey Municipal League, a group unconnected – totally – to fashion. "I told the person on the telephone that I didn't have time for jokes and hung up," he said.

Mr. Cucci has yet to assess the political damage from his selection to the best-dressed list but wants residents of Jersey City to know that he is as surprised as they are and "that this does not necessarily mean that I am a bad person. I don't want them thinking I'm more interested in image than substance."

Mr. Cucci, a former vocational-education teacher, said he saw the award as an honor to his wife, Anna, who washes and irons his shirts and helps him shop for clothes. He said that he owned four or five off-the-rack suits – all made in America. He swore that he had never even been to Europe.

Mrs. Cucci said that for leisure wear Mr. Cucci favored his Police Athletic League of Jersey City jacket and, during the warmer months, "perhaps just a T-shirt for a trip to the mall."

"I shop the sales," Mr. Cucci said. "No silks, no way. I go for the polyester blends that hold up. I stay away from checks and plaids," he added, showing a fine fashion sense for someone five feet seven inches and 184 pounds, with a thirty-eight-inch waist.

"I even wear unmatched socks sometimes," he said, recalling a time on the subway when everyone was staring at his unmatched socks and he had to stand up so they wouldn't show.

"This is Jersey City," he said. "I have not ruled out the possibility that this honor is a political smear tactic."

Mr. Richman said that he had weathered many a brouhaha over the years and was standing firm on Anthony R. Cucci. "I had the mayor of Yonkers on one year. We lived through that."

NEW WRINKLES
IN THE WAR
ON AGING

"CEMENT?" LIVIA SYLVA, the self-proclaimed "World Famous Skin Care Expert," shrieked into the telephone. "Darling, this is terrible. And very ridiculous!"

Miss Livia, as she is known at her East Side beauty clinic, has heard of women putting potato peelings and tea bags on their eyelids — "oh, sure" — but this woman on the phone has put cement on her face as a cosmetic mask and cannot remove it. What should she tell this woman in cement? To dress up like a jockey and stand on the lawn?

The American population is aging, and people are wrinkling up all over the place. "They are desperate," said Miss Livia, who said she is a former Transylvanian Ping-Pong champion who escaped Hitler's Bergen-Belsen concentration camp. "Someone says 'cement,' they use cement. It is unbelievable, darling."

None of that hocus-pocus at the Livia Sylva Clinic de Beauté on East 54th Street. Miss Livia does not use cement. She uses Rumanian bee pollen. Why? "Because," she said dramatically, in a Rumanian accent, "there is no pollen like Rumanian bee pollen."

In the heat of this wrinkle frenzy facial salons are opening around town as fast as plastic surgeons' offices these days. Madame Ilona of Hungary offers whipped quail eggs and bull-blood wine treatments, and not for brunch either. Princess Marcella Borghese is partial to Italian mud.

Magazines are chockablock with ads for Age Response System Gelee (two ounces for $35), Cellular Recovery Complex,

Anti-Aging cream, Activating Serum With Trace Elements, Line Preventor, Wrinkle Eradicator, Lift Serum, B. H-24 Bio-Rhythmic Skin Care, Skin-Responsive Hydrating Lotion, European Collagen Complex, Vaso-dilating Herb Extract, Firming Action Moisture Cream, Embryo Cell Extract and Terme di Montecatini mud.

Some doctors think it's all a lot of poppycock, a few don't. Claims are carefully worded. Ads say the creams and lotions "awaken the skin," "help restore a balance to the skin" and "encourage the skin." Let's go, skin!

There is much talk in the ads of mysterious beauty secrets of the pharaohs, of small Swiss clinics and of Hungarian springs discovered by Romans. Cleopatra, said Miss Livia, didn't know for sure about an afterlife, but she stocked her tomb with bee-pollen beautifier just in case.

One salon offers electroshock to make the skin products penetrate deeper. Others offer a volcanic-ash mask and treatments of collagen and elastin. One reflexology skin salon suggests pressing on the bottoms of the feet with a ballpoint pen for twenty minutes each day, to cause better health and a better complexion (but also indelibly blue feet).

Miss Livia offers seaweed body wraps for $175, but mainly she offers Rumanian bee pollen. "I believe in bee pollen," proclaimed Romy Revson, emerging at Miss Livia's from a $75 top-of-the-line bee-pollen facial (by a qualified "esthetitician") and "rejuvenating paraffin treatments" of the hands and throat.

"Miss Livia is an example for us all," said Corinne, the receptionist, in reverential tones. Miss Livia was immaculately dressed, groomed and coiffed, and she assured us that her wrinkle-free skin looked at least ten years younger than her age — although she wasn't saying what that was.

She greeted and counseled the clients, sounding like a cross between Zsa Zsa Gabor and Billy Crystal's character Fernando. "Darling," she said, taking the hand of a young woman, "this is Livia talking to you now. You are concerned about your fingernails. I know you are. I am telling you to use the cotton wrap. I am sharing with you now my secret, darling."

This particular darling, Lynn Ingrassia, said she comes to

the salon because New York is a competitive place, socially and professionally.

"I'm going to be twenty-nine on Saturday," she groaned, saying she comes to Miss Livia for vegetable peels, seaweed wraps, leg waxing, manicures and pedicures.

"We see a lot of young women now," Miss Livia said. "None of them want to look like their mothers. Except my daughter, of course!" she hastened to add. "My daughter would love to look like her mother. And my daughter is beautiful.

"The young women come here and spend their last penny," she said, although the bulk of her clientele is older and quite well-to-do. Miss Livia said her clients still come to her after cosmetic surgery to keep their skin smooth and healthy. "The bee pollen makes those suture marks just fade away.

"Our clients come, actually, to be pampered and paid attention to," said Miss Livia, who often acts as their psychoanalyst, they say. Miss Livia is opposed to mental illness as being bad for facial appearance.

Of critics who say that most of the products and treatments provided by the growing skin-care industry don't do much good, Miss Livia sighed and said: "Yes, it is too bad that people without knowledge get into the business. The clients are willing to try anyway. New Yorkers are a combative people. You wouldn't expect them to just grow old gracefully."

WEIGHT
WATCHERS

"**A**LL RIGHT, PEOPLE. That's enough. Please!" Michael Filan sought to restore order at the Weight Watchers meeting.

After talking for an hour on the grim subjects of sacrifice and restraint this holiday season, about counting calories and portion control, one woman in the group, Penny Winograd, confessed that she has fallen totally off the wagon this week, consuming two slices of pizza – Ray's pizza, at that – Oreo cookies (the bag) and three pints of Haägen-Dazs ice cream.

"What kind? What kind?" the group clamored.

"Pistachio and chocolate-chocolate chip!" Ms. Winograd answered enthusiastically, sending the whole room into an uproar. There were "oohs" and "aahs" from the group of about thirty women and two men at the Weight Watchers center at Lexington Avenue and 58th Street, adjacent to Blimpie's.

"Tell about the cookies!" yelled one member of the group. And that's when Mr. Filan called for order, trying to get back to the subject at hand, which was resisting tomorrow's avalanche of Butterball turkeys; bulk-load stuffing; mountainous, ten-megaton mashed potatoes, holding back vast reservoirs of glutinous gravy; candied yams topped with melted marshmallows; and sticky pecan pies capable of inducing insulin shock.

This is a time for circling the wagons at Weight Watchers. In these final hours of the turkey thaw-down Mr. Filan gathered his dieters to exhort them on to greater and ever more glorious sacrifice.

"It's like a pregame pep talk for a football team," said Mr. Filan as his "team" went through their weekly weigh-in.

Then, in classic Knute Rockne style, he told them they would have to fight to win during this holiday season. He told them not to give an inch at waist or thigh. "I need this pep talk bad," said Ms. Winograd.

Several members of the group told of the "groaning tables" they would face on Thanksgiving. One woman was told that her family had best call in a structural engineer to test the load limits on the dining room table to avert disaster. Another was told she should probably have a *Guinness Book of World Records* representative on hand for the meal.

"My relatives eat until they're comatose," said Mr. Filan. "After three hours they're all slumped down in their chairs with one hand in the nuts."

"How come the pilgrims in all those pictures look so thin?" one member of the group asked.

"They wore black skirts," answered another.

Mr. Filan said that before their Thanksgiving dinners they should drink what sounded like several cubic yards of water. And he suggested they try some of his holiday recipes, such as his low-calorie cauliflower pudding or his carrot-pineapple dish. "You put carrots and pineapple in a blender, then put it in a pan and bake it," he explained.

"Then what?" snapped a woman named Jean. "You don't eat it, I hope."

"People lose weight on my recipes," Mr. Filan retorted, and Jean said she wasn't surprised.

Mr. Filan warned the group about holiday drinking, noting that eggnog has the power to devastate a diet. "Also," said Ann-Marie Larkin, a dieter, "if you have several drinks, you really don't care how fat you get." Someone else wondered, however, if it might not be a good strategy to have several drinks and pass out before eating dinner.

"The holidays kill me," said Susan Lehman, recalling all of the cookies, candies and cocktails. "I can gain ten or twelve pounds. I have Thanksgiving, followed by a Jewish wedding with the reception at an Italian restaurant. The relatives say, 'Eat, eat, you look thin,' no matter how fat you are."

"I turn into one gigantic Swedish meatball from all the parties," said another woman. But another said it was worse not to get invited, "Because I get depressed and stay home and eat cookies."

Ms. Lehman confessed that she, too, had fallen off the wagon this week. "I ate Crunch 'n Munch," she said.

"Crunchy what?" someone across the room asked.

"Crunch 'n Munch!" came a chorus of condescension, as if the questioner had just landed from the planet Anorexia or something.

"How much did you eat?" Mr. Filan asked Ms. Lehman.

"The box," she answered, in a tone suggesting that his question hadn't exactly been College Bowl caliber either.

Ms. Lehman confessed further to breaking up Girl Scout cookies and putting them in ice cream. "Mmmmmmm," said the woman sitting in front of her.

And that wasn't all. On the Weight Watchers plan dieters may opt for "food exchanges," such as substituting a half cup of peaches for a half cup of orange juice or half of a banana. Ms. Lehman confessed she had eaten a large apple, a large, caramel-covered apple at that, rolled in chopped nuts. "Could that be considered," she asked Mr. Filan, "a fruit exchange?"

Mr. Filan shook his head, indicating that it could not and indicating disbelief. He said that they could all have some turkey and stuffing but in amounts that some in the group considered microscopic.

Mr. Filan smiled and greeted members of the group as they came in by name, applauded them if they had lost weight and consoled them if they'd gained. Most of the women were not what would be called "fat" but were rather normal-looking women who said they needed to lose ten or twenty pounds. Mr. Filan said that Weight Watchers women are thinner in New York.

He greeted one woman who made no reply. She confessed later that she hadn't opened her mouth, because she didn't want him to see that it was filled with Hershey's kisses.

He encouraged them to dust off those exercise bikes, the ones buried under piles of clothes. "Exercise makes me ravenous," said Ms. Lehman.

He told them to avoid "Trigger foods," which he explained were foods that triggered overeating — foods that made them eat like a horse.

"I think I'll go have my picture taken," said one class member on the way out. "I won't be this thin again until the day before Thanksgiving 1987."

"My brother is coming home for Thanksgiving," Ms. Winograd announced.

"How lovely," said a woman doing some knitting.

"He's a chef!" barked Ms. Winograd.

"Oh no!" gasped the knitter.

"He cooks for three days!" said Ms. Winograd. "He makes chocolate-mousse pie!"

"Mmmmmm," said the group.

Mr. Filan looked concerned.

THE
STAGESTRUCK...

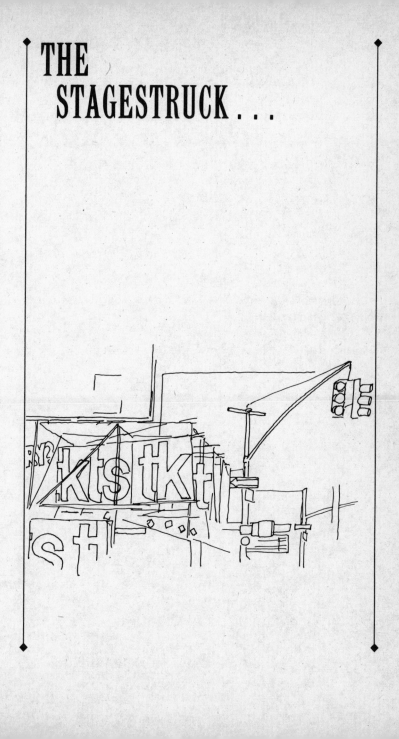

LIBERACE

SURE, LIBERACE COULD get by with using chintzy rhinestones. But he doesn't. Liberace uses the finest rhinestones available in the world today, multifaceted, hand-cut Austrian rhinestones.

"I only use the best of everything," Liberace explained. "People know a phony."

There were those who suggested that New Yorkers might just be a little too sophisticated for Liberace, and a couple of them may very well be, but more than 103,000 others have purchased tickets to see the Lord High Poobah of Glitz at Radio City Music Hall during a seventeen-day engagement that opens tomorrow. It is a ticket sales record for Radio City.

Some people will attend as part of a package deal that includes dinner at Mama Leone's, but probably not Diana Vreeland, Walter Cronkite, Christopher Walken, Glenda Jackson, Sammy Cahn, Ashford and Simpson, the cast of *Saturday Night Live*, Cicely Tyson and Chuck Zito, a chieftain of the Hell's Angels – some of the luminaries expected to attend opening night.

"The older people like the warm, sentimental, personal touch," said Liberace, between practice kicks with the Rockettes, "and the young audiences love the crazy clothes. It reminds them of rock stars. Kids like glitz."

To watch preparations yesterday for Liberace's show was to worry about Austria's economy – an entire nation so dependent on one man. One of the four cars used in his show is completely covered with hundreds of thousands of Austrian rhinestones, as is one of the pianos. As for his wardrobe, ticket holders might wish to acquaint themselves with the early warning signs of retina damage.

Liberace will open in a cape of silvery plum lamé, festooned with waves of shimmering multicolored sequins. And that's the lining. The outside? Don't ask, but it includes an eight-foot train of pink feathers. Under the cape is a suit that makes Liberace look as if he were dipped in glue and rolled through the precious stones department at Kmart. The baubles, bangles and bright shiny beads are literally set on top of one other.

Advances in technology since Liberace began back in the 1940s have given him even greater flamboyance capability, Dancing Waters being the primary example. The device appears to be a Palm Springs—size lawn sprinkler, forty by fifteen feet, with eleven hundred jets spurting colored waters that dance to Strauss waltzes played on a revolving piano by Liberace. Not to worry, he can play Tchaikovsky's Piano Concerto Number 1 in four minutes, "by cutting out the dull parts."

It takes some doing to creat a splash in New York, but Liberace has. Aides working for him here sometimes wish the frenetic sixty-five-year-old would just get out of town so they could get some rest.

Since arriving a few days ago, Liberace has been seen here, there and everywhere, appearing on almost every known television talk show, showing up on *Saturday Night Live*, dancing with some Rockettes at a professional wrestling match, stopping in at the Rolls-Royce dealer to talk valve jobs and mink carpeting, buying a gold-plated shovel at Tiffany's (for ground-breaking ceremonies at a bigger and better Liberace Museum in Las Vegas) and shopping for groceries and Tupperware-like plastic food containers at the Pathmark. Of the latter, an aide said, "Liberace is just like you and me."

Explaining his participation in the wrestling match, Liberace, who was named Wladziu Valentino Liberace upon his birth in Wisconsin, said: "My mother loved wrestling. She would be very proud of me today." He told of appearing at professional wrestling matches in Indianapolis to promote his concerts, "because the fans were found to be one and the same." He said his mother was thrilled when he met Gorgeous George: "She said they used the same lavender rinse on their hair."

His bodyguard is now limping around after he tripped trying to catch up with Liberace in the Pathmark parking lot. The bodyguard sustained further damage when he stepped in front of an airborne professional wrestler on a collision course with Liberace at ringside.

A near disaster occurred when Liberace was dining at the Rainbow Grill and the comedian Billy Crystal stopped by the table, embraced Liberace and the two of them stuck together – no joke. Mr. Crystal had become entangled in the (real) gold and diamond jewelry that encrusts Liberace: pendants, medallions, bracelets and his big diamond grand-piano watch.

To shake his hand is to flirt with laceration. Left to right, we have the enormous topaz and gold ring, then the grand piano of diamonds and gold with the top that opens, followed by the simple hunk-of-amethyst ring. Moving to the right hand, there is the diamond candelabrum ring, the gold record-player ring with moving turntable, and a large gold structure of a ring that looks as if it were designed by Buckminster Fuller, possibly for human habitation.

Liberace intelligently leaves one finger on each hand open to avoid ring-lock.

He is staying in the model apartment at glittering Trump Tower, even though the place is a tad subdued for his tastes – certainly compared to his home in Las Vegas, with the Sistine Chapel-ceiling reproduction that includes the likeness of himself. Liberace said he is going to buy a condominium from Donald Trump, whom he describes as "a smart man who has a feel for what is going on."

Liberace is more popular than ever, and he hazards a guess why: "This is an age of glitter and flamboyance. People like Cyndi Lauper realize this. She is smart. She knows the flashier looking you are the better. Prince is smart, too."

A rock promoter backstage at the wrestling spectacular, which featured appearances by Liberace, Muhammad Ali, Billy

Martin and Mr. T, spoke reverently of Liberace as "the sage of the glitter age."

Liberace recalled when he first realized that more attention was being paid to his tuxedo and candelabrum than to his piano playing. "I was not too thrilled about it," he said, "but then someone said, 'Hey, you've got something going there.'

"It was easy to be flashy in those days," he said, "but now everyone is doing it, and I have to have eight people sewing all the time."

KING KONG

INVARIABLY, THESE BIG apes that come to New York and hang on the top of the Empire State Building making spectacles of themselves run into trouble.

It happened to King Kong in 1933, and it's happening again to a three-thousand-pound model being tethered to the top of the building in commemoration of the film's fiftieth anniversary.

The eight-story nylon King Kong balloon, which had a blowout in an armpit during a test, developed a hole in his left shoulder yesterday during inflation and lay in a heap on the side of the building's mast. He appeared to the millions of metropolitan-area residents who had been anticipating yesterday's scheduled arrival of the ballyhooed beast to be more like a commemoration of another film, *The Blob*.

"Is that what all the fuss is about?" said Sheila Maxwell, walking to work along 34th Street and echoing the reaction of others who had hoped to see something more anatomically correct.

By late morning the bump on the southwest corner of the mast had been removed, and it was announced that King Kong was to make his debut in his seven-to-ten-day appearance today or tomorrow, after tethers were untangled and the hole repaired.

Near the building pedestrians bumped into one another as they strode briskly to work with their necks craned for a glimpse of the ape not present.

"Watch the cars!" Louis Silva, a traffic-control agent, screamed time and again from his post at the intersection of 34th

Street, Broadway and the Avenue of the Americas. "Everybody's looking up," he said, noting that this included motorists, who had experienced several near misses because of their gawking.

"Gastritis" was Mr. Silva's snappy retort to those who asked him, "Where's King Kong?" Many people had come to Manhattan just to photograph the balloon.

"What a disappointment," said Ruth Denard, from Long Island, who had come with her five-year-old daughter, Ann. Linda Meyer, here on a high-school trip from Affton, Missouri, seemed crushed. "I heard his fingernails were absolutely huge and awful," she said. "I have to see him."

Many Manhattan office workers skipped out for a while to observe the phenomenon and reported that groups of people in their buildings had been huddled by the windows all day looking upward. Everywhere in New York people seemed to be talking about the great ape, and King Kong rubbernecking was reported on expressways in Westchester County, New Jersey and on Long Island.

Visitors to the eighty-sixth-floor observation deck began practicing their Fay Wray screams and chanting, "We want Kong," as early as Wednesday afternoon.

Yesterday was somewhat embarrassing for promoters of the event, for which Kong's manufacturer and the owners of the Empire State Building have spent more than $100,000. The blowout was recorded by journalists from throughout the nation and several foreign countries.

Undaunted, the promoters continued the scheduled hoopla as if nothing had happened. As King Kong lay hemorrhaging in the cold air above, a news conference with at least twelve television cameras was held in the lobby, where officials of government agencies and companies donating services to the project spoke of it glowingly. In the lobby an exhibition of King Kong memorabilia was opened, and a week of continuous showings of the film began.

A gala reception of several hundred dignitaries and press representatives, consuming champagne and hors d'oeuvres, commenced as scheduled in the observatory. Reporters interviewed a man in a gorilla suit, and Harry Helmsley, an owner of the Empire State Building, thanked "the press for all it has done."

Two biplanes, symbolic of those that shot down King Kong a half century before, and perhaps having passed their fail-safe point before Kong sprang a leak, buzzed the building, dodging five helicopters that carried photographers and some jet airliners flying special routes to give passengers a view of the ape.

"King Kong deserves better than this," said Raymond Mitter, one of many aficionados at the building. "He shouldn't get punctured on his homecoming."

Indeed, this is a quite different King Kong from the one brought from the savage isle where he fought dinosaurs, to here, where he experienced considerable difficulty adjusting to our style of life. (How they sneaked him through customs is anybody's guess.) That Kong toppled buildings, hurled automobiles filled with passengers and tore down elevated train tracks in blatant disregard of the mass-transportation needs of the people, whom he often squished with his hairy feet. Some suggest he deserved to be shot.

But the new nylon Kong obtained permits to climb the building from the City Buildings Department and the Landmarks Preservation Commission. And when he went to the top, he took the elevator.

Perhaps more important, this Kong has a job. If he does well in New York, said Robert Keith Vicino, his creator, he will take Kong on a world tour of tall buildings. Mr. Vicino's business, Robert Keith & Company, of San Diego, is the manufacturer of such promotional devices as big balloons in the shape of six-packs of beer, packs of cigarettes and other products.

Film experts at the reception said *King Kong* was viewed as a triumph of technological innovation and, by many of the experts, a profound cultural statement. Asked to compare the balloon to the film, one expert said that although he would not yet label the vinyl-coated Kong a technological triumph, he would certainly go along with the part about the profound cultural statement.

Haruo Nakamura, a television technician who is a member of a crew covering the extravaganza for Channel 10 in Tokyo, recalled being in the city for the laser light show celebrating the fiftieth birthday of the Empire State Building two years ago that fizzled.

Of this King Kong spectacle, he said: "It is so American. It is big. It is, if I may say, crazy. And it doesn't work."

RADIO CITY'S MAGNIFICENT CHRISTMAS SPECTACULAR

GEORGE, A CAMEL, stepped on the foot of a Rockette; six sheep came off the elevator as three kings bearing gifts got on; human Christmas trees bumped into eight maids-a-milking at the water cooler and an elf came down with the flu.

As Christmas mania arrived in Manhattan on the day after Thanksgiving, the cast and crew of Radio City Music Hall's *The Magnificent Christmas Spectacular* had to pick up the pace, doing four shows yesterday to sold-out 5,874-seat houses.

Scrooge pushed past Mary Number 1 and Joseph Number 2 in the wings without so much as an "excuse me." Typical.

Between shows, Rockettes snoozed in their sleeping bags in uncharacteristically haphazard formations on dressing-room floors. An electrician unfolded a cot in his work area. Cathy Beatty, a Rockette who does seven costume changes in the ninety-minute extravaganza, ran out to the bank, begging passage through long, thick lines outside the Music Hall waiting for the next performance.

"We could no more miss this than Christmas mass," said Mary Santucci, attending the traditional show, which premiered in 1933, with her three children and her mother. Mrs. Santucci has attended almost every year for the past forty years, and her mother recalled seeing the show during World War II, when the Rockettes dressed as ration coupons.

The show was revamped last year by Robert Jani, who

among other things produces Super Bowl halftime shows, but he kept it true to tradition, rolling all of America's myriad Christmas icons – Scrooge to Santa, Nutcracker to nativity – into one glossy package.

Some New Yorkers see the show as sort of campy kitsch, while some others, Mrs. Santucci among them, call it "a religious experience." She noted the cathedral-like appearance of the Art Deco extraordinaire theater and the two gargantuan Wurlitzer pipe organs.

Call it what you will, this hardy annual is expected to draw seven hundred thousand people this year, more than ever before.

It is the job of Howard Kolins, stage director of the Music Hall, to ride herd on the backstage chaos in this zoo of animals, 117 cast members and 65 stagehands, making sure that somehow it is not reflected in the extravaganza onstage.

With a show in progress, Mr. Kolins was found yesterday speaking into a walkie-talkie in the subbasement, aboard a seventy-foot-by-forty-foot elevator without walls.

Down in the gray darkness, women in shimmering white chorus-girl outfits festooned with sequins and rhinestones stood here and there, looking out at the engine room and mammoth hydraulic shafts while doing stretching exercises. Occasionally one of the women kicked her leg astonishingly, almost inhumanly high. But of course. These were the Rockettes.

"Light the sleighs," Mr. Kolins ordered, and thousands of small white lights trimming red sleighs on the elevator lit the darkness. Mr. Kolins next ordered the Rockettes to board the sleighs. Then he ordered the elevator up from the subbasement to the stage. He hopped off the moving elevator as it passed a catwalk – occupied by a small flock of sheep – on the basement level. A turntable forty-three feet in diameter in the center of the elevator began to turn just eighteen inches before it reached stage level, the same point where the Rockettes began smiling. Then the crowd roared.

Mr. Jani calls the stage "a toy box," referring to the three-part stage elevator, the turntable and the traveling orchestra pit that moves up and down, as well as upstage and downstage. Ms. Beatty's father, Norman, who has played the trumpet in the

Christmas spectacular for thirty-five years, said the traveling orchestra pit can be hard on the lips. Ms. Beatty's sister, Carol, is
also a Rockette, as was their mother, Claire.

The hydraulics system was studied by the armed services
and copied for use on aircraft carriers, according to spokesper-
sons for the Music Hall, who said a government agent was stationed there throughout World War II to keep enemy agents from
copying the technology.

Some of the performers doing three and four shows a day say
they are starting to feel as though they are permanently stationed
at the Music Hall, napping on couches and in sleeping bags and
eating chicken nuggets delivered from Popeye's.

On their one day a week off — soon to disappear as the show
goes to seven days a week — cast members say all they can do is
sleep, deeply. The animals go home to the Dawn Animal Agency
in Colts Neck, New Jersey, where they unwind by rolling in the
mud.

Bambi Brook, an animal handler, walks the camels around
midtown between 6:00 and 7:00 each morning, drawing all sorts
of comments, such as: "The desert is that way, miss. Take the
Midtown Tunnel; it'll save you ten minutes."

"Other than slobbering on the Rockettes and an occasional
stampede in the wings," said Ellen Schiebelhuth, a spokesperson
for the Music Hall, "we haven't had any problems with these
animals."

"These are great animals," said Mr. Kolins, who recalled
years past when the camels would get tired of standing still during
the nativity scene and leave — "kind of destroying the moment" —
and when the donkeys would not leave the stage at all.

At a particularly hectic point in the show, when seventy-five
cast members were making sixty-second costume changes and
life-sized houses were hurtling on- and offstage, Mr. Kolins was
also being informed that an elf was getting sick, that plumbing
had backed up in a dressing room and that George, the camel,
had relieved himself on the pad the Rockettes fall back on in the
toy-soldier scene.

When things calmed down for a moment, Mr. Kolins, who
is thirty-three years old and has done shows at Radio City rang-

ing from Liberace to Twisted Sister, peeked out at the audience, comprised mainly of spellbound children. "I've done this show five hundred times," he said, "and I love it. It's . . . wonderful.

"We're going into Bethlehem now," he said into his headset. "Get the Rockettes out of Bethlehem.

"The show is just one crisis after another," he explained to an onlooker, "until, thank God, Jesus is born."

EAR, NOSE AND THROAT MAN TO THE STARS

"Yes, I was Marilyn Monroe's doctor," said Dr. Eugen Grabscheid, with a thick Viennese accent and a round mirror on his forehead. "She was some girl. She had terrible problems, of course. Sinus problems."

The office of Dr. Grabscheid — ear, nose and throat man to the stars — grows bustling and a little loony at this time of year, as colds and flu attack the vocal cords of New York's vast singing community.

"There would be no Broadway now without him," said Elizabeth Franz, an actress, in the waiting room.

"The opera would close!" proclaimed Vickie Phillips, a cabaret singer, also waiting to see the doctor.

"Half our company is coming to see him," said Ken Jenkins, a cast member of *Big River*.

"I feared I'd have to cancel," said Jan Shaulis, who is with the New York City Opera. "But he's a miracle worker. Other doctors say rest, take medicine and come back in three days. He gets you on."

Opera divas make dramatic entrances, sweeping into the old, cluttered office on East 96th Street, tossing their furs and scarves to valets, then sputtering into the open arms of their beloved eighty-two-year-old voice doctor.

Actors from Broadway, soap operas and television commercials crowd the waiting room, along with others whose livelihoods depend on the condition of their vocal cords: broadcast announcers, trial lawyers, classroom teachers and cantors, among them.

Dr. Grabscheid makes emergency calls backstage, restoring lost voices so that shows can go on. One prima donna flew back from London on the Concorde between performances to see him. Singers on the road call in from around the world, frantic for a cure. Some vocalists even ask his advice on what parts they can sing.

"The only performer not seeing him must be Marcel Marceau," said Michael Feinstein, who is singing at the Algonquin Hotel and was referred to the doctor by "Liza and Chita" – Minnelli and Rivera – who told him not to be concerned by the appearance of either office or doctor.

Many new patients are somewhat taken aback, according to Pauline, the receptionist-opera singer, who asked that her last name not be published: "The new patients say, 'Is *this* the doctor's office?' And then, 'Is *that* the doctor?'"

It seems the least Dr. Grabscheid could do is slip on a white lab coat. Even the guys selling aspirin on TV do that. Rather, the balding and bespectacled doctor wears a rumpled gray suit, blue Ultrasuede shirt, a well-worn, perhaps formerly yellow, cardigan sweater and running shoes.

The office does not inspire confidence. Dr. Grabscheid works out of the old office he has occupied for forty-five years, which is dimly lighted (one one-hundred-watt bulb in the examination room) and cluttered. Without questioning its effectiveness, it could be said that his equipment looks somewhat antiquated – less like state-of-the-art technology than like machinery used in black-and-white movies for the manufacture of laboratory monsters. He often doles out medication not by prescription but by pouring pills from a bottle into patients' hands.

The office is "a delightful little madhouse," as one patient put it, where the opera star Lucine Amara was seen on a ladder replacing a light bulb in the ceiling fixture. A young actress painted the office the last time it was needed. "No doubt," Pauline said, "because the doctor thought he could save a few bucks. Our typewriter doesn't work; he thinks that's just fine."

She said one actor told her that the office was better than

any situation comedy on television. *"Dummkopf!"* Dr. Grabscheid can be heard to yell at Pauline. "Quack!" Pauline, rather a feisty sort, replies.

"Some patients must come just to get autographs," said a man in the waiting room. "We get them all," said Pauline, rattling off the first few names that came to mind: Anthony Quinn, Matt Dillon, Bette Midler, Ashford and Simpson, Kenny Loggins, Donna Summer. She picked up a copy of *Opera News* and said all five of the singers shown on the cover were his patients: Ruggero Raimondi, Kathleen Battle, Carol Vaness, Thomas Allen and Frederica von Stade.

Pauline is an opera singer and sometimes has problems recognizing the rock stars. When the singer named Meat Loaf came in, she informed the doctor that "Meatballs" had arrived.

Dr. Grabscheid said that he had treated Sigmund Freud in Vienna and that one of his favorite patients was Vivien Leigh. Said Pauline, who does most of the talking for this doctor of few words: "Marilyn Monroe was always late. One time he stood her up. That's the way he is."

The drab walls are festooned with festive Broadway show posters, autographed: "To Wonder Doc," "The doctor of every girl's dreams," "My larynx thanks you," and even "Hope to see you soon." There are also photographs of German shepherds, which he breeds.

The doctor, who lives with his wife in Tenafly, New Jersey, sees as many as fifty patients or more at this time of year in the twelve-to-fourteen-hour days he puts in. He does not break for lunch and rarely sits down.

He tells the receptionists, Linda Kastl and Pauline, that they are too fat to take time off for lunch, and he does not give them vacations. He admits that he likes Pauline despite her "unreliability," although she has not had a day off for three years. "You'd treat us better if we were German shepherds!" Pauline yells at him.

"In spite of it all," she said, "we love him." She said the patients do, too, recalling that they had organized a birthday party for him and showed up wearing T-shirts with his picture on them.

In the waiting room the patients discussed all sorts of home remedies that performers use for their voices, from old socks wrapped about the throat to chewing garlic. "I chewed garlic for my voice when I was in a play with Noël Coward," recalled George Rose, who appears in Dr. Grabscheid's office as well as in *The Mystery of Edwin Drood* on Broadway. "And Mr. Coward went through an entire scene holding his handkerchief in front of his nose."

"There are all sorts of bizarre curatives," one actress said. Just then, Dr. Grabscheid walked in. The patients looked at him and then at each other and grinned.

Postscript: Pauline called to say, "Dr. Grabscheid received so many calls and letters from his patients after the article appeared that he somehow thought it a fitting ending to his career and went home for the weekend and died." She wasn't kidding.

BEA'S
BLOOMERS

"*Fantastic!*" – Ethel Feagley
"*A real stunner!*" – Dorothy Bartholet
"*A must see!*" – Mary Ellen Newman
"*Nice, I guess.*" – Margaret Stoffregen

BEATRICE SHUTTLEWORTH says
that people are coming from miles around – well, from a couple
of blocks away at least, and from virtually every floor in the building – to see her amazing blooming dracaena plant.

The youthful eighty-four-year-old woman was bustling from
her ringing telephone to her braying door buzzer as the living
room filled to overflowing with nine people – most of them
women getting on in years – who had come to witness the daily
opening of the bloom. "Lucky to get a seat," commented Marcy
Mortensen, from down the hall.

Mrs. Shuttleworth, a widow and a great-grandmother of
four, announced that she did allow the taking of photographs.
One woman suggested that she sell tickets and refreshments.

"Oh, my," said Mrs. Shuttleworth, walking carefully out
from the kitchen with a tray full of complimentary glasses of
orange juice, "I wouldn't do that."

About two weeks ago, she placed a photograph of her
flowering plant on the bulletin board in the lobby of her building
at 106 Morningside Drive, at 121st Street, inviting tenants to see
it in person. Word spread, and soon people were even coming
from outside the building and off the block.

She estimates that several dozen people have witnessed the
rare dracaena blossoms – an expert said perhaps only one in
twenty blossoms in New York – and said she was having so much

fun that she did not mind them tracking dirt in on the carpet. "Most come around suppertime," she said, "but what the heck."

She also contacted the press about her plant, and she seemed a mite peeved that a reporter did not show up until late this week. "You're a little late," she said, noting that most of the blooms were turning brown. "What took you so long?"

"We got here as soon as we could," she was told by this reporter. One elderly woman remarked: "Newspaper people aren't the smartest in the world. Sometimes it takes them a while to recognize the significance of things." Then she smiled sweetly and took a sip of juice.

"It's pretty," Mrs. Stoffregen, an elderly woman in a red hat, said of the plant, "but is it this important?"

"Well," said Mrs. Shuttleworth, "Charlie over at the New York Horticultural Society was certainly impressed. He said this is very rare.

"I've had that plant for forty years," she continued, "and it bloomed for the first time last year. Don't you see? That's what's newsworthy.

"I've certainly read less interesting things in the paper," she said, pushing her glasses up on her nose.

"You should see Ethel's ferns," said a guest. Mrs. Shuttleworth shrieked, "That's another story!"

"We just love Bea," Ms. Feagley, a sprightly ninety-one-year-old, said of Mrs. Shuttleworth, who displayed a disposition to match the crisp, sunny day. "She keeps things stirred up around here. She has little music concerts and parties in her apartment. The police called to thank her for something one day, and her one-hundred-year-old mother answered the phone and said, 'Now what has she done?'" The women had a good laugh at that.

"Shush, Ethel," said Mrs. Shuttleworth.

"Everyone is talking about this plant," Ms. Feagley said. "Everyone I know."

"A lot of people come in to see it," said Lois Adams, who works at the front desk in the lobby. "Some people won't though. They think this city is too sophisticated." She conceded she had not seen it and issued a lengthy, complex, ironclad alibi.

Mrs. Shuttleworth said she did not know why the plant had

bloomed. She said she saw a lot of corn plants – the nickname for this variety of dracaena, because of the leaf shape – in museums, banks and libraries.

"I ask the guards if their corn plants flower," she said. "They always say 'no,' and they sure raise their eyebrows when I say, 'Mine does.'"

The audience this afternoon watched three little white "pips," as Mrs. Shuttleworth calls them, opening at 5:00 to about the size of the tip of a pinkie finger. When the plant had been in full bloom, there had been thousands of pips forming many rounded flowers on an eighteen-inch branch that sprouted from the top of the seven-foot dracaena.

Mrs. Shuttleworth showed photographs of that and then invited guests forward to smell the "heavenly fragrance of these three little stars" and to taste the gooey, sweet nectar.

Mrs. Mortensen said when she saw the blossoms for the first time she began screaming, "La Dama de Noche! La Dama de Noche!" the name of the plant (Lady of the Night) in her native Philippines, where as a small girl she last saw one bloom. She describes this blooming in New York as "a miracle."

"But she's a little dramatic," Mrs. Newman explained to someone from outside the building, and they all laughed.

In the twilight, before the table lamps were turned on, the women sat in the living room, cluttered with knickknacks and family photographs, telling stories and giggling.

One of them talked of her trip to Atlantic City in 1914, and another spoke of New York in 1985: "You have to look around now and enjoy the things in your life, even little things like this plant. You can watch too much news on TV, and you can get to thinking life is grim here when really it isn't."

Then Mrs. Shuttleworth announced that it was time for them to leave, because she had to attend a disarmament rally at the church. "Oh, she's a troublemaker all right," said one woman. "She pickets and writes letters to presidents. She calls them warmongers."

"Did you notice, Margaret," Mrs. Shuttleworth asked, "how my pink button" – advocating human rights – "matches my dress so nicely?"

She told the women that if her plant kept blooming every year, they would make this an annual event, just like caroling in the corridors and parties in the lobby.

"I don't give a hoot about a plant," said one of the elderly women on her way out the door. "Being around Bea just makes me glad I'm still alive."

THE NEW YORK–MONTANA COMEDY CIRCUIT

GREAT FALLS, MONTANA — It seems cruel. Two New York comedians are booked into the wilderness of Montana and forced to live by their wits. All of their one-liners about the neuroses of East Siders, the aroma of the subway and the horrors of finding a decent apartment are useless to them here.

The farthest west that Steve Mittleman and Cathy Ladman, who are both twenty-seven years old and who both grew up in Queens, normally travel is to their apartments on West 96th and West 84th streets, respectively — no kidding. But they are proving to be a lot of laughs in Montana, intentionally for the most part.

In White Sulphur Springs the attendant at the gas station next to the Buck-a-Roo Bar laughed and shook his head at the very idea of somebody being sent several thousand miles from New York to make Montanans laugh. It sounded to him like some sort of federal humor program.

Their show in Great Falls made members of the audience laugh so hard they complained to the manager that their stomachs hurt. And when Mr. Mittleman went horseback riding and tried to command the horse by yelling, "Go," "Stop" and "Wait a second, wait a second," one of the ranch hands rolled in the dust with laughter.

Mr. Mittleman and Ms. Ladman, who are here on an eleven-day, four-city (that's almost all there are) tour of the state, are among hundreds of comedians that New York regularly exports to cities throughout the country to alleviate the current national comedian shortfall, caused by the huge demand for comedians in hundreds of new comedy clubs opening in cities large and small.

"New York is the comedy warehouse," said Jeff Schwartz, a New York agent, who keeps the names of comedians and their fees in a computer, making it easier to fill a growing number of orders coming in from about two hundred full-time comedy clubs and untold lounges and restaurants around the country. Jerry Stanley, who probably books more comedy acts than any other agent, describes the situation simply: "Too many comedians in New York and too few elsewhere."

To Ms. Ladman and Mr. Mittleman, the idea of playing Montana seemed as foreign as playing Belgium, although it might have taken them a little longer to fly here to Billings than to Brussels. They were relieved to find they had not been booked into Little Bighorn or any of Montana's ghost towns, but Monday night in Bozeman did not sound a whole lot better.

When Ms. Ladman, who has worked in the business just two years, told her friends in New York where she was going, they replied: "Montana? Are you playing to cows?"

She remained optimistic: "I expect to find people out there. Where is Montana, anyway?"

Mr. Mittleman, who has been in the business for six years and is recognized as one of the most promising young comedians in New York, has a joke in his routine about paying $3 a glass for Perrier that is poured over Hudson River ice cubes. He was concerned that there would be no polluted water in Montana and no one would get it.

"This is like vaudeville," Mr. Mittleman said as he and Ms. Ladman drove on a narrow road from Bozeman to Great Falls in a car provided by the chain of Black Angus restaurants they were playing. The car's odometer was lying by some multiple of one hundred thousand miles, and the car broke down on a Blackfoot Indian reservation.

But on the road to Great Falls, the car bounced along under the Big Sky (as advertised), between breathtaking mountain ranges, through dense and aromatic forests of tall pines and past golden fields of wheat swaying to and fro. A majestic bird, which local residents said was probably an eagle, took flight with the approach of the car, as did a small herd of antelope. A full rainbow appeared.

Ms. Ladman dozed in the backseat of the car, a victim of the constant traveling and of the fresh air that can prove crippling to urban residents. Mr. Mittleman played a tape recording of his Bozeman performance and took notes as he drove. It didn't matter that the car swerved all over the road as he wrote. Other cars were few and far between.

The show back in Bozeman (population 18,670), given in a lounge at the Best Western Motel, had gone well. A live comedy show was a first for the city, and *The Bozeman Chronicle* carried a headline reading NEW YORK COMICS COME TO BOZEMAN.

A tablecloth was placed over the jukebox for the occasion. Opening the show, Ms. Ladman received some laughs just for saying, "Hello," apparently because of her New York accent. Mr. Mittleman was in luck; the Bozeman water supply was being visited by parasites that caused something known here as "backpacker's diarrhea," and his Perrier joke went over big.

Jim Henneman, the lounge manager, said the crowd for the Sunday show had been disappointing, with most people in town attending the big sweet-pea festival. But there was a full house Monday, and no one was happier than the waitresses, who said they received tips for the first time in memory.

"I don't know why in the world they'd ever come here, but it was certainly worth the four dollars," said Jean Dunning, a member of the audience. "A movie costs that much. We've never had anything live in Bozeman but a hypnotist."

Mr. Mittleman's jokes about growing up Jewish fell on deaf ears, but the ones with sexual references about cows and sheep nearly brought down the house.

Zoe Ann Kaisler complained that there were no jokes about people from North Dakota, which are apparently a lot like the jokes Manhattanites tell about New Jersey residents.

Up in Great Falls the Black Angus is set amid the Burger King, Dairy Queen, Tire-Rama, Vacuum City and Fabricland — not a good sign, according to Mr. Mittleman.

As Ms. Ladman ravaged the salad bar, as is her custom upon entering any new city, the restaurant manager explained he had seen a good comedian at the state fair recently and nobody laughed. That was not a good sign either, according to Mr. Mittleman. The manager also said he had been turned down by the high school in his bid to obtain a spotlight for the show. Mr. Mittleman was also concerned about the rather advanced age of the people filing into the restaurant.

Some see irony in comedians leaving small towns for the bright lights of New York, only to be shipped out to small towns, but most of the comedians do not seem to mind.

They go to New York to be seen by agents and scouts, but there are so many comics in the city that the Improvisation, the club at 358 West 44th Street, for example, pays $10 and a sandwich, according to Mr. Stanley. He said the comedians he put on the road made an average of $1,400 plus expenses for seven shows.

Comics also say they enjoy the opportunity to do half-hour or hour shows on the road rather than the few minutes they are given at the New York clubs. Ms. Ladman said she had taken a number and waited four and half hours on a recent night at Catch a Rising Star, the comedy club on First Avenue near 79th Street, and never made it onstage.

Being on the road is also an opportunity to get out of the hip Manhattan clubs and try material on "real people," something crucial to those seeking lucrative jobs in television.

It can be terrifying. In Great Falls Ms. Ladman was greeted by polite applause fit for a church banquet, then stony silence. But her effervescent style and a performance shot through with local Great Falls references — garnered from a waiter — won the audience. People began laughing and howling and holding their sides, and they didn't stop throughout her act or Mr. Mittleman's.

When the show was over, the people of Great Falls came up to thank the comedians for coming "all that way," and some asked for autographs that at least one man was certain would be worth a lot of money someday. The next night, the place was packed, despite a frightful storm that blew in off the plains in one of the country's windiest cities.

All who saw Mr. Mittleman and Ms. Ladman seemed to agree that the two comedians were bound for glory and Johnny Carson.

Missoula was next.

...AND THE
CULTURALLY BENT

THE ART
OF ARTSPEAK

WHEN VIEWING WORKS of art in galleries and museums, avoid blurting out words and phrases like "incredible," "cool" and "totally awesome."

Even "interesting" is preferable — especially when uttered with the head cocked and a hand cupping the chin in a contemplative pose — although that old routine doesn't really fool many people anymore.

What to say?

William Quinn, artist and lecturer, talked yesterday about that problem as he joined the eager throngs streaming through the Metropolitan Museum on the opening day of the new Lila Acheson Wallace wing, where twentieth-century art is displayed.

Mr. Quinn, who paints large computer product codes on seven-foot-by-fourteen-foot canvases in SoHo, was uptown exploring the new $26 million, 40,000-square-foot museum addition because he takes students to museums as part of a course he teaches in New York on what to say about paintings — artspeak.

The course is titled "Meeting People at the Great Museums," and the "basic but critical vocabulary" that the course teaches is important in striking up conversations.

"The course teaches you," said a former student of his, "how to sound halfway intelligent about art when you're not. It's great."

"Culture is such an important part of life in New York," Mr. Quinn said. "New Yorkers like to feel sophisticated, and they just can't without knowing at least something about art.

"If they're at a dinner party and start talking about the Modigliani heads' being inspired by Brancusi," he explained, "other people at the table pay attention to them, no longer regarding them as just tea ladies or bond traders.

"Knowing art indicates breeding and sophistication," he said, "like knowing about wine."

"If I saw a Cézanne now," said William Fleck, another student, "I could talk about how it is fuzzier than Renoir."

"There is nothing more intimidating to some people," said Mr. Quinn, "than finding themselves in a room with some modern art. What do you do? Laugh? Cry? Weep?

"A blob of blue on canvas," he continued, "is all well and good, but when it is presented as a million-dollar art object, people wonder why. They can't grasp it."

The artwork in the new museum wing elicited a myriad of overheard responses yesterday. Mr. Quinn and museum reference materials suggest perhaps more impressive responses for those planning to visit the new wing.

"It just looks like a mess to me," said Janet Schroeder, looking upon Jackson Pollock's *Autumn Rhythm (Number 30)*. This is not an impressive response. Instead, the visitor might say: "Although the words 'poured' and 'dripped' are commonly used to describe Mr. Pollock's unorthodox creative process, they hardly suggest the diversity of Mr. Pollock's movements, namely flicking, splattering and dribbling."

See?

"The artist didn't even bother to erase his pencil lines," noted Bob Merlin, referring to *Nasturtiums and the Dance* by Henri Matisse. A little bourgeois, Bob. Others might want to try this: "Matisse played the violin, and this painting almost turns the figures into musical notes. The whole is positively symphonic. The colors are pale, yet luminous and masterfully combined."

"I love this," said Samuel Gersten, appreciating Pierre Bonnard's *The Terrace at Vernon*. This response is, of course, totally insufficient. Instead, one should speak of the boldness of interpretation and, if in the company of someone sophisticated, add: "He goes beyond the limits of color and the laws of natural perspective."

"This looks like something my kids brought home from nursery school," said Janice Bartolli, glancing at Marsden Hartley's *Cemetery, New Mexico*. This is an improper, somewhat hostile response, Ms. Bartolli. Try this: "It may seem naively done, but all the better to jolt the nerve endings of the viewer and make him think rather than merely appreciate a beautifully and smoothly rendered landscape."

"Seriously, what is this supposed to be?" asked a visitor, looking at Charles Biederman's *Number 18. Wood and Plastic*. Mr. Quinn offered no help on this one.

"The Sanibel Public Library should come and take their books back," said a man walking past three twelve-foot stacks of books — many of them stamped Sanibel Island Public Library in Robert Rauschenberg's *¼ mile or Two Furlong Piece*, which includes the old books, smashed fifty-five-gallon drums, shirts stuck to walls, photographs, collages and taped traffic noises.

"I could do that," said another visitor, referring to a display of polyurethane-soaked cardboard boxes in the Rauschenberg. "But you didn't," said Mr. Quinn.

"This whole thing is a mess," said another visitor to the Rauschenberg. Incorrect. Instead, say, as Mr. Quinn did: "The boxes recall Motherwell, and the books are of course a play on Brancusi's *Endless Column*."

As if we didn't know.

SCALPERS
OF THE OPERA

MONTY IS UNCOMFORTABLE with the word "scalper," finding it a rather indelicate description of the service he provides habitués of the opera.

The eighty-four-year-old ticket agent, sans booth, has provided this service to operagoers for decades, becoming something of an institution outside the Metropolitan Opera House. He was greeted at the gala opening of the new season this week by dozens of the gowned and the bejeweled as they stepped from limousines.

Most men wore tuxedos for opening night, but Monty opted for understatement, wearing a rumpled sport coat and a tie that appeared to be a palette for the complete Campbell's Soup line.

"It's good to see you back for another season," said a woman in a stunning black gown, who appeared from a distance to be wearing a string of Ping-Pong balls that turned out to be pearls, actually, once she got close. "Monty is such a dear. He saved my life once," she said recalling the time she desperately needed tickets for out-of-town guests for a sold-out performance and Monty found some.

Of her friendly nature, Monty remarked, "Only the poor ones are snobs."

"Monty is famous around here," said Yolanda V. Catapano, arriving for the opening-night performance of *Die Walküre*. "He is very reputable, and he knows more about the opera than practically anyone here tonight.

"Monty was at the old Met on Thirty-ninth Street," Ms. Catapano recalled. "Everything about the opera is worse now than it was then, except him."

Many of those who have done business with him for years do not even know his name is Monty, and virtually no one knows he is Joseph Muntefering of Jamaica Estates, Queens. Some people say they call him "Mr. Magoo" because of his appearance, and he said he doesn't mind that.

He is the dean of a coterie of these free-lance ticket salesmen, and he conducts business in a rather more dignified manner than the others.

"A-couple-a-honeys!" yelled one of the other salesmen holding up two tickets. "Thirty-five dollars each." That was the minimum face-value price for opening-night tickets, some of which cost $250 (buffet not included).

As a group, the six men engaging in outdoor sales on opening night were admittedly snobs. Five of them divorced themselves entirely from those scalpers who conduct business in such low-brow locations as football-stadium parking lots. The sixth seller, whom Monty called "Maroon Man" because of the color of his jacket, is known to sell tickets at athletic events and even rock-and-roll concerts.

"Him?" Monty said of Maroon Man. "He doesn't know a center parterre seat," ($90) "from a family-circle box," ($8.50). Everyone laughed. Monty said he had strayed from the Met on occasion to sell tickets at Carnegie Hall, "but only if they have something decent."

Before and after the rush of business, the salesmen stood beneath the towering marble columns and Chagall murals discussing the state of opera and swooning over bygone performances of Birgit Nilsson as Isolde, Renata Tebaldi as Desdemona and Risë Stevens as Carmen.

As sophisticated as some of the sellers might be, they are nevertheless subject to the indignity of arrest. Last year, Monty himself was arrested.

"There was an outcry from some very influential people when that happened," one of his customers said. The resale of tickets for more than their face value is illegal, but the police seem to take far more seriously the sale of fraudulent tickets, a practice Monty denounces.

He said most of the tickets he sold were from people who had purchased them months in advance, only to find that they could not attend. He contended that for the most part, he resold the tickets at face value, giving most of the proceeds to the original owners and keeping "a modest gratuity" for himself. Indeed, two people who said they were in just such circumstances gave Monty sets of tickets Monday evening and instructed him to sell them. They would collect their money from him when next they came to the opera.

"Of course," he said, "when Pavarotti or Domingo sing, tickets have been known to be sold for three, four, even ten times their face value," hastening to add, "so they tell me."

"Not much money around tonight," Monty said before *Die Walküre*. "This is a long, boring opera," he said.

As curtain time approached, the competition among the salesmen became more pronounced, with Maroon Man cutting in on another seller's pitch to a customer, offering better seats at the same price. Another salesman began loudly hawking his tickets.

"This is not appropriate," Monty said. "The guy in the green suit selling tickets has actually gone so far as to give away opera phonograph albums to people buying his tickets."

Monty said he earned less than $10 this night, but he seemed not upset in the least. At four minutes before the curtain, he adjusted his nutritious-looking tie, removed from his wallet an $8.50 standing-room ticket for the five-and-one-half-hour performance — "Me miss opening night, you kidding?" — and dived into the blur of tuxedos, diamonds and furs hurtling toward the door.

LOWER EAST SIDE
ART TOUR

"MILDRED!" MINNA KIRZENBAUM yelled to a companion on the Avant-Garde Art Tour of the East Village. "I could paint that!"

Mildred Kaplan gazed upon the one-foot-square monochromatic green painting that didn't look all that different from, say, a kitchen floor tile and dissolved in laughter that turned every head in the gallery.

What was wrong with Mildred Kaplan? Couldn't she read? It explained right in the brochure that these paintings "evince synthetically a peculiar characterology: their static or virtually 'minimalistic' (hyper image defused) mode effects a counterexpressionistic attitude, even while this mannered reductive mode psychologically inflects itself," and so on for a full page of fine print. But Mildred wasn't buying it.

"The tour people!" said one exasperated gallery owner. As the weather got warmer and the word spread that the East Village is the hot spot of the art world, a trickle of tourists began that is expected to become a flood before spring turns to summer.

A longtime resident enjoying a curbside cocktail from a brown bag said, "First came the artists" – about four years ago as he recalls – "and then came the ladies" – on the tours. "What next?" he asked, "souvenir T-shirts?"

In fact, LOWER EAST SIDE T-shirts were already selling at the neighborhood's newly opened souvenir shop. A boy named Luis said that he and his friends were thinking about selling Kool-Aid on weekends, although a white-wine-spritzer stand might be more appropriate.

"You see whole busloads of them sometimes," said Gracie Mansion, the owner of a gallery in the neighborhood. "They wear those stickers on their fur coats that say, 'HELLO, I'M so and so.' I've thought about getting a bullhorn to use when I greet them. Some of them say things like 'Does anybody really *buy* this stuff?'"

Mrs. Kirzenbaum and Ms. Kaplan, both from Kendall Park, New Jersey, had dined with their tour group on chilled chicken and snow-pea salad in a real artists' loft on Lafayette Street before they headed into the very bowels of the East Village.

Eileen Guggenheim, head of Art Tours Associates, based in Princeton, New Jersey, and their guide, told the group of middle-aged suburban women that if there is an East Village style, it is neo-surrealism.

By the end of the day, they all agreed with her, having traipsed through a funky neighborhood of artists, motorcycle-gang members, middle-class families, real-estate speculators with briefcases, burned-out buildings, a woman hopping in and out of her limousine as the car inched from gallery to gallery, a man putting a 1964 Chevy up on concrete blocks and a smattering of drug pushers.

Some of the people seeking a glimpse of "the newest experimental outpost," as the East Village is described in the tour brochure, got more than they bargained for.

"God, it's so depressing," said Ilene Cohen, a tour member, as she viewed the burned-out buildings on Avenue B. Ms. Guggenheim recalled the time a tour member picked up a syringe from the sidewalk and asked, "Hey, what's this?"

Before the tour began, Ms. Guggenheim explained that the neighborhood was rapidly gentrifying, just as happened in SoHo. "We'd better get going then, that happens awfully fast," said Susan Hockaday, rising from lunch in the loft. She asked if she should bring along a loaf of French bread for protection.

Walking along on a warm spring day, the women pointed to various sights in the neighborhood, and some residents standing on sidewalks or enjoying the weather on the fire escapes pointed right back at them.

"Hmm, maroon and orange hair," said one woman, as a denizen walked past, "a combination I had not considered."

"Watch out for dog-do," Ms. Guggenheim chirped.

As the group arrived at the first gallery, Piezo Electric, the owner, Elizabeth McDonald, greeted them with "This is unlike anything you have seen before." And so it was: paintings done with photographic chemicals on Cibachrome paper that seemed to glow.

"They're just terrible," said Ms. Kaplan. "I wouldn't want them in my house." Then she added: "At least they're different. SoHo has become so ho-hum."

Dr. Lila Nachtig, another member of the tour, clutched her purse tightly and said: "What amazes me is that people can buy valuable art and walk out on these streets with it."

At the Vox Populi Gallery the group rather liked the deteriorating walls better than the art, and one woman seemed faint when told one of the works sold for $4,000. "For that?" she replied.

"Is the emperor wearing clothes?" Diane Unruh, an associate of Ms. Guggenheim's, said as the group strolled along. "That's the question you keep asking." As they walked past the New Comers Motorcycle Club, a man in a car yelled: "Hey, *chiquitas!*" One woman was offended; another said it made her day.

"What is that on top of that car?" said one of the women, pointing to a car a few feet away at the stop sign. "Art!" yelled a man in the passenger seat, referring to a pile of black rubber with lots of red pencils stuck in it. "I couldn't tell," the woman said.

"Is it or isn't it?" said Ilene Cohen. "That seems to be the question of the day."

At the Sharpe Gallery, the owner asked if there were questions, and one of the women said: "Yes. Where did you get these lovely glass doors? I'd love to have them in my home."

At the Gracie Mansion Gallery, an artist named David Sandlin was putting the final touches on one of his works when the group trooped in and Ms. Guggenheim said: "Look! A real artist,

live and in person!" The women all gathered around, and Mr.
Sandlin ran out the door.

"Museum fatigue," as Ms. Guggenheim called it, began to
set in with Ms. Kaplan and some of the others straggling far
behind. Ms. Kaplan perked up, however, when she passed a psychiatrist's office between the souvenir store and a gallery featuring
paintings of monsters. She began laughing again and said, "Boy,
I'll bet they do a business in there!"

In the gallery of monster works, Mrs. Kirzenbaum started
discussing a painting with the person next to her but suddenly
realized it was a stranger she was talking to, a man with a spiked
Mohawk hairdo.

"You are not with us," she said.

"I am not with you," he replied.

MORRIS KATZ—
FASTEST BRUSH
IN THE CATSKILLS

Loch Sheldrake, N.Y. — There is a legend in these hills, the Catskills, of a man they say can paint a landscape in under two minutes and frame it in eight seconds flat.

"And the heck of it is, it's true!" said Roberta Liebling, who made the pilgrimage today from New York to Brown's Hotel here to witness the legendary Morris Katz performing the miracle.

"I have heard," chimed in her companion, Ruth Simons, "that he once painted a landscape in the dark." Also true. How did it look, Mr. Katz was asked. "A guy bought it," he answered.

The women watched with about a hundred others in the lobby as Mr. Katz "schmeered," to use his expression, a landscape on a 20-by-24-inch canvas in 1 minute 46.5 seconds, shattering the 2-minute barrier, if not breaking his own world record of 90 seconds.

Mr. Katz invented "Instant Art" in 1956 and has gone on to become the most prolific painter alive, according to the *Guinness Book of World Records*, with about 143,000 paintings to his credit.

He said he perfected his technique by doing six thousand paintings at something of an art factory in Mississippi. Mr. Katz does not use paintbrushes because they are "too slow and hard to clean." Instead he paints with the palette knife, often straight from the paint can, and with lots of toilet paper. "What miracles I can do," he said, "with a full roll of toilet paper and a good head of steam."

In the summer of 1985, as Pete Rose makes his celebrated quest to break Ty Cobb's all-time record for base hits, Morris

Katz is closing fast on Pablo Picasso's record of 147,800 works of art. He could break it this year, barring injuries.

The sixty-three-year-old Mr. Katz, a Polish immigrant, rose at dawn today in his Bronx home and did his daily exercises, which he said he needs to stay strong enough to carry loads of paints and frames and to keep his eighteen-hour days. He is a burly man with a easy smile and with long, wiry salt-and-pepper hair, which he tucks under a green beret. He wears paint-splattered pants and T-shirts that read MORRIS KATZ — WORLD'S MOST PRO-LIFIC ARTIST.

He loaded his overworked van, with 160,000 miles on it, and drove to work in the Catskills — the lobby of Brown's in the morning, the Pines in the afternoon and Kutsher's at night. He did not expect to be home until after 1:00 A.M.

He is to spend next week in Jerusalem, working the hotels along the Dead Sea. "This is what you have to do," he said.

On Monday he appeared on the *Joe Franklin* television talk show, painting landscapes. The director, Bob Diamond, said Mr. Katz was always welcome because he has "such a huge following."

After the show Mr. Katz went to his Greenwich Village studio. With an electric fan behind him to hasten drying of the oil paint, he knocked off three landscapes, framed them and tied them together with a rope in ten minutes, like some rodeo event.

"There!" he exclaimed. "Put those on a gallery wall on Madison Avenue, under a spotlight, with a refined woman saying sophisticated things about them, and they'd sell for three thousand dollars apiece."

The studio looks like an art-supply warehouse. He buys his oil and acrylic paints not by the tube but by the gallon, his frames by the hundreds and his canvases by the thousands. He spends $1,000 a year on the staples alone that affix canvas to frame. He actually wears out palette knives. He is thinking of coming out with his own longer, faster and tougher palette knives bearing his autograph.

Also in the studio are videotapes of his appearances on public-access television and copies of his new book, *Paint Good and Fast*, which tells busy people how to paint masterpieces in minutes, just as he contends Picasso and Monet did.

"Life goes faster and faster," he writes. "The fine arts must keep pace. This art will one day be viewed as prophetic." His is the true modern art, he says, "fast, democratic and to the point."

"Oh my God!" said Bobby Brachman of New York City as Mr. Katz executed two clown paintings at the same time in Brown's lobby, then completed three seascapes in under five minutes. He was asking up to $200 for his paintings but usually settled for less than $50.

"The prices are low," said Mr. Katz, who keeps up a repartee in English and Yiddish with his audiences while he paints, "because I want to sell my paintings now, not when I'm dead. Some painters waited five hundred years to sell their work. Some are still waiting — on tables, in the dining room."

"You're beautiful, Morris Katz," said Elaine Finkelstein of Cambridge, Massachusetts. "You bring art to the lay people."

In his studio, Mr. Katz, who said he trained in Europe and at the Art Students League of New York, has finally painted some portraits, each representing months of detailed brushwork. He went broke doing this kind of work in 1969, "so I put on a beret, came to the Catskills to do these little shows, where I paint to order and play the fool." His idea was to make enough to buy some time to do fine artworks, "but I cannot seem to ever get enough ahead."

He did not break his world record of 90 seconds (98 seconds, framed) today, but his 1:46.5 for a landscape complete with mountains, a river, trees with leaves, a house, birds and not one but two human figures was a feat that stunned the audience.

Mr. Katz has a dazzling finish, whipping the painting from easel to frame and holding it high over his head while stapling it with one of several loaded staple guns he keeps at the ready.

Max Goldstein of Norfolk, Virginia, took a photograph of the painting and said, "Wait until they see this back home."

"What's the title of that last one?" someone yelled.

"That's entitled, *My Home in Poland*," Mr. Katz answered softly.

"I'll bet it is!" someone else yelled mockingly. "And I suppose that's you by the river holding hands with your daddy."

"It is, yes," said Morris Katz, and he began packing up his paintings for the next resort.

COAT CHECKING
AT THE PHILHARMONIC

"One of the finest things you can do in life, I believe, is check your coat. In this way, you don't have to sit on it."
— Albert Golub, 50-year veteran of the coat-check profession

THIS IS A time of siege in coat-check rooms around the city.

Overwhelmed coat-room attendants have been observed breaking down emotionally under the avalanche in Januarys and Februarys, and some seem to virtually disappear in the swell of down and fur.

But Ralph Burger, veteran coat-check professional, is keeping things well in hand at the Avery Fisher Hall coat room.

The fifty-three-year-old Mr. Burger runs the coat room alone in warmer months but has a staff of four helping him now in his time of need. And during the recent snowstorms, when galoshes and other paraphernalia clogged his checking system, he was forced to call in emergency relief. He closely monitors weather reports for approaching storms.

After the New York Philharmonic Orchestra completed its performance Thursday night, Mr. Burger's coat room kicked out 110 coats in ten minutes, or one coat every 5.45 seconds. Sixteen more coats went to stragglers.

"You do a fantastic job," said one patron of the arts. "Why do we have to wait so long?" asked another. "That's New York," shrugged Mr. Burger, who is from Wyoming.

Mr. Burger, a tall, amiable man hailing from Casper who sometimes greets customers with a "Howdy," arrived in New York twenty-six years ago to be a famous actor – only to wind up in the coat room. This happens. "I'm not at all cast down about it," he said.

"Nor should he be," said Mr. Golub, president of Golub Brothers Concessions, which operates many coat rooms and is Mr. Burger's employer. "This is an exciting business that keeps you young. Ralph Burger is in a class by himself in the coat-check profession."

Mr. Burger brings fresh-cut flowers to the coat room almost every day, along with cookies and cake for the employees, and he always makes a pot of coffee.

"This is practically my home in the winter," he said. "We had a Christmas tree." On a table is a photograph of his wife, Mary Ann, who died several years ago of heart disease. "I met her here," he said. "She checked her coat with me and one thing led to another.

"She hung around the coat room. She always listened to the old people who checked their coats and wanted to talk on and on. I learned something from that. Everything doesn't have to advance commerce."

After twenty-two years, Mr. Burger is considered an expert at predicting coat volume. He predicted the coat load Thursday night at 130 because of these factors: the Philharmonic was playing, the conductor was Kurt Masur, the music was by popular composers (including Brahms and Schumann), the night was Thursday, and the weather was clear and 27 degrees with no precipitation. There were 126 coats.

Mr. Golub makes fine distinctions, such as fewer people checking coats for a violin soloist than a piano soloist, but has no idea why. Mr. Burger keeps records on every performance. He pulled an index card at random from his file, and this card was on a performance at the hall by the Average White Band on May 2, 1978 ("sunny and dry, a little cool," the card recalled), a night when an astonishingly low eight coats and eight cameras were all that were checked. "The young don't check their coats," he explained.

"Only three to nine percent of all audiences do check," he

said. "Checking is mandatory in many European theaters for acoustical reasons." Indeed, some performers complained in the peak of the quilted down-coat trend in New York that all those goose feathers were absorbing the sound and diminishing their performance.

"The popularity of the down coat is on the decline, I'm happy to say," he said, noting that down coats take up an inordinate amount of precious space.

"Before the down-coat problem, there was the problem with those huge maxicoats," he said, noting that now there is the great fur coat glut clogging New York coat rooms.

People attempt to check any and all things in New York, from parakeets to cellos. "We are undaunted," Mr. Burger said. "We take everything in.

"This is also an information center," he continued, taping to the counter a copy of the program with the estimated number of minutes each segment would last: Matthus, twenty minutes; Brahms, thirty-three; intermission, twenty; Schumann, thirty.

"I was at rehearsal this morning, and I think Brahms will be more like thirty-six minutes," said a patron.

"Really?" replied Mr. Burger, most concerned.

It is also a service center, supplying change for the phone, two aspirin for those with a headache, matches and so on.

"We've had whole novels written by employees," Dan Zittel, a coat-room employee, said in reference to the lull between checking coats in and out.

"Ralph has become extremely well versed over the years in classical music and discusses it with customers," Mr. Zittel said.

"This is my niche," said Mr. Burger. "It could be upsetting to some people, I suppose, to wind up in the coat room, but I enjoy trying to do something well.

"This is not foolishness, this is helping people," he said, listening to the closing strains of Schumann, before the onslaught of coat owners. "Those of us with less glorious ambitions belong in New York, too."

When the rush was over, Mr. Burger said to his staff: "Thank you for your valued participation, gentlemen. You may depart for your chambers."

He sorted the coat-check numbers for reuse and recorded the number of coats checked, as well as the number of boxes of Milk Duds, Raisinets and lemon drops (they suppress coughs in the theater) sold. Then he stepped out in the cold, between the lines of limousines, and waited for the No. 29 bus home.

THE STATUE OF LIBERTY CELEBRANTS

THE STATUE OF LIBERTY
WORK CREW

T HE SMALL COFFEE shop at South Ferry was shoulder to broad shoulder at 7:00 A.M. with construction workers from locals 3, 825, and 1536. Most wore sleeveless undershirts that revealed tanned, muscular arms — arms that had never been hooked up to machines at health clubs, the men will assure you; arms with plenty of latitude for tattooed panthers, hula dancers and snakes.

The men drank coffee — black — and passed around photographs, which someone or other seems to carry with him every morning. There were photographs of someone's Datsun 280 ZX and of children and friends, but most of the photographs were of "The Lady," as the men refer to her — the Statue of Liberty.

These workers are on the crew that is rehabilitating the statue. One of them, Bob Conmy, says his nine-year-old daughter, Robyn, takes the photographs to school to show to her classmates. Mr. Conmy is on the crew that built the scaffolding surrounding the statue. He was one of the first people in ninety-eight years to look her right in the two-and-a-half-foot eye. When he did, he gave her a kiss.

At 7:30 the men boarded a boat that took them to the work site. They have made this trip every day for months, but still most of them face forward, gazing at the green copper statue showing through their shiny aluminum superstructure. Joseph Romano, a young general laborer, said this was an exciting job, because people asked him about it and because he gets to ride a boat to work. Fred Harris, who has operated a forklift for thirty-five years, insisted, "It's really just another job."

Paul Gabriel, an electrician for twenty-five years, said he liked the job, "because supervisors don't like to come out to an island where there aren't any good places to eat lunch. There is no need for supervision. This is something we want to do. She is all ours for a while."

It is just another job in some respects. There is straining and sweating these hot, humid days. There is the sound of clanging iron, of whirring power saws and of jackhammers busting things up.

Inside the statue temperatures reach 120 degrees, punctuated by occasional blasts of burning cold — liquid nitrogen at minus 350 degrees Fahrenheit is sprayed by Mr. Romano and others on a century of paint and corrosion, causing it to fall in flakes like autumn leaves.

There are cuts and bruises and the danger of far worse as men dangle out thirty stories above Liberty Island and Upper New York Bay, with winds whistling through the twenty-five-story, freestanding aluminum scaffolding.

Final preparations are hurriedly being made for a Fourth of July ceremony, when the old corroded torch will be removed by a hoist, with Lee Iacocca, chairman of the Statue of Liberty-Ellis Island Foundation, and other dignitaries in attendance. Elmut Leonardelli, of Local 1536, explains through a big wad of chewing tobacco that he always wears his stars-and-stripes sweatband on this job and plans to wear suspenders to match on the Fourth.

Fred Harris of Paterson, New Jersey, will be the man of the moment. Mr. Harris, an operating engineer for thirty-five years, has been selected for the exacting job of operating the hoist that is to lift off the old torch. "Just another lift," he said. "I'll have to work the Fourth, and my wife doesn't like that. At least I won't have to stay home and barbecue and work around the house. And it's a double day," a reference to premium pay.

On the other side of a wire fence around the construction site, the *Miss Freedom* of the Circle Line continues to deposit visitors. A park ranger, Mike Kusch, who leads tours, still gets a little choked up when he tells of immigrants arriving on ships and being greeted by the Statue of Liberty. A group from the Camp Fire Girls organization in Fairfax, Virginia, asked him how they could go about contributing $5 each to the restoration fund.

Angelo Bommarito, labor foreman on the project, immigrated from Italy eighteen years ago, at the age of seventeen. "Get moving with that!" he yells to one of the workers, in the midst of telling the story of his arrival on a ship from Italy at 3:00 A.M. and of seeing the Statue of Liberty for the first time. "I cannot talk about my feelings," he said. "To me, the job is a little special. I come from the other side."

Mr. Gabriel hung from the very top of the thin aluminum scaffolding to attach aircraft warning lights. The forty-five-year-old electrician from Matawan, New Jersey, talked of suddenly being an important person to family and friends interested in the project. "Normally, I am just an electrician," he said. "I hope my boss puts in a good bid for the remainder of this work," he said. "I want to finish the job. I have worked on a lot of jobs, including the World Trade Center. Working on The Lady here, you realize that the trade center was just a tall building."

Tom Snodgrass, supervisor of the project for the general contractor, Lehrer/McGovern, Inc., has a reputation among the men for toughness. He talked of arriving on the island at 6:30 A.M., before any of the other workers. "It is very quiet," he said. "You can take the time to notice little things about her, the little creases in her hands, the spots on her arms and little welts in her throat that need to be tended to. She is a different color in the morning light. It is quite a sensation to touch her face. Very few people have done that."

Joe Fiebiger works inside the statue making molds of each one of the twelve hundred corroded armatures that attach the superstructure of the statue to the copper skin and hold its shape. Each one must be replaced. Each is different, following the contour of the flow of the robes, the slant of the nose and the like.

"I guess," said Mr. Fiebiger, "whether we admit it or not, we are all in love with her, for different reasons. I don't want to sound foolish. I'm a blacksmith."

EIGHT HUNDRED
CAR DEALERS
SALUTE LIBERTY
AND LEE IACOCCA

THE SCENE IN Upper New York Bay yesterday seemed one of almost biblical proportion.

As teams of jet fighters swooped, several blimps floated and squadrons of helicopters hacked away at the skies, thousands of vessels of every conceivable size and shape — inflatable raft to aircraft carrier — thickened on the waters until it seemed for a moment that mortal men might walk across the hulls to New Jersey.

Into this mad cauldron steamed the eight hundred, eight hundred Chrysler and Dodge dealers, making a grand entrance for this weekend of excess aboard the *Queen Elizabeth 2*, flying a one-hundred-foot-wide American flag, releasing twenty-five hundred red, white and blue balloons and saluted by fireboats spraying red, white and blue geysers as the ship sailed beneath the Verrazano-Narrows Bridge.

Catching a first glimpse of the Statue of Liberty brought tears and goose bumps to these passengers. "Awesome statue, Buck!" Sharon Sloan, of Waxahachie, Texas, yelled to her dealer husband.

Lee A. Iacocca, chairman of the Chrysler Corporation and the Statue of Liberty-Ellis Island Foundation, had commissioned the entire ship for these chosen salesmen — men who grappled with their sales quotas and came out on top — and their guests, about sixteen hundred in all. More than one thought there should be a matching statue in the harbor of Mr. Iacocca, who has raised about $250 million for the restoration by accepting nickels and dimes from schoolchildren as well as charging $1 million for his speaking engagements and $100,000 to have a picture taken with him.

Just as Beverly Wullenweber, whose husband, Clyde, is a dealer in Cincinnati, was saying that things could not possibly be more perfect, a steward arrived with a tray of champagne — 7:45 A.M., but what the heck. Her group swept the tray clean and toasted the dramatic view, made all the more so because none in this group had ever seen New York or the Statue of Liberty.

There was much to celebrate, including this "trip of a lifetime," as Walter Parr, a dealer from Santa Monica, California, put it. Dealers also tipped their glasses to Chrysler's strong resurgence after the assault by Japanese imports, the fuel crisis, various recessions and Chrysler's near collapse. "Now," exclaimed Mr. Parr, tossing back another glass of champagne as the ship blasted her horn, "we are ridin' high!"

To these car dealers, the resurgence of sales and the resurgence of patriotism go hand in hand. They credit Mr. Iacocca with saving Chrysler and with saving the Statue of Liberty.

"Lee Iacocca is today's ultimate American hero," said Maddy Miller, whose husband, Wendell, owns three dealerships.

One dealer, Anthony Curiale, of New Rochelle, New York, said it was inappropriate that the Fuji Film blimp was flying over this American celebration. "Those jets ought to blow it out of the sky," he said.

The dealers and guests lined the ship's railings, cameras clicking away, and tossing red, white and blue carnations overboard in some symbolic gesture. Out on the deck a ten-piece orchestra struck up "I'm a Yankee Doodle Dandy" and other patriotic numbers as Eva Franchi spun about dancing on the deck. She is the wife of Sergio Franchi, who was on board and who is far and away the favorite singer of many of these salesmen. Why? He sang "Volare" in the Plymouth Volare commercial, that's why.

Asked how she liked traveling with eight hundred car dealers, Mrs. Franchi said she absolutely adored it. "We're a fun group," Buck Sloan commented, bragging that they had drunk a few bars on the ship completely dry on the passage. Ship personnel confirmed this.

Victor Potamkin strolled the decks, socializing and passing out real dollar bills with his picture pasted over George Washington's. Mr. Potamkin sells Cadillacs in New York, but Chryslers elsewhere in the country, and is described in these circles as a "mega-dealer."

"I have been fortunate in life, in America, to have more than one dealership," he said, looking out through purple-lensed glasses. How many? "Thirty-five."

Mr. Iacocca flew the sixteen hundred to Paris for dinner, at the Palace of Versailles, a couple of weeks ago, then sent them on to London and Southampton, England, where they boarded the ship for Bermuda and New York.

"We got a feeling what it must have been like for the immigrants crossing," said Mary Lou Karg, whose husband, Ken, owns a dealership in Strongsville, Ohio. "Going into Bermuda, we got sick as dogs."

"I didn't like Paris," bellowed Stew Smith, an Orlando, Florida, dealer, wearing one of the green foam-rubber Lady Liberty crowns so popular with the group. "People there don't smile enough. I like America."

THE PRIDE IS BACK read the Chrysler slogan on several jackets. Jennie Kuhn proclaimed loudly that she is proud of her husband, Howard, because "he did one hundred seventy-nine percent of his quota. If you want to buy a new or used car, or are looking to lease or buy or just want the best service, come to Future Dodge in Jackson Heights."

"This trip is ten times better than Christmas," said Mrs. Wullenweber, who wore a large Statue of Liberty commemorative pin that she had purchased from her Avon representative. She said this was the best bonus trip they had ever been on, including the cruise to Alaska, which she said "was as good as opening a *National Geographic.*"

Mack McClendon of Dallas sat inside, proudly watching on the big-screen Mitsubishi a network television broadcast of the arrival of the QE 2.

"You're not going to believe this," Mr. Wullenweber confided. "But tomorrow this ship will be parked right next to the *U.S.S. Iowa* that President Reagan's going to be on."

He was ready to bet the farm that Lee Iacocca had something to do with that. And as for the sudden clearing in the weather? He wouldn't be a bit surprised if Lee had a hand in that either.

CHOPPED LIVERTY

"**I** ACTUALLY BELIEVE New York may be even a little weirder than usual," Kevin Simons said yesterday, referring to the hoopla over the Statue of Liberty centennial celebration.

Mr. Simons made his observation while hanging upside-down in gravity boots from his fourth-floor fire escape at Second Avenue and 30th Street.

Casual empiricism around town tended to support his hypothesis. Minutes later, Leo Steiner, of the Carnegie Delicatessen, ceremoniously presented William D. Fugazy, chairman of the State Statue of Liberty Centennial Commission, with a sixty-pound chopped-liver Statue of Liberty. It was just the upper torso, and someone blurted, discourteously, that it looked more like a bulldog to him. Such is art.

In brief remarks Mr. Fugazy said he has been hearing a lot of people complain lately that the Liberty Weekend celebration is being overcommercialized and that he was sick and tired of hearing it. Mr. Steiner concurred.

Mr. Fugazy, who graciously accepted the sculpture, entitled "Chopped Liverty," said he was also fed up with the charges of "tackiness." He said that officials of the celebration had licensed tasteful products – to include official Statue of Liberty charcoal briquettes, dry-roasted peanuts and chewing tobacco – and that "they cannot control street vendors who go off making T-shirts and things."

He said he had just discussed the problem with David L. Wolper, executive producer of Liberty Weekend, who has lined up one thousand tap dancers and two hundred Elvis Presley look-alikes, among others, for the closing ceremonies in the Hackensack Meadowlands.

The city's first campers have begun arriving, some wondering if perhaps they should have bought additional gear — hand grenades, for example — for camping outdoors in New York. To the amazement of Parks and Recreation Department officials, Mayor Ed Koch exuberantly announced recently that to handle the expected overflow crowds for Liberty Weekend, he would throw open the parks to tent campers and recreational vehicles for the first time in city history. Shooting their reputations for sanity in their hometowns, more than a thousand campers from throughout the world are expected.

Christina Cox, who said she was just another aspiring actress in New York until she proclaimed herself "Miss Liberty," said she was part of the closing ceremonies, too. She was breathless, having just returned from France, and was off to be fitted for a gown for an appearance today at a Nathan's hot-dog restaurant.

Gladys Shelley was walking her five Chihuahuas down upper Fifth Avenue yesterday in the sunshine, singing "My Country's Been Good to Me." It has been very good from the looks of things.

Mrs. Shelley, who lives in a spacious apartment overlooking Central Park, said she wrote the song to express how she felt about her country and wished more people could hear it.

"It is available on records and tapes," said Mrs. Shelley, who noted that, unlike America, "some very talented people in Czechoslovakia live in one-room apartments" — with no views at all.

Burt Rubin was busy yesterday telling potential customers that his telescopes make "the best gift for your clients, as a fine remembrance and useful tool during the 1986 Statue of Liberty festivities." Mr. Rubin manufactured sixty thousand Halley-scopes, the better to see Halley's comet, and said he has "a nice inventory" left over, because American consumers were "too lazy" to go out and look for the comet. He hopes Americans aren't as unpatriotic as they are lazy.

At the Sheraton Centre the director of security, Vince Russo, has been giving courses to employees this week as part of "Liberty Weekend Preparedness" training at the hotel. He told the employees to look for worn shoe heels and dirty fingernails as signs of criminality. Some employees sneaked glances at their own.

On the radio yesterday "Save the Lady" advertisements for room air conditioners were playing, and appearing in a newspaper were advertisements reading LET'S CELEBRATE MISS LIBERTY WITH MEAT-O-MAT BEEF PATTIES, along with an advertisement for Carmine Marlino, "creator of fine men's hairpieces in Sheepshead Bay." Mr. Merlino has a "Statue of Liberty Special – dye and recondition your old hairpiece for $50."

On the streets a vendor said he was about to rotate his stock, from Rolex-like watches and tube socks to more patriotic goods, such as the popular foam-rubber Statue of Liberty crowns. A man with a six-foot Statue of Liberty cutout was seen yesterday letting people stick their faces through a hole where Miss Liberty's should be and taking their photographs for $5.

A pastry Statue of Liberty and a tree pruned in the shape of the statue were reported on Second Avenue, and the announcement came that a thirteen-foot, fifty-five-hundred-pound chocolate Statue of Liberty model is en route from Paris.

Peter Rocha is to arrive in town this week to make four-square-foot jellybean mosaics of Miss Liberty. Melody Weir has purchased one for "several thousand dollars." Ms. Weir, a party organizer, was busy putting finishing touches on the party last night for Governor Mario Cuomo's fifty-fourth birthday, where Mr. Steiner's "Chopped Liverty" was to be presented to the governor.

Mr. Steiner has previously sculptured Richard M. Nixon, Elvis Presley and Mae West. "I have also done many patriots," he said. "Washington, Lincoln and Youngman" (Henny). CBS News, NBC News and ABC News all videotaped the sculpture, and Mr. Steiner said there was no argument from ABC – as there has been over much of the celebration – over exclusivity vis-à-vis the commemorative chopped liver.

A group of Fifth Avenue shoppers sat on folding chairs inside

Lord & Taylor on Fifth Avenue, sipping complimentary coffee and waiting for the store to open. At 9:55 A.M. the public-address system played "The Star-Spangled Banner," and the shoppers stood and sang. This does not have anything to do with Liberty Weekend; the store does this every day of the year.

Likewise, there was nothing special about the boys shouting, "Yo, fireworks!" to motorists on Canal Street. They sell their fireworks there every year.

Two chimpanzees, accompanied by the King Kong Kuties, six female models in scanty jungle outfits, protested yesterday outside the NBC studios that David Letterman would not let them be guests on his show to talk about the new King Kong attraction on the Universal Studios Tour in Hollywood.

"That was just normal day-to-day stuff in New York," said Neal Styron, who witnessed the demonstration and said it had nothing to do with the Statue of Liberty celebration. Dennis O'Donnell, his friend, disagreed, saying it had everything to do with it.

FAMILY SAILS
AMID HISTORY

SEVEN-YEAR-OLD Josh Curtis
wondered aloud yesterday what in the world the Statue of Liberty
would say if she could speak. His question was lost in the roar of
thousands of boat engines and the blare of their horns.

The boy had just entered New York Harbor, uttering a
"Wow!" as the family motorboat emerged from a tributary. He
beheld more boats than he had ever imagined existed – indeed,
perhaps more than have ever been assembled, with estimates
ranging from twenty thousand to thirty thousand vessels – as
they swirled about the statue's feet and swarms of blimps, sky-
writers, helicopters and fighter planes buzzed around her head.

Josh's family had slept aboard their well-traveled, twenty-
six-foot wooden boat at the New Elco Marina in Bayonne, New
Jersey, for an early getaway on this historic occasion. With American flags unfurled, the family buzzed across Newark Bay and
down the Kill Van Kull, lined with salvage yards and oil tankers, a
dreary approach that made the harbor view all the more dramatic.

His father, Skip Curtis, dressed in a red, white and blue
LIBERTY PARK, NEW JERSEY T-shirt, had enthusiastically loaded
the family – Josh, his mother, Ellen, and Matthew, his ten-year-
old brother – aboard, along with two Styrofoam coolers so full of
beer, soda, cold cuts and nacho cheese chips that their sides were
splitting. Also on board were a sack of fireworks and a radio playing rock-and-roll oldies.

Mr. Curtis, forty-two, said he wanted them to be "present

and part of an unforgettable moment in American history." All they could do was hope this turned out better than Halley's comet, which he had also been excited for them to see.

Mrs. Curtis went along reluctantly on the pilgrimage to the refurbished Statue of Liberty. Matthew had suggested to his father a little fluke fishing instead.

"They told us at school we had to contribute five dollars to the statue," Matthew said, "or we'd be in trouble."

But now they were all excited — if occasionally afraid for their lives — as Mr. Curtis deftly wove them through this assemblage of virtually every type of vessel conceived of to pay homage to the statue.

There were sloops, hydrofoils, junks, carriers, brigantines, the *Queen Elizabeth 2*, Jet-Skis, an oil barge with bleachers, schooners, water taxis, a submarine, a battleship and a thousand and one would-be Don Johnsons in sleek Cigarette boats.

The parade of breathtaking tall ships, the ostensible reason for the gathering of the masses, seemed but a sideshow at times.

The Curtis family, of North Bergen, New Jersey, beheld two seemingly crazed people out in a kayak in this hull-to-hull traffic. There was even a car, one of those small convertible automobiles that run on land or water, with waves breaking over the windshield wipers.

They also came upon what appeared to be a four-foot-high remote-controlled model of a battleship, which turned out to have a husband and wife from California inside, peeping out through a hole in the bridge to pilot the craft.

So closely spaced were the vessels, in tricky waters, that when a man sneezed aboard the *Nauti But Nice*, passengers on the *Ship of Fools* and the *Banker's Away* yelled, "Gesundheit!"

"Taxi!" yelled a man with his hand raised as if he were on a corner in midtown Manhattan rather than bobbing on a boat. The two cabbies driving the *South Bay Water Taxi*, a small outboard boat, reported that business was brisk, what with running people to shore for dinners and Broadway shows. The fare was $25 a passenger.

Other boaters reported that water vendors had come around in boats hawking ice and fuel and that they were finding buyers among the throngs, some of whom had been anchored in prime viewing positions for four or five days.

"All part of the Fourth," Mr. Curtis said as he towed a disabled outboard boat carrying a distraught family of four to shore. Moments later, Mr. Curtis's own engine conked out, and he was on hands and knees with his tools. He managed to fix the engine, even while the boat pitched and yawed wildly.

Other members of the family worried that they might soon be dashed upon some pilings. Indeed, they had to hold the boat off the pilings with poles. The hatch cover came down hard on the back of Mr. Curtis's head. Josh managed to slip his father a beer, despite Mrs. Curtis's attempts to interdict the supply line.

Mrs. Curtis, whose parents immigrated from Czechoslovakia and whose father became a Pennsylvania coal miner, said she was surprised to find herself "getting choked up" when she watched the relighting of the statue on television the night before.

"Forget immigrants," said Mr. Curtis, one-upping his wife by noting that his great-grandfather was a Blackfoot Indian.

Mr. Curtis said that he believed, absolutely, in the American Dream and that his boat, which he purchased for $3,000 and fixed up, is part of that dream for him. He had a sixteen-footer before this, and eventually he would like a twin-engine fishing boat that costs $120,000. He said he believes that if he works hard, he'll get it.

He quit his job with Roto-Rooter a few years ago and started his own drain- and sewer-cleaning business, Drain Power, in North Bergen. "I don't make a lot of money," he said. "I pay my bills. I help people with problems and I get satisfaction from my work."

He described himself as "patriotic but not a love-it-or-leave-it guy." He lost part of his right foot to a land mine in Vietnam as a member of the 101st Airborne. His boat is named *Airborne*.

"I don't belong to any veterans organizations or any of that stuff," he said. "I told my boys never to get involved in a fight that isn't their fight, never to get into wars like Vietnam and to watch out about Central America."

His greatest love, he said, is fishing with his sons, whom he has taught to steer the boat, fillet the fish and fetch him a beer. He hopes that fishing will keep them occupied and out of trouble.

Looking over the scene yesterday, Mr. Curtis said that he had been at Woodstock, another unforgettable experience, and that he wondered if all those people from Woodstock were in the harbor now, drinking beer on their boats and waving the flag.

As these sons and daughters of immigrants continued to mill about the Statue of Liberty in their pleasure boats, Josh began to look a little weary and asked his father impatiently, "Are we part of history yet?"

FOR THE BEST IN PAPERBACKS, LOOK FOR THE Ⓟ

In every corner of the world, on every subject under the sun, Penguin represents quality and variety—the very best in publishing today.

For complete information about books available from Penguin—including Pelicans, Puffins, Peregrines, and Penguin Classics—and how to order them, write to us at the appropriate address below. Please note that for copyright reasons the selection of books varies from country to country.

In the United Kingdom: For a complete list of books available from Penguin in the U.K., please write to *Dept E.P., Penguin Books Ltd, Harmondsworth, Middlesex, UB7 0DA.*

In the United States: For a complete list of books available from Penguin in the U.S., please write to *Dept BA, Penguin,* Box 999, Bergenfield, New Jersey 07621-0999.

In Canada: For a complete list of books available from Penguin in Canada, please write to *Penguin Books Canada Ltd, 2801 John Street, Markham, Ontario L3R 1B4.*

In Australia: For a complete list of books available from Penguin in Australia, please write to the *Marketing Department, Penguin Books Australia Ltd, P.O. Box 257, Ringwood, Victoria 3134.*

In New Zealand: For a complete list of books available from Penguin in New Zealand, please write to the *Marketing Department, Penguin Books (NZ) Ltd, Private Bag, Takapuna, Auckland 9.*

In India: For a complete list of books available from Penguin, please write to *Penguin Overseas Ltd, 706 Eros Apartments, 56 Nehru Place, New Delhi, 110019.*

In Holland: For a complete list of books available from Penguin in Holland, please write to *Penguin Books Nederland B.V., Postbus 195, NL–1380AD Weesp, Netherlands.*

In Germany: For a complete list of books available from Penguin, please write to *Penguin Books Ltd, Friedrichstrasse 10–12, D–6000 Frankfurt Main 1, Federal Republic of Germany.*

In Spain: For a complete list of books available from Penguin in Spain, please write to *Longman Penguin España, Calle San Nicolas 15, E–28013 Madrid, Spain.*

In Japan: For a complete list of books available from Penguin in Japan, please write to *Longman Penguin Japan Co Ltd, Yamaguchi Building, 2-12-9 Kanda Jimbocho, Chiyuoda-Ku, Tokyo 101, Japan.*